21

FOTOTORST

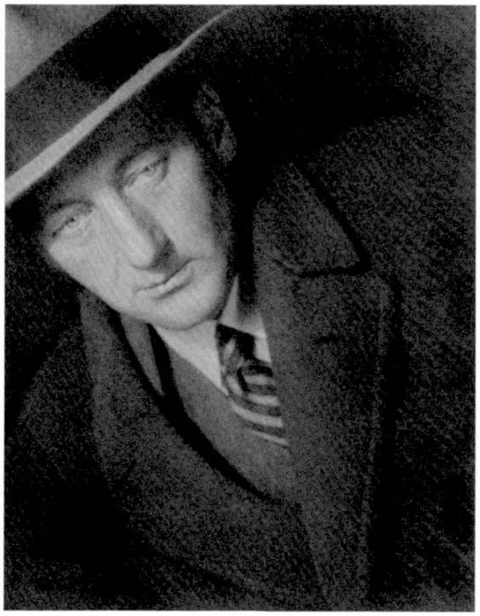

VLADIMÍR BIRGUS

Eugen **Wiškovský**

TORST

Kniha byla vydána ve spolupráci s Ministerstvem kultury České republiky.

Acknowledgments:
For their extraordinary help in the preparation of this book the author is most grateful to Eva Kafková and Hana Wiškovská, the daughters of Eugen Wiškovský. He also thanks Wiškovský's grandson Jiří Kafka and Anna Fárová, for their having lent him valuable material about Wiškovský.

Poděkování:
Mimořádnou pomoc při přípravě této knihy poskytly dcery Eugena Wiškovského Eva Kafková a Hana Wiškovská. Autor děkuje také vnukovi Eugena Wiškovského Jiřímu Kafkovi a Anně Fárové za zapůjčení cenných materiálů o Eugenu Wiškovském.

ISBN 80-7215-266-1

Although works by Eugen Wiškovský have appeared at most exhibitions of Czech avant-garde photography from the 1930s to the present, only one small book, by Anna Fárová, published in 1964, was, till now, devoted purely to his work. The first solo exhibition of his photographs was held 21 years after the publishing of that book at the Turin photography festival. Wiškovský's first exhibition in Prague took place in the Prague House of Photography in 1993. And yet, Wiškovský's photographs are among the most original, most forward-looking Czech contributions to the development of modern photography from the period between the two world wars. His theoretical writings from the 1920s, '30s, and '40s, in many respects anticipated trends that did not begin to make themselves felt in the theory of photography till subsequent decades. Wiškovský's photographic *oeuvre* is not large, and its range of topics is not wide, yet it is extraordinarily important owing to its depth of ideas and innovativeness. Even though his works are now part of collections in such important institutions as the Museum of Modern Art, New York, the Museum of Fine Arts, Houston, the Pompidou Centre, Paris, and the IVAM, Valencia, these holdings, with the exception of larger sets of prints he made himself, which are deposited in the Museum of Decorative Arts, Prague, and the Moravian Gallery, Brno, each comprise only several photographs. One reason is that Wiškovský never exhibited much and he therefore had little reason to make exhibition-format prints. Consequently, originals of his photographs are now exceptionally rare and there are far fewer of them in collections, public and private, than there are of works by František Drtikol, Josef Sudek, and Jaromír Funke. That is also one of the reasons his work – like that, for instance, of Jaroslav Rössler, another important Czech avant-garde photographer – has yet to be fully appreciated internationally.

Although Wiškovský had been making photographs intensively for many years, he never became a professional in this field. Nor was he alone in this respect. After all, modern Czech photography was not formed only by people who made their living as photographers, for example, Drtikol, Rössler, and Sudek, but also by forward-looking amateur photographers like the Czech-

-American physician Drahomír Josef Růžička, the chemists Jan Lauschmann and Jiří Sever, and the soldier Jiří Jeníček. Indeed, another amateur without formal training in photography became the most important Czech avant-garde photographer – Funke, who began to make his living with photography only after becoming a teacher at the School of Decorative Arts in Bratislava. Whereas in the USA or Germany, for example, the development of photography in the interwar period was driven mainly by professional photographers and artists, in Czechoslovakia at this time many important photographs were being made by people who for various reasons remained amateurs.

Among them was Wiškovský. For most of his life he made his living as a teacher at a secondary school, devoting himself to taking photographs and writing about photography only as a hobby. (The only exceptions were a calendar he made for the Interfarma pharmaceutical company and a set of postcards of flowers.) Wiškovský was born in a respected middle-class family in Dvůr Králové nad Labem, Bohemia, on 20 September 1888. His father, Alois Wiškovský, was the manager of the Dvůr Králové hospital. His mother, Eugenie Wiškovská, née Hotovcová, was the daughter of the regional council leader. Eugen had three brothers – Alois, a year his senior, Otakar, a year his junior, and Bedřich, two years his junior. All four brothers received university educations. Eugen graduated from secondary school in Dvůr Králové, and in 1906 began to study French, German, and psychology at the Czech university in Prague. He spent the winter semester of his last year, 1909–10, on a scholarship at the University of Geneva. After graduating, he

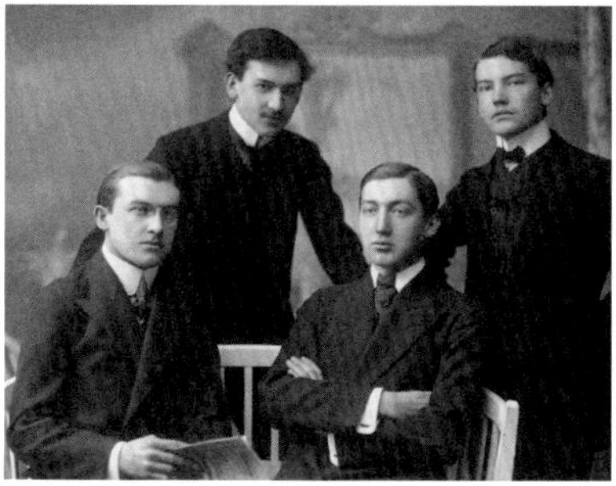

J. Rublič: Wiškovský Brothers

spent many years teaching at various secondary schools, the longest period was at the *realgymnasium* in Kolín, where he taught until 1937, except during the First World War, when he fought as a soldier in the ranks of the Austro-Hungarian army at the front in Italy and Russia. After being wounded a second time, he was stationed with troops behind the lines in Česká Lípa, north Bohemia. In April 1917 he married the 23-year-old Anna Streitová. In 1918 their daughter Eva (d. 1997) was born, followed, a year later, by their second daughter Hana (d. 1985).

Eugen Wiškovský was an educated man of many talents and interests. He devoted himself to the reform of teaching foreign languages at the secondary-school level, was a co-author of a Czech-German dictionary, worked with the Alliance Française, was a member of the Czech Psychological Society, translated Symbolist works by Maeterlinck as well as the writings of Freud and Jung. He was also profoundly interested in *belles-lettres* and the fine arts, played tennis competitively, and devoted time to swimming, skating, athletics, and camping. Wiškovský's work as a teacher at the secondary school in Kolín was recalled by his former pupil Anastáz Opasek, later Arch-abbot of Břevnov in Prague: "He was a unique teacher. I have truly excellent memories of him, and believe that not only I, but also the other students do as well. [...] With the inspectors and school council he was always having trouble. He did not, for example, have a class report-book, only an attendance sheet. When he entered the class, while still standing at the door he threw a book on the table – just to see if he could manage it –, then he sat down on the bench and immediately began to talk French to us. It was clear that he had spent some time in France. He treated us as a father treats his own children. Sometimes he lost his temper; it was in his nature. But he never hurt anyone. He was neither pedantic nor officious. He also had problems because he was a sportsman, and trained for competitive track-and-field."[1]

Wiškovský inherited his interest in photography from his father. While still a little boy, he used his father's 13 × 18 cm camera to take various family photos. At the age of fourteen or fifteen he got a more flexible camera, for 9 x 12 cm plates, but photography gradually gave way to other hobbies. He returned to it for a while toward the end of the First World War, making portraits of his wife and first daughter. He did not really begin to treat photography seriously, however, till the end of the 1920s, when in Kolín he began to make friends with a former student – Jaromír Funke (1896–1945). At that time Funke was already a leading Czech avant-garde photographer. Many years later, in October 1962, Wiškovský, in a letter to Anna Fárová, a historian of photography, recalled his work with Funke: "Not that he explained anything theoretical to me – that wasn't his way. He didn't like to express himself verbally about his work. That was because of shyness stemming from a slight speech defect, and also because he didn't want to expand on the matter when I was in the midst of experimenting. We used to go out into the field together, to the building site of a power plant, to places nearby, to the tower of the Business School [Obchodní akademie], and we photographed the "New Objectivity" – stocks of concrete rings, rails, Mannesmann line pipes, and so forth. Funke soon gave that up, because he saw that it was what I was specializing in, and he was also doing it more realistically than me. His greatest help to me was that I could print the good negatives in his darkroom (in the bathroom), since I didn't have my own at the time. On the one hand, I learnt enlarging techniques and good composition; on the other hand, the simple geometric forms revealed the potential that black-and-white photographs have to make things abstract by excluding color and emphasizing form. (And, like every introverted person, I was concerned solely with form, not color.) They were pure motifs, so it was easy to exclude disturbing, incongruous elements. This was a matter of form changed by the lens with a rather short focal length, where the parallel lines of pipes or rails ran together into a single point and created a flat design."[2] Wiškovský was also acquainted with another famous photographer from Kolín, Funke's contemporary, Josef Sudek (1896–1976). But whereas he had much in common with Funke intellectually and socially (both were respected inhabitants of Kolín), Sudek's intentionally accentuating his being one of the common people, particularly at first, was a certain barrier. Later, in an interview with the photography historian Jaroslav Anděl, Sudek himself responded to the question of whether he had associated with Wiškovský: "Not too often. It was mainly Funke who associated with him. This is how things were with Wiškovský: when Funke and I were still taking photographs in Kolín, Funke was a tennis player and Wiškovský too. Wiškovský saw us taking photographs, caught a whiff of it, and from then on began to take photographs too. His turf was Kolín, and when he was in Prague, it was the Hlubočepy district. His orientation was also more literary. He was an intelligent gentleman. He tended to associate with Ehm rather than with me, which is interesting."[3]

Even in his early works, in the late 1920s and early '30s, Wiškovský showed himself to be an original artist. Although he participated now and then in the work of the Kolín photographic society, he was little interested in typical amateur photographic activity, like discussions about the best developers, enthusiastically sending off works to various photo galleries, and great competitions for medals. On the other hand, as early as May 1930 he showed work in the "New Czech Photography" exhibition held in the gallery of the Aventinum publishing house (Aventinská mansarda), Prague. On the model of the acclaimed 1929 Stuttgart exhibition, "Film und Foto," the Prague exhibition was organized by the young photographer and film-maker Alexandr Hackenschmied and his friends. Wiškovský's photos at this first group exhibition of Czech avant-garde photographers in Prague were shown next to works by Funke, Rössler, Jiří Lehovec, Ladislav Emil Berka, and Sudek, as well as a number of scientific photographs. A year later he exhibited in a similar show at the same venue, and in 1933 had works in the "International Exhibition of Social-documentary Photography" in Prague, which was organized by the Cinema and Photography (Film-foto) Group of the Left Front (Levá fronta). Three years later, five of his photographs (*Insulator*, *Turbine Detail*, *Leftover Ice*, *Casing*, and *Bottom of an Antenna in Liblice*) were accepted for the "International Exhibition of Photography" in the Mánes Gallery, Prague, where they appeared next to works by Man Ray, Lászlo Moholy-Nagy, Hans Bellmer, Raoul Hausmann, Alexander Rodchenko, and other leading avant-garde photographers from around the world. Although his works were included in important avant-garde photography exhibitions, Wiškovský himself never joined any avant-garde group. One reason for this was his introversion; he was not a person who would have indulged in heated debates on art in cafés and wine bars.

Wiškovský himself stated that apart from contacts with Funke, a great inspiration for him was a book about Man Ray. He soon shared both Funke's enthusiasm for the "New Photography," which applied the principles of Constructivism, Functionalism, and New Objectivity, and his aversion to the survivals of Impressionist and Art Nouveau pictorialism, which imitated painting and graphic art and used oil prints, bromoil prints, carbon prints, and other pigment processes while suppressing the many features specific to photography. In the 1920s, battles raged in the USA and many countries of Europe between traditional pictorialists, who used pigment processes, and proponents of pure photography, promoted by Alfred Stieglitz, Clarence H. White, and other members of the Photo-Secession group, battles which had long been won by the opponents of pigment processes. In Czechoslovakia, however, the style of direct-photo processes, which rejected any additional manipulation of the negative, did not win out till 1921 at the exhibition of Růžička, one of White's pupils and, like his teacher, an opponent of pigment processes. Even later, however, when some young Czech photographers, for example, Funke, Sudek, Adolf Schneeberger, Lauschmann, and Arnošt Pikart, adopted this principle, pictorialist genre motifs predominated in their photographs, many of which accented atmospheric lighting and used soft-focus.

In his first important article on art photography, published in *Foto* in 1929, Wiškovský, undoubtedly under the influence of Funke's writing on theoretical aspects of photography, clearly rejected painterly efforts, stressing instead features specific to photography. He writes: "If [photography] is to have any justification, however, its creations must achieve their aims in a way that cannot be achieved by any technique other than a photographic one."[4] In accord with the views of the Russian Constructivists and the German Functionalists, Wiškovský emphasizes the search for new aesthetic values in apparently unphotogenic objects of modern technical civilization. "Whether machines or buildings, furniture or clothes, they always have the quality of functional simplicity, free of all ornament. And the more they correspond by their own pure forms to certain elementary geometric forms, the more amenable they are to us."[5]

Wiškovský wrote these words when he was at the beginning of his own serious photographic work and had only a few serious photos to his credit. None the less, even these works totally adhere to the principles of New Objectivity, a trend whose leading proponents, for instance Karl Blossfeldt, Albert Renger-Patzsch, Charles Sheeler, Paul Strand, and Edward Weston, had directed attention to the question of elementary forms and structures, the photographically most perfect, most effective expression of the essential features of the depicted objects, the discovery of aesthetic qualities in apparently unaesthetic objects, and, in the area of form, maximum sharpness and richness of tone of the photographic image. New Objectivity, whose essential features had already appeared in German and American photography as early as during the First World War, stood in opposition to romanticism, lyricism, sentimentality, and the frequently contrived quality of Impressionist and Art Nouveau pictorialism. In Czech photography of the 1920s, too, it already had several important proponents, particularly Funke, Sudek, Rössler, and Lauschmann, who, in the next decade, were then joined by many others, including Ehm, Vladimír Hipman, Jindřich Hatlák, Jaroslava Hatláková, Marie Rossmannová, Jindřich (Heinrich) Koch, Josef Voříšek, Emil Vepřek, and Karel Kašpařík.

In the late 1920s and early 1930s, Wiškovský could directly follow on from Funke's photographs of parts of cog-wheels and metal barrels as well as the general enthusiasm that a number of avant-garde artists had for modern technical civilization. In his own apparently simple, but in fact carefully thought-out, compositionally refined, photographs of line pipes, bundles of iron rods, bolts, insulators, sifters, or close-ups of turbines, light bulbs, and mortars he found artistically cogent forms. He presented ordinary, often-seen objects, which he could easily find at home or at the building-site of the Kolín power plant, in novel ways, surprising the viewer and demonstrating to the viewer that his or her eye had become tired and dim. He ingeniously used large details, which take the depicted objects out of their usual spatial contexts and often also change perspective and scale. With the move from the color original to the black-and-white photograph, with cropping and masterful work with light, he freed the main motif from superfluities and thus let the most important lines and tones stand out. He often used multiplication and the rhythmic repetition of geometric forms or whole objects, as is evident, for example, in the photos of eggs, corrugated iron, ceramic pipes, or spindles with wool. With extraordinary invention, artistic feeling, and technical precision, he thus put into practice his conviction that "the less unusual the content, the more unusual the presentation has to be."[6] Wiškovský's photographs in the style of New Objectivity are rigorously rational while being full of imagination. The objectivity of the perfect depiction of details of the surrounding world is blended with the subjectivity of the photographer's personal way of looking at things, his thinking, feeling, intellect, inner world. It differs strikingly from the reality that it depicts; in these photographs reality is artistically defamiliarized. The photos are distinctive works of art with the easily recognizable signature of the photographer. Wiškovský selected and photographed the kinds of objects with which he could express his idea. He writes: "Photography makes the invisible visible, that is to say, [it shows] what the photographer was feeling while looking at the object and what he wants the viewer to feel when looking at the photograph."[7]

Quality always takes priority over quantity in Wiškovský's work. To be sure, that was probably also owing to the fact that when the lightweight Leicas for 24×36 cm roll-film first appeared he was usually working with an Ica Ideal fitted with a Tessar 4.5/105 lens for 6.5×9 cm negatives. He initially photographed on glass plates. According to his friend Ehm he had only 12 cassettes, so that on his photographic excursions he really had to economize with the material.[8] Later, he got himself a Rolex cassette for film. He also had a square, single-lens Ensign Special Reflex for 9×9 cm plates, which was fitted with a 4.5/5 inch Aldis--Butcher lens. This camera, which he used when making, for example, a number of the photos of the Kolín power plant,[9] is now in the collections of the National Technical Museum, Prague. Simply owing to these inflexible cameras he tended to choose mainly static motifs and rarely took photographs of people. When people do appear in his photographs, they tend to be only figurines on the landscape or cityscape or in a Constructivist composition. The exceptions are the portraits he made of his wife, daughters, and friends, as well as experimental portraits using the play of light and shadow, for example, *Portrait of a Composer*, 1930, or the untitled portrait of a girl, 1932, on whose face the shadow of a net falls, photos of children at play, campsites, or, truly unique in his work, a set of documentary photos of the Prague Uprising in May 1945.

Wiškovský's photographs from the New Objectivity period are few in number and often depict various views of the same object. Unlike Funke, Wiškovský often returned to individual motifs, photographing until he was completely satisfied with the results. Whereas Funke, it is said, did not try in the *Time Persists* series to get a technically superior shot of the Surrealist photograph juxtaposing a Baroque statue of an angel in a Kolín cemetery with the smokestack of a power plant, because he felt this one was already finished, in Wiškovský's work we sometimes find more than ten negatives with various versions of the same shot, often made over a longish period. According to his daughters and Ehm, Wiškovský often spent hours setting up one shot, or would even leave home with his camera but end up not taking a single photograph.

His "definitive" shots in the style of New Objectivity are without a doubt among the best of their kind in this area of Czech photography. Among the typical features are set rules and inventive compositions in which secondary elements are suppressed. Wiškovský was convinced that "beauty is not absolute simplicity, but simplified complexity."[10] Despite all the rationality and formal mastery he was often concerned with more than just the artistically unusual depiction of simple and often apparently unaesthetic objects and the solution to problems of the visual minimum or relations between the whole and its parts; he was also concerned with the photographic expression of objective relations as well as his own impression of them, and often, as well, the search for analogies in form and metaphorical meaning. More than once he managed to go beyond a terse optimal description of reality typical, for example, of many of the works of Renger-Patzsch, Aenne Biermann, and other leading practioners of New Objectivity, and to create photographs with a more symbolic effect, whose metaphorical quality has much in common with Edward Weston's photographs of seashells or artichokes. The objects in some of Wiškovský's photographs are depicted with the aim of stripping them of their identity. The analogies of form and metaphor do not, however, appear in all Wiškovský's photographs, yet where they do appear they often play an important role. (Thus, for example, the shot of corrugated metal evokes an image of long hair worn loose or the surface of a seashell, the shot of rhythmically arranged eggs brings to mind fish scales, and a detail of sugar-refinery waste floating on dirty water can suggest a map of South-East Asia or an arabesque.) This is most striking in *Lunar Landscape* (which sometimes also goes by the curt title *Collars*) from 1929, in other words from the very beginning of his serious photography. The composition with stiff shirt collars was transformed by suppressing the scale and isolating repeating details, by inventive lighting using a bulb placed among the collars, and, in a later version of the photo, the addition of the silhouette of a coin placed in the background onto the photographic paper like a picture of the Earth, into an imaginative picture of the cratered surface of the Moon. About this frequently published photo Wiškovský himself writes: "The collars led me to the possibility of the double meaning in photography: the actual and the metaphoric. The omission of color and the simplification of the visual sensation by projecting into the surface of the format enable certain similarities to emerge, which are [otherwise] masked by the color and the sculptural nature of real perception. These similarities, even in the realistic presentation of the subject matter, cannot be denied if one has even just a bit of imagination."[11] Elsewhere he defines the possibilities of metaphoric photography as follows: "It consists in the fact that the shot emphasizes the similarity between the depicted object and some other object that is, however, a typical source of the emotion the photograph should evoke. Emphasizing this similarity increases the power of suggestion of the subject."[12]

In the early 1930s Wiškovský, apart from details of small objects, often photographed the new ESSO power plant in Kolín. This modern Functionalist piece of architecture by Jaroslav Fragner provided him with a number of motifs for unusual photographs, which were often modeled on works by Rodchenko, El Lissitzky, and Moholy-Nagy, with striking low-angles or dynamic diagonal compositions. The building was also photographed several times by Sudek as well as by the Bauhaus graduate Jindřich (Heinrich) Koch, whose shots are, however, far more static and conventionally composed. Photographs by Funke, who often accompanied his older friend on photographic excursions to the building-site of the power plant, also have much in common with Wiškovský's Constructivist photos. Works by both these photographers were used to illustrate Fragner's article about the ESSO power plant, which was published in the fourth issue of *Volné směry* in 1931. Some of their diagonal shots of the power-plant smokestack are so similar that it is often difficult at first glance to determine which is by whom. On closer inspection, however, it becomes clear that Wiškovský tends to put more emphasis on geometrical qualities of the basic elements of the construction of the building, works more with details, and has even created the more original shot – namely, the photograph of the factory smokestack with its reflection in the surface of the river, composed in a rhomboid. Whereas the parallels of the photos made from striking low angles and other unusual perspectives appear in Russian Constructivism and German Functionalism, the rhomboid shot symmetrically depicting a factory and its reflection is a true one-of-a-kind. It is the most eloquent example of the fact that Wiškovský was not only a modern depicter of modern architecture, but also its interpreter. At the same time, however, it is also evidence that for him the architecture itself was often merely a starting point and inspiration for his own art, and it is largely unimportant what building appears in the photograph. Evidence of that is in Wiškovský's photos taken around the power plant, for example those which, from a high angle, juxtapose details of metal structures, human figures, and sharply cast shadows. Some are reminiscent of André Kertész's photographs of the Eiffel Tower and reflect the interest that a number of other avant-garde photographers had in motifs of modern metal lookout towers and radio towers, for instance in the work of Rodchenko, Moholy-Nagy, Germaine Krull, and Rössler.

Neither for Funke nor for Wiškovský, however, was the Kolín power station the only Functionalist structure to be depicted. Funke, for example, took photographs for a publication about the Masaryk Halls of Residence in Brno, which were designed by another leading proponent of Czech Functionalism, Bohumil Fuchs,[13] and he also captured from unusual angles other Functionalist buildings in Bratislava, Kolín, and Prague. Wiškovský made, for instance, an exemplar photograph called *Functionalist Architecture*, of a new apartment building, and several photos with the motif of the swimming pool, designed by Václav Kolátor, and the Barrandov Terraces restaurant designed by the architect Max Urban. With café tables on terraces above a swimming pool, this photogenic spot on the edge of Prague was among the most popular subjects of Czech photographers in the interwar period. It has been photographed in various ways by Sudek, Růžička, Ehm, Lauschmann, Funke, Pikart, Julius Tutsch, and others.[14] Whereas most of them, however, have depicted it with a high-angle shot of the semicircle created by the tables and umbrellas, and some, like Růžička and Lauschmann, even used a lyrical soft focus, Wiškovský stresses the contrast between the terrace and the swimming pool below it, in which he achieves a striking change of perspective and scale. No other photographer obtained from this location more radical shots capturing the very essence of modern architecture or even the modern age in general. Constructivist compositions also appear, however, in other photographs by Wiškovský, for example the well-known *Game* (1929), which captures from a high angle his two daughters sitting on a diagonally depicted staircase, in the unpublished photo taken from above of boys tossing coins, or in the unusual composition of *Canoe*, about which one may reasonably wonder whether its erotic metaphor does not reveal the fact that Wiškovský had translated works by Sigmund Freud.

In 1937 Wiškovský and his family moved to Prague, where he taught at a secondary school in Ječná ulice and another for girls in Libeň. In Prague he continued to associate with Funke, who had been teaching photography at the State School of Graphic Art since September 1935. He also made friends with Funke's colleague Josef Ehm (1909–1989), another important photographer of technically precise works depicting architecture and sculpture, classic landscapes, portraits, and more experimental photos based on the principles of New Objectivity and responding to Surrealism. Ehm told me the following about his friendship with Wiškovský: "There was a twenty-year age-difference between us. We didn't address each other with the familiar *Ty* form, but I did not have to call him Professor, only Mister, and he called me Ehm. We used to meet mostly on Saturdays or Sundays, often with our wives. He had quite a complicated attitude to life, and used to suffer from depression, and was also being treated for it. We often went on walks together. He needed to be with someone with whom he could chat about his problems and photography. It was a really valuable friendship, and I got a lot out of it. On the other hand, I was able to repay Wiškovský a bit in that I knew much more about technique than he did. He usually printed in the postcard format, and often used to get me to print some photo for some exhibition. I also adjusted some of his negatives with reducer, even though he and Funke used to claim that the negative was inviolable."[15]

Whereas in the small-town milieu of Kolín he mainly photographed industrial buildings, details of technical objects, and modern architecture, in Prague Wiškovský began, somewhat paradoxically, to be concerned chiefly with landscape photography. He already had some experience in this area, for example, his masterfully composed photograph of the path through a field near Police nad Metují, made as early as 1933, and the diagonally depicted high-angle shot of the River Sázava with the Scout camp, made about a year after that. He later justified his interest in landscape photography in the article "Proč fotografujeme krajiny" (Why we photograph landscapes): "The land, the soil, the earth, attracts us precisely because of what is lasting in it as opposed to the fleeting and changing nature of everything else in our lives. For us, it is the greatest satisfaction and greatest consolation to find in it harmony with our inner selves. The land, like our inner selves, is similarly manifold, and has idyllic nooks for a blissful dreamer, just as a stormy sea and rocky cliffs have for the romantic misfit."[16] In the landscape photos, in which he emphasizes the subjective contribution of the photographer, Wiškovský was interested chiefly in elementary geometric forms, unusual surface textures, and phantasmagorical images. For his motifs he did not have to travel to foreign lands, usually finding them in the few places he had been visiting on foot for many years and was intimately familiar with. Mainly, it was in Hlubočepy, on the western edge of Prague, whose picturesque cliffs and valley (the Prokopské údolí) had attracted many other photographers as well. Wiškovský also photographed the monumental cliffs of Hlubočepy in romantic late-afternoon light, but more often depicted details of them stripped of their true dimensions, revealing natural sculptures, elementary geometric forms, and sometimes also metaphorically effective analogies of forms. He was fascinated also by the irregularity of the terrain there and the bizarre shapes of the fields, which he sculpturally accented in his photographs using light. (Some of these photos have much in common with Funke's landscape photographs from areas around the towns of Kolín and Louny.) With great patience he photographed identical landscape motifs again and again until he was satisfied with the composition, capturing the texture and the moods created by light. Among other places Wiškovský enjoyed photographing in Prague and its environs was the area of Vidoule in the Jinonice district. There he found, for example, the motif of the field and path, which he shot from above, whose form brings to mind a fluttering banner and mast. In most cases these were landscapes that had been strikingly reshaped by people, and are evidence of the relationship between man and Nature.

Wiškovský made his most original landscape photos around the Šalamounka farm in the Prague district of Smíchov. There, he photographed in many variants a small section of land with a hillock and house: sometimes he was fascinated by the contoured little rows of mowed grass, other times by the geometric forms of haystacks or the menacing shadow of the neighboring hill, which made a ghostly symbolic image. The zenith of Wiškovský's landscape work is the metaphorical photo of lodged wheat with the protruding roof of a farmhouse, suggesting a ship sinking in a stormy sea. This almost Surrealist meshing of reality and imaginary vision is intensified by the title *Disaster*, under which the photograph was later published. (The original title was *Wheat*). In the set of Wiškovský postcards published by Orbis in 1963, *Disaster* is dated 1943. In the first book of Wiškovský's work, published in 1964, it is dated 1940. It was, however, most likely made in 1939, to judge both from what Ehm claimed and from the fact that it was apppeared in the July 1940 issue of *Fotografický obzor*. Although it does not belong to the works made during the Second World War, the oppressive period of the end of democratic Czechoslovakia and fears about the coming of another great war may have played a role in its making. A similar interpretation is plausible for the photo *Landscape near Prague*, which captures the encroaching oval shadow of the neighboring hill, and was printed in the June 1940 issue of *Fotografický obzor* (this photograph was later presented under the title *Shadow*), and for the less well-known photograph *Specters* from 1939, which is a detail of a living-room with two chairs draped in white fabric, giving the impression of intimately familiar things that have now been abandoned. These works also demonstrate that Wiškovský was sometimes inspired by Surrealism far more than is usually acknowledged when discussing his work.

The late 1930s and early 1940s were the most important period of Wiškovský's theoretical writing.[17] This was thanks mostly to Ehm and Funke. In October 1939 Ehm became the new editor-in-chief of *Fotografický obzor*, and invited Funke to join him to work on the magazine. They gradually managed to turn this conservative monthly of the Association of Czech Amateur Photographic Societies into a modernly conceived specialist journal, increasing its print-run in a short time from 4,000 copies to almost quadruple that number. This was also thanks to Wiškovský, who at the time had published in *Fotografický obzor* not only a number of his photographs, but also four of his original theoretical essays: "Tvar a motiv" (Form and motif), "Dezorientace názorů na fotografii" (A confusion of opinions about photography) "Zobrazení, projev, sdělení" (Depiction, expression, communication), and "Oproštěním k projevu," (Expression by way of simplification) which together with articles by Funke and Karel Teige form the basis of modern Czech photography theory. In them, as in several other articles published in 1946–48, Wiškovský first tried to deduce the principles of photographic composition from the process of perception on the basis of Gestalt psychology. He was concerned with questions about the point of photography, and sought to use his knowledge of information theory to construct a new theory of photography. Owing to their depth, originality, and precise formulation, these articles were unique in Czech photography theory, and were therefore not understood by most readers interested in photography. It would be decades before they were finally appreciated. At the same time, however, it must be said that in them and other articles by Wiškovský the same ideas are sometimes repeated, even if formulated a bit differently; for example, the idea that high-quality photography was a visual adventure guaranteed to be reality. (The belief, so frequently presented by Wiškovský, that the depicted image is reality itself, has now been completely undermined by the comparatively recent advent of digital technology.)

The most important of Wiškovský's theoretical writings is "Tvar a motiv" (Form and motif), published in the October 1940 issue of *Fotografický obzor*. In this article Wiškovský considers the pictorial quality of photographs and how it is perceived by the viewer. He applies here various elements of Gestalt psychology, chiefly the priority of the whole over the parts. This principle had already long been known from "Über Gestaltqualitäten" (1890) by the pioneer of Gestalt psychology, the Austrian psychologist, philosopher, and professor at the German university in Prague, Christian von Ehrenfels, but it had not been thoroughly applied in the area of photographic theory till Wiškovský did so. In this article, Wiškovský writes: "If we therefore want to penetrate to the essential signs of the motif, let's start from the undeniable and generally acknowledged principles that a good photograph must be a unified whole. If we employ here the way of looking at things and the terminology of what is known as Gestalt psychology, we say that there must be a formation (form), that is, a multiple articulated whole, whose individual parts in themselves are not independent, but are mutually linked by a firm inner bond (as opposed to mere plurality, co-existence, a random cluster of singularities."[18] The photographer's main role in making the photo is in the choice of subject matter and in its photographic transformation into a motif. "The motif is a case of real visual unusualness (or something foreseen by the photographer on the finished print), which can be photographically isolated and thereby intensified to an impression of surprisingness against a background of absolute realness, created by a well-presented structure." Wiškovský himself divides motifs into three basic groups: motifs, in which unusualness is purely external, visual, a matter of form, such as plurality, similarity, regularity, movement, and definition of form; motifs whose differentness from ordinary seeing stems from the particular potential of photography, for example, distortion of perspective by a short focal length, large depth of field, changes in the black-and-white tonal scale by the use of colored filters, size achieved by enlarging or reducing the field of view, or unusual angles; and, lastly, motifs, whose unusualness is based on the feeling of novelty stemming from other emotional content, for example visual metaphors emphasizing the similarity the depicted object has with another object, or the juxtaposition of two elements, from which a symbol emerges, in which they somehow clash. Only the motifs of the third group are directly dependent on the photographer. In conclusion, Wiškovský writes: "...transformation is the actual essence of aesthetic photography. Transformation, not, however, deformation of reality. Transformation, that is to say, the simplifying, the purging, of reality from all that is superfluous and inappropriate, which would have disfigured the picture of our idea – the motif

– which should be clearly reflected in the mirror of the photograph."[19] In "Tvar a motiv" Wiškovský anticipates later attempts to apply Gestalt psychology to the area of the fine arts, as practiced, for example, by the German-born theorist of film Rudolf Arnheim in his *Art and Visual Perception* (1954). Despite all its originality, depth of thought, and precision of formulation, this fundamental article by Wiškovský did not meet with unanimous approval. This is clear, for example, from the criticism by Karel Hermann, Editor-in-Chief of *Fotografie*, in his article "Učme se dívat fotograficky" (Let's learn to look photographically)[20] to which Wiškovský quickly responded with the article "Desorientace názoru na fotografii" (A confusion of opinion about photography).[21]

Ehm and Funke ran *Fotografický obzor* as a high-quality, daring periodical, and as late as November 1940, that is, a year and eight months after the beginning of the German occupation, faced with the Nazi opinion that avant-garde work is "degenerate art," they managed to publish a special issue devoted to experimental photography. In early 1941, however, in view of increasing denunciatory statements from some Czech photographers, they gave up the editorship, and Wiškovský thus lost, till the end of the war, a place to publish his articles on theory. He did, however, continue to take photographs. He continued with his abstract-making details of the Hlubočepy cliffs and variations of photographs with the motifs of the Šalamounka farm, as well as taking almost impressionistic photos of the little fields above the valley, in which the late-afternoon or early-evening light emphasizes their undulating terrain, he photographed trees with back-lighting, which separates them from their surroundings, and depicted the architecture of Prague. At the very end of the war, during the Prague Uprising, he made documentary photos of the building of barricades and their defense. These photos are the exception in his otherwise thoroughly static *oeuvre*. They tend, however, to be descriptive shots, largely lacking in drama, and do not compare with the far more dynamic, emotionally effective photos of the same event taken by a number of other Czech photographers. Shortly after the war Wiškovský also made several photographs of German women and Czech women who, having collaborated with the German regime, were forced – often humiliatingly painted with swaztikas – to clear way barricades and debris. Apart from these photographs, the topic of war also present appears in the symbolic *After an Air Raid*, which shows a bent cross on a pile of rubble.

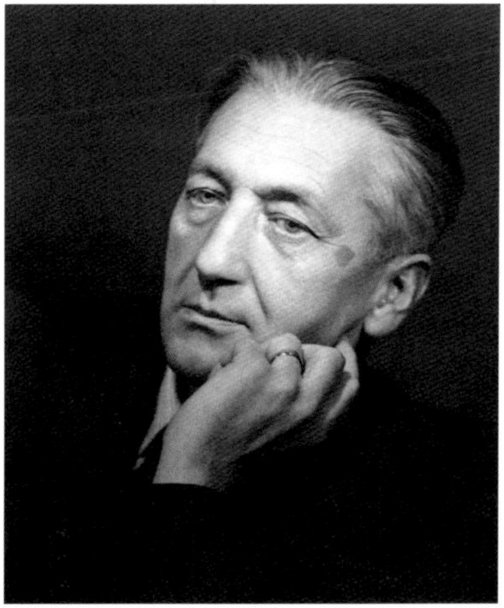

Josef Ehm: Eugen Wiškovský, 1946

In the short period of relative freedom and democracy between the end of the Second World War and the Communist seizure of power in February 1948, Wiškovský published other articles on theory in the periodicals *Fotografie*, *Československá fotografie*, and *Zpravodaj fotografů*. In parallel with his theoretical writing he made other landscape photographs in Hlubočepy, static photos of Prague, and details of various natural motifs, for example, the well-known *Chestnuts*. In this period he also showed works in several important group exhibitions, in particular "Modern Photography in Czechoslovakia," which was first held in Vienna in late July 1947, and later in Zurich. It was a major exhibition of works by leading Czech and Slovak photographers, for which Orbis published a catalog with 24 plates and an article by Teige providing an outline of the development of Czechoslovak photography. Wiškovský also had work in the "Fourth International Photography Salon," held in Prague in 1948, which then traveled to Brno, Bratislava, and Ostrava. In 1947 several of his photographs appeared in Jiří Jeníček's *Fotografie jako zření světa a života* (Photography as a vision of the world and life). Nineteen of his photographs, including the well-known *Banner* and one of the Barrandov Terraces restaurant – but also photos of tennis matches at the Štvanice island in Prague and of a graduation ceremony in the Karolinum of Charles University – were included in a work by Ehm and the art historian V. V. Štech with the pathos-filled title *Krásy plná, slávou i kletbou bohatá...Praho!* (Full of beauty, rich in glory and curses ...O, Prague!), published by Družstevní práce in 1948.

Soon after the Communist regime established itself in Czechoslovakia in early 1948, the propagandistic role of photography in the style of Socialist Realism was officially asserted above all others. Consequently, there was no room on the officially sanctioned scene either for creative experiments or for profound articles on theory based on Gestalt psychology. In the years of the most rigid Stalinism of the Communist regime led by Klement Gottwald (till his death, several days after Stalin's, in early 1953) articles appeared in photographic periodicals questioning whether landscape photographs without tractors could be anything but a bourgeois holdover. Wiškovský at the time quit teaching, publishing and exhibiting. One piece of evidence of his distancing himself even from moderate expressions of Marxist ideology is, for example, his ironic remarks written in pencil on the margin of Lubomír Linhart's introduction to his copy of *Josef Sudek. Fotografie* (1956) and many articles in *Československá fotografie*. In his photographs in the 1950s, Wiškovský devoted himself primarily to work on the large series of imaginative photographs *From the Old Jewish Cemetery in Prague*, where he sought to juxtapose crumbling tombstones with the bizarre shapes of the surrounding trees and shrubs, contrasting the man-made and the natural worlds. He wrote about this to Fárová in 1962: "At the Jewish cemetery I tried to capture tombstones in interesting light or to link them with dying Nature. I managed to capture the cemetery in its original form, completely overgrown with grass, ferns, shrubs, before its later repairs, which then took away many nice motifs."[22] He also often focuses on details of various reliefs and carved in-

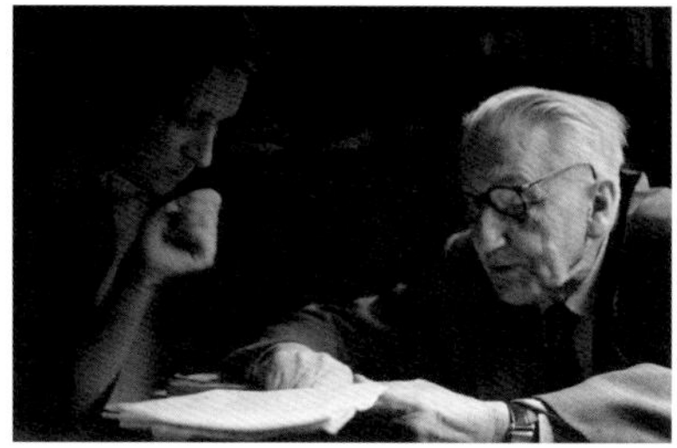

Miroslav Jodas: Anna Fárová with Eugen Wiškovský, 1963

scriptions, in which he accents their signs and symbols. Cemetery motifs have of course attracted a number of other Czech photographers, including Jindřich Štyrský, Sudek, Funke, Vilém Kříž, Tibor Honty, and Jindřich Brok, but none of them was as devoted to them as Wiškovský. None the less, unlike the photographs from the period of New Objectivity and Constructivism, these shots of Wiškovský's do not have the visual power or ability to reveal. Many of his photos of the Old Jewish Cemetery seem highly descriptive and some motifs repeat themselves. Although they demonstrate the depth of his ideas and his mastery of composition, they also indicate his decline as an artist, his dwindling ability to take the viewer on new visual adventures.

In this period Wiškovský also photographed historical architecture of Prague, flowers (which came out on several postcards), inventive abstract-making details of ficus leaves or lemons in water, and genre shots of people walking in a park or children on an outing. He also returned, however, to the old motifs of the juxtaposition of Nature and the changes man makes to it. In the Hlubočepy quarry (lom U svatého Prokopa) he captured the counterpoint of the cliffs and rails, in Hlubočepy he juxtaposed the romantic landscape with the nearby factories and houses. When illness (a prostate operation in 1958 and a subsequent infection) eventually prevented him from taking longer trips in search of landscape motifs, he traveled by tram from his flat at Malátova ulice no. 17, in the Smíchov district of Prague, to Petřín or Karlovo náměstí (Charles Square), and photographed there. It was on Karlovo náměstí that he made several outstanding photographs (for example, the bold composition with the fragment of two old men on a bench or the poetic shot of a monument to the nineteenth-century nationalist poet, librettist, and feminist essay writer Eliška Krásnohorská, suggesting the specter of a woman standing under a stately black locust tree), which constitute the dignified culmination of his photographic work. He was at the time gravely ill, forgotten by the wider public, and on the margins of photographic life, but he still tried to remain true to his conviction that "modern photography should be the representation of some idea or some emotion with the help of the specifically photographic depiction of the chosen subject matter rather than the mere capturing of objects as such."[23] The only substantial recollection of his personality, photographs, and writings was an article by Jeníček in the April 1957 issue of *Československá fotografie*, accompanied by three of Wiškovský's photographs.[24]

The credit for truly rediscovering Wiškovský's work in the early 1960s is due to Fárová. Her fascination with his modern photographs in back issues of *Fotografický obzor* and the *Československá fotografie* annual led her to ask other photographers to help her find Wiškovský. For a while it seemed that no one knew him, but finally, she was taken to Wiškovský by Jeníček. He warned her first, however, that Wiškovský did not have enough photographs to turn into a small volume for the SNKLU photography series in which she had published her books about Henri Cartier-Bresson, Werner Bischof, and Jeníček. For Wiškovský, already living long in isolation with his family, not associating with any photographers or theorists, and suffering from a sense of having been forgotten, that meeting, followed by a number of others, was a great boost and inspiration. He himself wrote as much to Fárová in a letter of December 8, 1963: "With an emotional smile I often recall the day you and Jeníček came, and in the mess of my prints performed that 'pêche miraculeuse,'[25] separating the wheat from the chaff. After all, up to that point I hadn't even dared to think it could ever be a book, partly because of the difference between my things and what was then accepted, and also, indeed mainly, because the things are scattered over a period of some 30 years and the contexts are now lost, whereas you, having a true aim in front of you, could tell. [...] I now see how miraculously you figured me out from those plates in [*Fotografický*] *Obzor* and the yearbooks. Actually, you knew me as photographer better than I knew myself, which is surely a very interesting phenomenon psychologically. (Just as was, on the other hand, the lack of interest of those who knew my photographs but didn't lift a finger to help them see the light of day.)"[26] The first fruit of the collaboration between Fárová and Wiškovský was a set of twelve postcards with copies of his photographs and a short, but cogent article by Fárová, which came out in the "Profily" (Profiles) series of the Orbis publishing house, Prague, in July 1963. Wiškovský did not, unfortunately, live to see the small book Fárová compiled and edited as the 23rd volume in the Umělecká fotografie (Art photography) series of the SNKLU publishing house, Prague, in June 1964 in a print-run of 5,000. He died on 15 January 1964 at the age of 75 of peritonitis after a belated appendectomy. A small group of family and friends paid their last respects in the chapel of the Strašnice crematorium in Prague.

The publishing of Fárová's little book with a good selection of photographs and an informed, analytical-interpretational essay finally awakened interest in the work of Wiškovský. After being ignored for years, the art and artists of the interwar avant-garde now began to be more intensively exhibited once again, and articles by their leading theorists and artists began to be published as books and in periodicals. A year after Wiškovský's death, a competition exhibition of landscape photography, called "The Eugen Wiškovský Memorial Exhibition" was organized in Hradec Králové. As early as 1966, John Szarkowski, the director of the Photography Department of the Museum of Modern Art, New York, mediated the purchase of four photographs by Wiškovský for the Museum collections. The most important set of his works, however, were acquired for the Museum of Decorative Arts in Prague by Fárová, the first curator of its Photography Department. Another important set was acquired for the Moravian Gallery in Brno by Antonín Dufek, head of its Photography Collection. In 1967 Rudolf Skopec included works by Wiškovský in a traveling exhibition called "Czechoslovak Photography between the Two World Wars." In 1973 Fárová included works by Wiškovský in the exhibition "Great Czech Photographers, Part I." In 1981 Wiškovský occupied an important place in the exhibition "Czech Photography, 1918–38: From the Collections of the Moravian Gallery, Brno," which was curated by Dufek and traveled in a reduced form to Łódź, Essen, Frankfurt on Main, and Vienna. Since that time, works by Wiškovský have been presented abroad at many major exhibitions of Czech photography and Czech fine art, for example "Czech Photographers, 1920–50" at the Centre Pompidou, Paris (1983), "Czechoslovak Photography, Yesterday and Today" in Frankfurt on Main (1986), "Czech Art of the 1920s and '30s" in Darmstadt (1988), three large exhibitions of Czech avant-garde works in Houston (1989–90), Valencia (1993), and Dijon (1997), and the exhibition "Modern Beauty: Czech Photographic Avant-Garde 1918–1948" in Barcelona, Paris, Lausanne, Prague, and Munich (1998–99). The very first solo exhibition of works by Wiškovský was organized by the author of the present essay in the Galleria d'Arte Narciso, Turin, in 1985, as part of the international "Torino Fotografia '85" festival. Since that time there has been no other solo exhibition abroad of his works.

In the 1980s I worked intensively with Wiškovský's two daughters on two books about their father, but none was published because, by coincidence, both the "Mezinárodní fotografie" (International photography) series of portfolios of bromographs published by Pressfoto and the large "Fotografie – – Osobnosti" (Photographs and photographers) series published by Panorama were discontinued before our two books were supposed to appear in them. I am delighted that now, after so many years, the assembled material has found use in this little book devoted to Wiškovský. It is but a small payment on a debt that the historiography of Czech photography owes him.

Wiškovský's work is today no longer forgotten and it is recognized as essential to the history of Czech photography. None the less, it still awaits its well-deserved place in the international context.

Notes

1 Anastáz Opasek, *Dvanáct zastavení*, Prague: Torst, 1992, pp. 20–21.
2 Letter from Eugen Wiškovský to Anna Fárová, October 1962, archive of Anna Fárová, Prague, p. 5.
3 Jaroslav Anděl, *Josef Sudek o sobě*, Prague: Torst, 2001, p. 41.
4 Eugen Wiškovský, "O obrazové fotografii," *Foto*, 1929, no. 12, p. 184.
5 Ibid., p. 185.
6 Eugen Wiškovský, "Zobrazení, projev, sdělení," *Fotografický obzor*, 1941, no. 1, p. 2.
7 "Eugen Wiškovský o fotografii," Notes from the archive of Anna Fárová, Prague, *c.* 1962, p. 2.
8 Author's interview with Josef Ehm, Prague, 28 August 1983.
9 Jiří Janda, *Kamery obskury: Fotografické přístroje z let 1840–1940*, Prague: Nakladatelství dopravy a spojů, 1983, p. 198.
10 Eugen Wiškovský, "Je fotografie uměním?" MS, archive of Anna Fárová, Prague, *c.* 1962, p. 15.
11 Letter from Eugen Wiškovský to Anna Fárová, October 1962, archive of Anna Fárová, Prague.
12 Eugen Wiškovský, "Tvar a motiv," *Fotografický obzor*, no. 10, 1940, p. 113.
13 Bohuslav Fuchs, *Masarykův studentský domov*, Brno: Fuchs, 1930.
14 See Vladimír Birgus (ed.), *Česká fotografická avantgarda 1918–1948*, Prague: Kant, 1999, pp. 128–29, published in English as *Czech Photographic Avant-Garde 1918–1948*, Cambridge, Mass.: The MIT Press, 2002; see also Jaroslav Anděl, *Nová vize: Avantgardní architektura v avantgardní fotografii 1918–1938*, Prague: Slovart, 2005, pp. 182–85.
15 My interview with Josef Ehm, Prague, 28 August 1983.
16 Eugen Wiškovský, "Proč fotografujeme krajiny," *Československá fotografie*, no. 6, 1947, p. 81.
17 See, for example, Jaroslav Anděl, "Teoretické přístupy a interpretace – Eugen Wiškovský," *Československá fotografie*, 1974, no. 1, pp. 6–8, no. 2, pp. 56–57; Evžen Sobek, "Teoretické práce Eugena Wiškovského," extended essay for B.A. course, Institute of Creative Photography, Silesian University, Opava, 1998; Evžen Sobek, *Teoretické práce české fotografické avantgardy*, Opava: Silesian University, 2004.
18 Wiškovský, "Tvar a motiv," p. 109.
19 Ibid., p. 111.
20 Karel Hermann, "Učme se dívat fotograficky," *Fotografie*, 1940, no. 22, p. 348.
21 Eugen Wiškovský, "Desorientace názorů na fotografii," *Fotografický obzor*, 1940, no. 12, pp. 125–26.

22 Letter from Eugen Wiškovský to Anna Fárová, October 1962, Archive of Anna Fárová, Prague, p. 12.

23 Anna Fárová, "Imaginární rozhovor s Eugenem Wiškovským," *Československá fotografie*, 1964, no. 5, p. 150.

24 Jiří Jeníček, "Eugen Wiškovský," *Československá fotografie*, 1957, no. 4, pp. 41–42.

25 "Miraculous draught of fishes" (Luke 5: 1–11).

26 Letter from Eugen Wiškovský to Anna Fárová, 8 December 1963, archive of Anna Fárová, Prague, pp. 2–3.

Přestože díla Eugena Wiškovského nechyběla na většině výstav české avantgardní fotografie od 30. let 20. století až do současnosti, byla mu dosud věnována pouze jediná drobná knižní monografie Anny Fárové z roku 1964. První samostatná výstava jeho tvorby proběhla o jedenadvacet let později v rámci fotografického festivalu v Turíně a první autorská expozice v Praze se uskutečnila v Pražském domě fotografie až v roce 1993. Přitom Wiškovského snímky patří k nejoriginálnějším a nejprogresivnějším českým příspěvkům k vývoji moderní fotografie z období mezi dvěma světovými válkami. Jeho teoretické práce z 20.–40. let v mnoha směrech předjímaly trendy, které se v teorii fotografie začaly masověji prosazovat až v následujících desetiletích. Wiškovského fotografická tvorba není velká rozsahem ani tematickou šíří, ale je mimořádně důležitá myšlenkovou hloubkou a novátorstvím. I když je dnes zastoupena v tak významných institucích, jakými jsou Muzeum moderního umění v New Yorku, Muzeum výtvarných umění v Houstonu, Pompidouovo centrum v Paříži či IVAM ve Valencii, s výjimkou rozsáhlejších souborů dobových autorských zvětšenin v Uměleckoprůmyslovém museu v Praze a v Moravské galerii v Brně jde vždy jen o několik snímků. Eugen Wiškovský totiž za svého života příliš nevystavoval, a neměl tedy důvod zhotovovat větší počet výstavních zvětšenin. Proto jsou dnes originály jeho fotografií mimořádně vzácné a ve veřejných i soukromých sbírkách je jich nesrovnatelně méně než fotografií Františka Drtikola, Josefa Sudka či Jaromíra Funkeho. I to je jedním z důvodů, proč jeho dílo – podobně třeba jako tvorba dalšího významného představitele české avantgardní fotografie Jaroslava Rösslera – zůstávalo a stále ještě zůstává mezinárodně nedoceněné.

I když se Eugen Wiškovský mnoho let intenzivně zabýval fotografií, nikdy se v této oblasti neprofesionalizoval. Nebyl ostatně sám. Vždyť moderní českou fotografii neformovali jenom lidé, kteří se fotografováním živili, jako František Drtikol, Jaroslav Rössler či Josef Sudek, ale i progresivní fotoamatéři – třeba lékař Drahomír Josef Růžička, chemici Jan Lauschmann a Jiří Sever, nebo voják Jiří Jeníček. Ostatně fotoamatérem bez fotografického vzdělání byl i nejvýznamnější představitel české fotografické avantgardy Jaromír Funke, jenž se začal fotografií živit až jako pedagog Školy uměleckých řemesel v Bratislavě. Zatímco třeba ve Spojených státech nebo v Německu vývoj meziválečné fotografie posouvali kupředu především profesionální fotografové a výtvarníci, v Československu řadu významných fotografií vytvořili autoři, kteří si z různých důvodů zachovávali postavení fotoamatérů.

Patřil k nim i Eugen Wiškovský, který se po většinu svého života živil jako středoškolský profesor a fotografování a psaní o fotografii se věnoval jen jako své zálibě (jedinými výjimkami byl kalendář pro farmaceutickou firmu Interfarma a soubor pohlednic květin).

Narodil se 20. září 1888 ve Dvoře Králové nad Labem ve vážené středostavovské rodině – otec Alois Wiškovský byl správcem královdvorské nemocnice, matka Eugenie Wiškovská, rozená Hotovcová, byla dcerou okresního hejtmana. Měl tři bratry – o rok staršího Aloise a mladší sourozence Otakara a Bedřicha, kteří se narodili v ročních intervalech po něm. Všichni čtyři bratři získali vysokoškolské vzdělání. Eugen absolvoval gymnázium ve Dvoře Králové a v roce 1906 začal studovat francouzštinu, němčinu a psychologii na Filosofické fakultě české Karlo-Ferdinandovy univerzity v Praze. Zimní semestr v posledním školním roce 1909–1910 strávil jako stipendista na univerzitě v Ženevě. Po ukončení univerzity se mnoho let věnoval výuce na různých středních školách, nejdéle na Státním reálném gymnáziu v Kolíně, kde učil až do roku 1937 s přestávkou během první světové války, kdy bojoval v řadách rakousko-uherské armády na italské a ruské frontě a po dvojím zranění působil u týlového vojska v České Lípě. V dubnu 1917 se oženil s tehdy třiadvacetiletou Annou Streitovou, v roce 1918 se jim narodila dcera Eva (1918–1997), o rok později druhá dcera Hana (1919–1985).

Eugen Wiškovský byl vzdělaný muž mnoha talentů a zájmů: věnoval se reformě vyučování cizích jazyků na středních školách, byl spoluautorem česko-německého slovníku, spolupracoval s Alliance Française, zabýval se psychologií, působil v České psychologické společnosti, překládal symbolistická díla Maurice Maeterlincka i Freudovy a Jungovy psychologické spisy, měl hluboký zájem o literaturu a výtvarné umění, závodně hrál tenis, věnoval se plavání, bruslení, atletice a tábornictví. Na Wiškovského pedagogické působení na kolínském gymnáziu později vzpomínal jeho bývalý žák Anastáz Opasek, arciopat břevnovského kláštera v Praze, ve své knize Dvanáct zastavení: *„Byl* *to jedinečný pedagog. Mám na něho skutečně skvělé vzpomínky a myslím, že nejen já, ale i ostatní studenti. (...) S inspektory a školním dozorem měl stálé konflikty. Neměl například notes, nýbrž jen seznam žáků. Přišel do třídy, od dveří hodil knihu na stůl – schválně, jestli se mu to povede –, sedl si na lavici a hned s námi začal mluvit francouzsky. Dobře se poznalo, že nějakou dobu strávil ve Francii. Jednal s námi jako otec s vlastními dětmi. Někdy byl vzteklý, protože to měl v povaze, ale nikdy nikomu neublížil, nebyl pedant, nebyl byrokrat. Měl potíže i proto, že byl sportovec, že pěstoval závodně lehkou atletiku.*“[1]

Zájem o fotografii zdědil Eugen Wiškovský po otci. Už jako chlapec používal pro různé rodinné snímky otcovu kameru na negativy formátu 13 × 18 cm. Ve čtrnácti či v patnácti letech dostal pohotovější fotografický přístroj na desky o rozměrech 9 × 12 cm, ale fotografování postupně ustupovalo před jinými zálibami. Znovu se k fotografii na čas vrátil ke konci 1. světové války, kdy vytvářel portréty své ženy a první dcery. Vážněji se však fotografickou tvorbou začal zabývat až koncem 20. let, kdy se v Kolíně sblížil se svým bývalým žákem z gymnázia Jaromírem Funkem (1896–1945), jenž už tehdy patřil k nejvýznamnějším představitelům české fotografické avantgardy. Wiškovský o mnoho let později na spolupráci s Funkem vzpomínal v dopise Anně Fárové z října 1962: „*Ne že by mi něco teoreticky vysvětlil – na to on nebyl. Nerad se ústně o tom, co dělá, vyjadřoval. Byl to u něho jakýsi ostych kvůli malé vadě v řeči, ale také protože se nechtěl o věci šířit, když já byl v plném experimentování. Chodívali jsme spolu do terénu, na stavbu elektrárny. Do okolí, na věž Obchodní akademie – a fotografovali tzv. „novou věcnost“ – skládky cementových skruží, kolejnic, mannesmannových vodovodních rour atd. Funke toho brzy nechal, neboť viděl, že se na to specialisuji, také to dělal realističtěji než já. Nejvíce mi pomohlo, že jsem – nemaje tehdy zvětšovák – s ním v jeho temné komoře (koupelně) zvětšoval naše zdařilé negativy. Jednak jsem se přiučil zvětšovací technice a dobré komposici, jednak jsem na těchto celkem prostých geometrických formách poznával onu abstrahující schopnost černobílé fotografie, která vyloučením barev zdůrazňuje tvar (a o tvar jedině, ne o barvu, se mi jednalo jako každému introvertovanému člověku). Byly to čisté motivy, kde bylo velmi snadné vyloučit rušivé, nesourodé prvky. Zde šlo o tvar pozměněný optikou spíše krátkého ohniska, kde rovnoběžky rour nebo kolejnic se sbíhaly do jednoho bodu a vytvářely plošné obrazce.*“[2] Znal se také s dalším slavným fotografem z Kolína a Funkeho vrstevníkem Josefem Sudkem (1896–1976). Zatímco však k Funkemu měl blízko intelektuálně i společensky (oba patřili k váženým místním občanům), Sudkovo záměrně akcentované plebejství zejména v počátcích tvořilo určitou hráz. Sám Sudek později odpověděl v rozhovoru s Jaroslavem Andělem, zda se stýkal s Wiškovským: *„Poměrně málo. S ním se stýkal hlavně Funke. S Wiškovským to bylo tak: Když já jsem chodil ještě s Funkem fotografovat v Kolíně, Funke hrál tenis a Wiškovský taky. On nás viděl fotografovat, taky k tomu čuchl a od té doby začal fotografovat. Jeho oblast byla v Kolíně, a když byl v Praze, tak v Hlubočepích. On měl taky zaměření víc literární. Inteligentní pán to byl. Spíše se stýkal s Ehmem než se mnou, to je zajímavý.“*[3]

Eugen Wiškovský se už ve svých raných dílech z přelomu 20. a 30. let projevil jako originální tvůrce. I když se sporadicky účastnil činnosti kolínského fotoklubu, typické fotoamatérské aktivity, jako byly diskuse o nejlepších vývojkách či horlivé obesílání různých fotosalónů a honba za medailemi, mu byly cizí. Zato se už v květnu 1930 zúčastnil výstavy *Nová česká fotografie* v Aventinské mansardě v Praze, uspořádané po vzoru slavné přehlídky moderní fotografie Film a foto ve Stuttgartu z roku 1929 mladým fotografem a filmařem Alexandrem Hackenschmiedem a jeho přáteli. Wiškovského snímky se na tomto prvním společném vystoupení české fotografické avantgardy v Praze ocitly v sousedství děl Jaromíra Funkeho, Jaroslava Rösslera, Jiřího Lehovce, Ladislava Emila Berky či Josefa Sudka i řady vědeckých fotografií. O rok později vystavoval v podobné expozici na stejném místě, v roce 1933 byl zastoupen na *Mezinárodní výstavě sociální fotografie* v Praze, uspořádané Film-foto skupinou Levé fronty, a o tři roky později bylo pět jeho snímků (Izolátor, Detail turbíny, Zbytky ledu, Šalování a Spodek antény v Liblicích) přijato na *Mezinárodní výstavu fotografie* v pražském Mánesu, kde se ocitly vedle děl Man Raye, Lászla Moholy-Nagye, Hanse Bellmera, Raoula Hausmanna, Alexandra Rodčenka a dalších předních reprezentantů světové fotografické avantgardy. Přestože však Wiškovského práce byly vystavovány ve významných expozicích avantgardních fotografií, sám se nikdy nestal členem nějaké avantgardní skupiny. Přispěla k tomu i jeho introvertnost. Nebyl člověkem, který by se vyžíval ve vzrušených uměleckých debatách v kavárnách a vinárnách.

Wiškovský sám uváděl, že kromě kontaktů s Funkem byla pro něj velkou inspirací Man Rayova monografie. Brzy přejal Funkeho nadšení pro tzv. novou fotografii, v níž se uplatňovaly principy konstruktivismu, funkcionalismu a nové věcnosti, i jeho odpor k přežívajícímu impresionistickému a secesnímu piktorialismu, napodobujícímu malířské a grafické vzory, používajícímu olejotisky, bromolejotisky, uhlotisky a další takzvané ušlechtilé tisky a potlačujícímu řadu specifických rysů fotografie. Ve 20. letech byl ve Spojených státech i v mnoha evropských zemích boj mezi tradičními piktorialisty, používajícími tvárné procesy, a zastánci čisté fotografie, propagované Alfredem Stieglitzem, Clarencem Hudsonem Whitem a některými dalšími členy skupiny Fotosecese, dávno dobojován ve prospěch odpůrců ušlechtilých tisků. V Československu se však styl přímé fotografie, odmítající jakékoliv dodatečné zásahy do negativů, prosadil až v roce 1921 na výstavě Čechoameričana Drahomíra Josefa Růžičky, který se řadil k Whiteovým žákům a po jeho vzoru odmítal ušlechtilé tisky. Avšak i potom, kdy mladší čeští fotografové Jaromír Funke, Josef Sudek, Adolf Schneeberger, Jan Lauschmann, Arnošt Pikart a další přijali tuto zásadu, dominovaly v jejich fotografiích piktorialistické žánrové motivy a mnohé záběry akcentovaly světelnou atmosféru i mírné rozostření.

Eugen Wiškovský ve svém prvním významnějším článku o umělecké fotografii, uveřejněném v časopise *Foto* v roce 1929 a nepochybně ovlivněném předchozími teoretickými texty Jaromíra Funkeho, jednoznačně odmítl snahy o napodobování malířských vzorů a akcentoval specifičnost fotografie, o níž napsal: *„Má-li však míti vůbec nějaké oprávnění, musí její výtvory dosahovati svého účelu takovým způsobem, jehož nelze docíliti žádnou jinou technikou nežli fotografickou.“*[4] Shodně s názory ruských konstruktivistů a německých funkcionalistů kladl důraz na hledání nových estetických hodnot ve zdánlivě nefotogenických objektech moderní technické civilizace. *„Ať to jsou stroje nebo stavby, nábytek nebo šaty, mají vždy charakter účelné jednoduchosti prosté všeho ornamentu. A jsou nám tím milejší, čím více odpovídají svými čistými formami určitým základním tvarům geometrickým.“*[5]

Tato slova Wiškovský napsal v době, kdy stál na počátku své seriózní fotografické tvorby a měl na svém kontě jenom několik výrazných děl. Přesto i ta dokonale naplňují principy nové věcnosti, směru, jehož představitelé Karl Blossfeldt, Albert Renger-Patzsch, Charles Sheeler, Paul Strand, Edward Weston a další obrátili pozornost na fotograficky co nejdokonalejší i nejpůsobivější vyjádření podstatných rysů zobrazených objektů, na objevování estetických kvalit ve zdánlivě zcela neestetických objektech, v oblasti formy pak na maximální ostrost a tonální bohatství fotografického obrazu. Nová věcnost, jejíž podstatné rysy se objevily v německé či americké fotografii už kolem první světové války, stála v opozici k romantismu, lyričnosti, sentimentalitě i časté vyumělkovanosti impresionistického a secesního piktorialismu. Také v české fotografii 20. let už měla několik výrazných představitelů, zejména Jaromíra Funkeho, Josefa Sudka, Jaroslava Rösslera a Jana Lauschmanna, k nimž se v následující dekádě připojili mnozí další, například Josef Ehm, Vladimír Hipman, Jindřich Hatlák, Jaroslava Hatláková, Marie Rossmannová, Jindřich (Heinrich) Koch, Josef Voříšek, Emil Vepřek či Karel Kašpařík.

Na přelomu 20. a 30. let mohl Wiškovský bezprostředně navázat na Funkeho snímky fragmentů ozubených kol či plechových sudů i na obecné nadšení řady avantgardních tvůrců z moderní technické civilizace. Ve svých zdánlivě jednoduchých, ve skutečnosti však neobyčejně pečlivě promyšlených a kompozičně vycizelovaných fotografiích rour, svazků železných prutů, šroubů, elektrických izolátorů, sít nebo detailů turbín, žárovek či hmoždířů nacházel výtvarně působivé tvary. Mnohokrát viděné obyčejné objekty, které často nalézal doma nebo na stavbě kolínské elektrárny, ukazoval nově a neotřele, překvapoval diváky a usvědčoval jejich zrak z únavy a otupělosti. Dokonale promyšleně užíval velkých detailů, vytrhujících zobrazené objekty z obvyklých prostorových souvislostí a mnohdy rovněž měnících perspektivu a měřítko. Hlavní motiv oprošťoval převodem z barevného originálu do černobílé fotografie, výřezem a mistrovskou prací se světlem od zbytečných podružností a nechával tak vyniknout nejdůležitějším liniím a tónům. Často užíval zmnožení a rytmické opakování některých linií nebo celých předmětů, jak to můžeme vidět například na snímcích vajíček, vlnitého plechu, keramických rour nebo vřeten s vlnou. S mimořádnou nápaditostí, výtvarným citem a technickou precizností tak realizoval své přesvědčení, že *„čím méně nevšední je obsah, tím nevšednější musí být způsob jeho předvedení"*.[6] Wiškovského fotografie ve stylu nové věcnosti jsou přísně racionální a současně plné fantazie. Prolíná se v nich objektivita dokonalého zobrazení detailů okolního světa se subjektivitou autorova pohledu, jeho osobitého vidění, myšlení a cítění, intelektu, vnitřního světa. Výrazně se liší od skutečnosti, kterou zobrazují, realita je v nich výtvarně ozvláštněna, jsou to svébytná umělecká díla s jasně rozeznatelným autorským rukopisem. Wiškovský si vybíral a fotografoval takové objekty, kterými mohl vyjádřit svou představu. Psal: *„Fotografie dělá viditelným neviditelné, totiž to, co fotograf cítil při pohledu na objekt a co chce, aby pozorovatel pocítil při pohledu na fotografii."*[7]

Ve Wiškovského díle vždy převládala kvalita nad kvantitou. Jistě k tomu přispěla i skutečnost, že i v době nástupu lehkých kamer Leica na kinofilm 24×36 cm většinou pracoval s fotoaparátem Ica Ideal s objektivem Tessar 4,5/105 na negativy formátu 6,5×9 cm. Původně fotografoval na skleněné desky (podle svědectví jeho přítele Josefa Ehma měl jenom dvanáct kazet, takže při fotografických výpravách musel velmi šetřit materiálem),[8] později si pořídil rollkazetu Rolex na film. Měl také jednookou čtvercovou zrcadlovkou Ensign-Special-Reflex na desky formátu 9×9 cm, osazenou objektivem Aldis-Butcher 4,5/5 palců, která je dnes ve sbírkách Národního technického muzea v Praze (s tou pořídil například řadu snímků architektury kolínské elektrárny).[9] Už vzhledem k těmto málo pohotovým přístrojům se zaměřoval především na statické motivy, a snímky lidí pořizoval spíše výjimečně. Pokud se na jeho fotografiích objevovali lidé, měli většinou jenom roli stafáže v krajině či v městském prostředí nebo v konstruktivistických kompozicích. Výjimkou jsou portréty manželky, dcer a přátel, experimentální portréty využívající hry světel a stínů (například Portrét komponisty, 1930, či o dva roky mladší bezejmenný portrét dívky, na jejíž tvář dopadá stín sítě), záběry hrajících si dětí, snímky z trampských táborů či v jeho tvorbě zcela ojedinělý soubor reportážních záběrů z Pražského povstání.

Wiškovského fotografií z období nové věcnosti není mnoho a navíc často zobrazují různé pohledy na stejné objekty. Wiškovský se na rozdíl od Funkeho k jednotlivým motivům často znovu vracel a fotografoval je tak dlouho, dokud nebyl s výsledkem spokojen. Zatímco o Funkovi se traduje, že nepořídil technicky kvalitnější záběr surrealistické fotografie z cyklu Čas trvá, konfrontující barokní sochu anděla z kolínského hřbitova s komínem elektrárny, protože pro něj už byla tato fotografie hotova, ve Wiškovského pozůstalosti najdeme někdy i více než deset negativů s různými variantami téhož snímku, mnohdy pořízenými i ve větších časových odstupech. Wiškovský prý přitom podle vzpomínek jeho dcer i přítele Josefa Ehma často záběr připravoval celé hodiny, mnohdy si také vyšel s fotoaparátem a neudělal jedinou fotografii.

Jeho „definitivní" snímky ve stylu nové věcnosti nepochybně patří k tomu nejlepšímu, co v této oblasti v české fotografii vzniklo. K typickým rysům patří pevný řád a invenční obrazová skladba, potlačující podružné prvky. Wiškovský byl přesvědčen, že *„krása není naprostou jednoduchostí, nýbrž zjednodušenou složitostí."*[10] Přes veškerou racionalitu a formální mistrovství mu často nešlo jenom o výtvarně nevšední zobrazení jednoduchých a mnohdy zdánlivě neestetických předmětů a řešení problematiky obrazového minima či vztahů celků a detailů, ale i o fotografické vyjádření předmětných vztahů stejně jako vlastního dojmu z nich a nezřídka i o hledání tvarových analogů a metaforických významů. Nejednou se mu podařilo překonat strohý optimální popis skutečnosti, jaký je typický třeba pro mnohé práce Alberta Rengera-Patzsche, Aenne Biermannové a dalších významných představitelů nové věcnosti, a vytvořit symboličtěji vyznívající fotografie, jejichž metaforičnost má v některých aspektech blízko třeba k fotografiím mušlí nebo artyčoků od Edwarda Westona. Objekty na některých Wiškovského fotografiích jsou zobrazeny se záměrnou ztrátou své identity. Tvarové analogy a metafory nenajdeme ve všech Wiškovského snímcích, ale v některých hrají důležitou roli (například záběr vlnitých plechů evokuje obraz rozpuštěných dlouhých vlasů nebo povrchu mušle, fotografie rytmicky poskládaných vajíček připomíná rybí šupiny, detail cukrovarnického odpadu na špinavé vodě může sugerovat mapu jižní Asie i arabesku apod). Nejvýraznější je to u fotografie Měsíční krajina (uváděné i pod strohým názvem Límce) z roku 1929, tedy ze samotných začátků jeho vážné fotografické tvorby. Kompozice s tvrdými košilovými límci byla transformována prostřednictvím potlačení měřítka, izolování opakujících se detailů, důmyslného osvětlení s žárovkou položenou mezi límci a přidáním obrysu mince, položené v pozdější variantě snímku na fotografický papír coby obraz Země, v imaginativní obraz měsíčního povrchu s krátery. Sám o tomto mnohokrát publikovaném snímku napsal: *„Límce mne přivedly na možnost dvojího smyslu fotografie: vlastního a metaforického. Odpadnutí barvy a zjednodušení zrakového vjemu promítnutím do roviny formátu umožňuje vznik jistých podobností, které barva a plastičnost skutečného vnímání zastíraly. Tyto podobnosti se i při realistickém podání námětu nedají odmítnout, má-li člověk jen trochu fantasie.“*[11] Jindy možnosti metaforické fotografie definoval takto: *„Záleží v tom, že záběrem je zdůrazněna podobnost zobrazeného objektu s objektem jiným, který je však typickým pramenem citu, jejž fotografie má vyvolat. Zdůrazněním této podobnosti se evokační síla námětu zvyšuje.“*[12]

Začátkem 30. let Wiškovský kromě detailů drobných předmětů často fotografoval i novostavbu elektrárny ESSO v Kolíně. Moderní funkcionalistická architektura Jaroslava Fragnera mu poskytla řadu motivů neobvyklých fotografií, často využívajících po vzoru Alexandra Rodčenka, El Lisického či Lászla Moholy-Nagye výrazných podhledů nebo dynamických kompozic do úhlopříčky. Stejnou stavbu několikrát fotografoval také Josef Sudek, stejně jako absolvent Bauhausu Jindřich (Heinrich) Koch, jejichž záběry však jsou daleko statičtější a klasičtěji komponované. Velmi blízko k Wiškovského konstruktivistickým záběrům měly fotografie Jaromíra Funkeho, jenž nezřídka svého staršího přítele na fotografických výpravách na staveniště elektrárny doprovázel.

Snímky obou těchto fotografů byl ilustrován Fragnerův článek o elektrárně ESSO, publikovaný ve 4. čísle Volných směrů v roce 1931. Některé jejich diagonální záběry elektrárenského komína jsou tak podobné, že u nich bývá obtížné na první pohled určit autorství. Při podrobnějším zkoumání je však zřejmé, že Wiškovský více akcentoval geometričnost základních prvků konstrukce stavby, více pracoval s detaily a vytvořil i nejoriginálnější záběr – do kosočtverce komponovaný snímek továrního komína s jeho odrazem v hladině řeky. Zatímco paralely snímků fotografovaných z výrazných podhledů a z nezvyklých úhlů najdeme v ruském konstruktivismu i v německém funkcionalismu, kosočtvercový záběr se symetrickým zobrazením továrny a jejího odrazu je skutečným solitérem. Je to nejvýmluvnější příklad toho, že Wiškovský nebyl jenom moderním zobrazovatelem moderní architektury, ale také jejím interpretem. Současně však jde také o důkaz, že samotná architektura mu často byla jenom východiskem a inspirací pro volnou tvorbu, v níž příliš nezáleželo na tom, jaká konkrétní stavba je na fotografii zachycena. O tom ostatně svědčí i další Wiškovského záběry z prostředí elektrárny, například snímky, které z nadhledu konfrontují detaily kovových konstrukcí, lidské postavy a ostré vržené stíny. Některé připomínající fotografie z Eiffelovy věže od Andrého Kertésze a zapadají do kontextu zájmu řady avantgardních fotografů o motivy moderních kovových rozhleden a rozhlasových vysílačů, jak je známe třeba z děl Alexandra Rodčenka, Lászla Moholy-Nagye, Germaine Krullové či Jaroslava Rösslera.

Pro Funkeho ani pro Wiškovského nebyla kolínská elektrárna jedinou funkcionalistickou stavbou, kterou zobrazovali. Funke je například autorem fotografií pro publikaci o Masarykově studentském domově v Brně, navrženém dalším protagonistou českého funkcionalismu Bohumilem Fuchsem,[13] a zachycoval z neobvyklých úhlů pohledu i jiné funkcionalistické stavby v Bratislavě, Kolíně nebo v Praze. Wiškovský vytvořil třeba přímo ukázkovou fotografii novostavby činžovního domu Funkcionalistická architektura a několik záběrů s motivem koupaliště, navrženého Václavem Kolátorem, a restaurací Terasy na Barrandově, postavených podle návrhu architekta Maxe Urbana. Toto fotogenické místo s kavárenskými stolky nad plaveckým bazénem patřilo k nejoblíbenějším motivům meziválečných českých fotografů. Různým způsobem ho fotografovali Josef Sudek, Drahomír Josef Růžička, Josef Ehm, Jan Lauschmann, Jaromír Funke, Arnošt Pikart, Julius Tutsch a další.[14] Zatímco však většina z nich zobrazovala z nadhledu půlkruhy vytvořené stoly a slunečníky a někteří, jako třeba Růžička či Lauschmann, dokonce ještě použili lyrizující jemné rozostření, Wiškovský zdůraznil kontrast mezi terasou a pod ní ležící plovárnou, v němž docílil pronikavé změny perspektivy a měřítka. Žádný jiný fotograf nevytěžil z tohoto prostředí radikálnější záběry, vystihující samotnou podstatu moderní architektury a v obecnější rovině i moderní doby. Konstruktivistické kompozice se ovšem objevovaly i v jiných Wiškovského fotografiích, například ve známém snímku Hra (jindy Děti na schodech) z roku 1929, zachycujícím z nadhledu jeho dvě dcery sedící na úhlopříčně zobrazeném schodišti, v nepublikovaném snímku zeshora snímaných chlapců vyhazujících mince nebo v neobvyklé kompozici Kánoe, u níž se můžeme dohadovat, zda se v její latentní erotické metaforice projevila skutečnost, že Wiškovský překládal spisy Sigmunda Freuda.

V roce 1937 se Wiškovský se svou rodinou přestěhoval do Prahy, kde postupně učil na reálce v Ječné ulici a na dívčím reálném gymnáziu v Libni. V Praze se dál stýkal s Funkem, který tam od září 1935 vyučoval fotografii na Státní grafické škole. Spřátelil se i s jeho kolegou Josefem Ehmem (1909–1989), dalším významným fotografem, autorem technicky precizních snímků architektury a soch, klasických krajin, reprezentativních portrétů i experimentálnějších děl vycházejících z principů nové věcnosti a reagujících i na surrealismus. Josef Ehm mi o svém přátelství s Wiškovským řekl: *„Mezi námi byl dvacetiletý věkový rozdíl. Netykali jsme si, ale já mu nesměl říkat pane profesore, jenom pane, a on mi říkal Ehme. Scházeli jsme se většinou v sobotu nebo v neděli, mnohdy i s manželkami. On měl dost komplikovaný vztah k životu a trpíval depresivními stavy, kvůli nimž se také léčil. Často jsme spolu chodili na procházky. Měl potřebu mít někoho, s kým by si mohl popovídat o svých trablech a o fotografii. Bylo to velice cenné přátelství a hodně jsem z něho těžil. Zase jsem to Wiškovskému trochu vracel v tom, že jsem byl technicky daleko fundovanější než on. On sám většinou zvětšoval do formátu pohlednice a často za mnou přišel, abych mu nějaký snímek zvětšil na výstavu. Některé jeho negativy jsem také upravoval zeslabovačem, i když on a Funke tvrdili, že negativ je nedotknutelný.“*[15]

Zatímco v maloměstském prostředí Kolína Wiškovský fotografoval hlavně industriální objekty, detaily technických předmětů a moderní architekturu, v Praze se začal poněkud paradoxně zabývat především krajinářskou fotografií. Měl v tomto směru už určité zkušenosti, vždyť například jeho mistrovsky komponovaná fotografie polní cesty u Police nad Metují vznikla už před rokem 1933 a diagonálně zobrazený nadhled na Sázavu se skautským táborem o rok později. Svůj zájem o krajinářskou fotografii později zdůvodnil v článku Proč fotografujeme krajiny: „*Krajina, půda, země nás přitahuje právě tím, co je v ní trvalého proti prchavosti a měnivosti všeho ostatního v našem životě. Je to pro nás největším zadostiučiněním a největší útěchou, nalezneme-li v ní souhlas se svým nitrem. Je stejně jako ono mnohotvárná a má idylická zákoutí pro blaženého snílka, tak jako rozbouřené moře a skalní útesy pro romantického rozervance.*“[16] V krajinářských snímcích, v nichž zdůrazňoval subjektivní autorský přínos, ho zajímaly hlavně jednoduché základní linie, neobvyklé struktury povrchu a fantaskní obrazy. Za svými motivy nemusel jezdit do cizích zemí, ale obvykle hledal na několika málo místech, kam chodil celá léta a jež důvěrně znal. Především to byly Hlubočepy na západním okraji Prahy, které svými malebnými skalami a Prokopským údolím přitahovaly i mnohé jiné fotografy. Také Wiškovský fotografoval monumentální hlubočepské skály v romantickém podvečerním osvětlení, ale ještě častěji zobrazoval jejich detaily zbavené reálného měřítka, v nichž objevoval přírodní skulptury, geometrické tvary a někdy i metaforicky vyznívající tvarové analogy. Zaujaly ho rovněž tamní terénní nerovnosti a bizarní tvary polí, které ve svých fotografiích akcentoval plastickým osvětlením. (Některé z těchto snímků mají velmi blízko k Funkeho krajinářským fotografiím z okolí Kolína a Loun). Jedny a tytéž krajinářské motivy s velkou trpělivostí fotografoval znovu a znovu, dokud nebyl spokojen s obrazovou skladbou, zpodobením struktury a se zachycením světelné nálady. K dalším místům, která v Praze a jejím okolí Wiškovský s oblibou fotografoval, patřila oblast jinonické Vidoule, v níž našel například motiv pole a polní cesty, připomínající z nadhledu svým tvarem vlající prapor s žerdí. Ve většině případů šlo o krajiny výrazně přetvořené lidmi, které dokumentují vztah člověka a přírody.

Nejoriginálnější Wiškovského krajinářské snímky vznikly kolem smíchovského statku Šalamounka. Malý krajinný úsek s kopcem a domem tam Wiškovský fotografoval v mnoha obměnách: jednou ho zaujaly vrstevnicové řádky posečené trávy, podruhé geometrické tvary kupek sena a jindy zase hrozivě vyhlížející stín vedlejšího kopce, který vytvářel přeludný symbolický obraz. Vrcholem Wiškovského krajinářského díla je metaforický snímek slehlého obilného pole s vyčnívající střechou statku, sugerující obraz potápějící se lodi na rozbouřeném moři. Toto téměř surrealistické prolnutí reality a imaginární vize ještě umocňuje název Katastrofa, pod nímž ovšem byla fotografie publikována až později (původní název byl Obilí). I když Katastrofa vznikla pravděpodobně už v roce 1939 (a nikoliv v roce 1943, jak byla datována v souboru pohlednic Eugena Wiškovského, vydaném Orbisem v roce 1963) nebo 1940, jak je uvedeno v první Wiškovského monografii z roku 1964 (svědčí o tom tvrzení Josefa Ehma i skutečnost, že snímek slehlého vysokého obilí byl publikován v červencovém čísle Fotografického obzoru v roce 1940) a nepatří tak k dílům vzniklým přímo během druhé světové války. Je ale možné, že při jeho vzniku sehrála svou roli dusná doba konce demokratického Československa a obavy z vypuknutí děsivého válečného konfliktu. Podobná interpretace se ostatně nabízí u snímku Krajina u Prahy, zachycujícího útočící oválný stín sousedního kopce a otištěného v červnovém čísle Fotografického obzoru ve stejném roce (ostatně později byla tato fotografie uváděna s názvem Stín), ale také u méně známé fotografie Přízraky z roku 1939, zobrazující detail obývacího pokoje s dvěma křesly zahalenými do bílé látky a sugerujícími dojem opouštění důvěrně známých a blízkých věcí. Jsou to také doklady, že Wiškovský byl v některých dílech inspirován surrealismem daleko více, než se v souvislosti s jeho tvorbou většinou uvádí.

Přelom 30. a 40. let byl nejvýznamnějším obdobím Wiškovského teoretické činnosti.[17] Přispěli k tomu především jeho přátelé Ehm a Funke. Ehm se v říjnu 1939 stal novým šéfredaktorem časopisu Fotografický obzor, k jehož redigování přizval Jaromíra Funkeho. Postupně se jim podařilo z tohoto konzervativního měsíčníku Svazu českých klubů fotografů amatérů vytvořit moderně koncipovaný odborný časopis, jehož náklad se během krátké doby zvýšil z původních 4000 výtisků na téměř čtyřnásobek. Zásluhu na tom měl i Wiškovský, který tehdy publikoval ve Fotografickém obzoru nejen řadu svých fotografií, ale také čtyři originální teoretické stati: Tvar a motiv, Desorientace názorů na fotografii, Zobrazení, projev, sdělení a Oproštěním k projevu, které spolu s texty Jaromíra Funkeho a Karla Teigeho vytvořily základ moderní české teorie fotografie. Wiškovský se v nich (podobně jako v několika dalších článcích publikovaných v letech 1946–1948) poprvé pokusil odvodit zásady skladby fotografického obrazu z průběhu vnímání na základě tvarové psychologie, zabýval se otázkami smyslu fotografie a snažil se využít poznatků teorie informace pro výstavbu nového systému teorie fotografie. Svou hloubkou, originalitou a formulační precizností byly tyto články v tehdejší české fotografické publicistice natolik ojedinělé, že zůstaly širší fotografickou veřejností nepochopeny a na své ocenění čekaly celé desítky let. Současně je však třeba uvést, že se v nich i v dalších Wiškovského statích někdy opakují jinak formulované stejné myšlenky, například o tom, že kvalitní fotografie je zrakovým dobrodružstvím se zárukou skutečnosti (přitom právě toto Wiškovským tolikrát uváděné divákovo přesvědčení o tom, že zobrazené je skutečnost, zcela zpochybnil nedávný nástup digitálních technologií).

Nejzávažnější z Wiškovského teoretických textů je Tvar a motiv, publikovaný v říjnovém čísle Fotografického obzoru z roku 1940. Wiškovský v něm řeší otázku obrazové kvality snímků a jejího působení na diváka z hlediska percepce. Aplikuje zde různé poznatky tvarové psychologie, především prioritu celku před částmi. Tento princip byl znám už z díla Über Gestaltqualitäten (O celostních kvalitách) od průkopníka tvarové psychologie, rakouského psychologa a filosofa, profesora německé univerzity v Praze Christiana von Ehrenfelse, ale v oblasti teorie fotografie ho důsledně uplatnil až Wiškovský. Ve svém textu Wiškovský píše: *„Chceme-li tedy proniknout k podstatným znakům motivu, vyjděme od nepopiratelné a všeobecně uznávané zásady, že dobrá fotografie musí být jednotným celkem. Použijeme-li tu nazírání a terminologie tzv. psychologie celků, řekneme, že musí býti útvarem (tvarem), tj. mnohotným členěným celkem, jehož jednotlivé části, samy o sobě nesamostatné, jsou vzájemně spojeny pevnou vnitřní vazbou (proti pouhé mnohosti, koexistenci, náhodnému shluku jednotlivin.“*[18] Hlavní autorův podíl na realizaci snímku tkví ve volbě námětu a v jeho fotografické transfiguraci v motiv. *„Motiv je případ skutečné zrakové neobvyklosti (nebo fotografem na hotovém tisku předvídané), kterou lze fotograficky isolovati a tím stupňovati k dojmu překvapivosti na pozadí naprosté reálnosti, vytvořeném dobře podanou strukturou.“* Sám motivy dělí do tří základních skupin: na motivy, u nichž jde o nevšednost čistě vnější, zrakovou, tvarovou, jako je mnohost, stejnost, pravidelnost, pohyb a tvarová vyhraněnost, dále na motivy, jejichž odlišnost od běžného vidění vzniká ze specifických možností fotografické techniky, například perspektivního zkreslení kratšími ohnisky objektivů, velké hloubky ostrosti, změny valérů černobílé škály použitím barevných filtrů, velikosti dosažené zvětšením či zmenšením zorného pole či nezvyklých úhlů pohledu, a konečně na motivy, jejichž nevšednost tkví v pocitu novosti vyplývajícího z jiných citových obsahů, kam patří třeba obrazové metafory, zdůrazňující podobnost zobrazeného objektu s jiným objektem či konfrontace dvou prvků, z jejichž spojení vyplyne symbol, v němž si nějak odporují. Pouze motivy třetí skupiny mají primární závislost na autorovi. V závěru stati Wiškovský píše: *„...proměnění je vlastní podstatou estetické fotografie. Transfigurace, ne však defigurace skutečnosti. Transfigurace, tj. oproštění, očištění skuteč-*

nosti ode všeho zbytečného a nevhodného, co by defigurovalo obraz naší myšlenky – motivu – který se má jasně odraziti v zrcadle fotografie.“[19] Ve stati Tvar a motiv Wiškovský předjímal pozdější pokusy aplikovat poznatky tvarové psychologie na oblast výtvarného umění, jaké vytvořil například německý teoretik filmu Rudolf Arnheim ve své knize Art and Visual Perception (Umění a vizuální vnímání) z roku 1954. Přes veškerou originalitu, myšlenkovou hloubku a formulační preciznost nebyl tento zásadní Wiškovského text přijat jednoznačně kladně, jak dokazuje třeba kritika šéfredaktora časopisu Fotografie Karla Hermanna v článku Učme se dívat fotograficky,[20] na kterou Wiškovský rychle reagoval ve stati Desorientace názoru na fotografii.[21]

Ehm s Funkem vedli Fotografický obzor velmi kvalitně a odvážně a ještě v listopadu 1940, tedy v době, kdy dávno platil oficiální německý pohled na tvorbu avantgardy jako na zvrhlé umění, se jim podařilo vydat speciální číslo věnované experimentální fotografii. Začátkem roku 1941 se však vzhledem k sílícím denunciantským projevům přímo z řad některých českých fotografů jeho redigování vzdali, a Wiškovský tak přišel až do konce války o publikační platformu pro své teoretické články. Dál však fotografoval. Pokračoval v abstrahujících detailech hlubočepských skal i v dalších variacích snímků s motivy statku Šalamounka, vytvářel téměř impresionistické záběry políček nad Prokopským údolím, v nichž pozdně odpolední či podvečerní světlo zvýrazňovalo jejich vlnitý terén, fotografoval stromy v protisvětle, které je vydělovalo z okolí, zobrazoval pražskou architekturu. Na samém konci války, během Pražského povstání v květnu 1945, vytvořil reportážní snímky ze stavby a obrany barikád a z nucených prací německých žen a kolaborantek těsně po skončení války, které jsou výjimečné v kontextu jeho vesměs staticky orientované tvorby. Jde však o popisnější záběry bez větší dramatičnosti, které neobstojí ve srovnání s daleko dynamičtějšími a emotivně působivějšími snímky stejných událostí od řady jiných českých fotografů. Tématu války je také věnován – kromě už zmíněných výjimečných živých snímků z výstavby barikád – symbolický snímek Po náletu, zachycující ohnutý kříž na haldě sutin.

V krátkém období relativní svobody a demokracie mezi koncem druhé světové války a komunistickým převratem v únoru 1948 Wiškovský publikoval další teoretické články v časopisech Fotografie, Československá fotografie a Zpravodaj fotografů. Paralelně s jeho teoretickými texty vznikaly i další krajinářské snímky z prostředí Hlubočep, statické záběry z pražského prostředí nebo detaily různých přírodních motivů, například známý snímek Kaštany. Tehdy se také zúčastnil několika významných skupinových expozic, především výstavy Moderní fotografie v Československu, která byla premiérově uvedena od konce července 1947 v Uměleckoprůmyslovém sdružení ve Vídni a později reprízována v Curychu. Šlo o reprezentativní přehlídku děl předních českých a slovenských tvůrců, k níž nakladatelství Orbis vydalo katalog se 24 reprodukcemi a textem Karla Teigeho, podávajícím nárys vývoje československé fotografie. Wiškovský byl rovněž zastoupen na 4. mezinárodním fotografickém salonu v Praze v roce 1948, jenž byl reprízován v Brně, Bratislavě a Ostravě. Jeho snímky se v roce 1947 objevily v knize Jiřího Jeníčka Fotografie jako zření světa a života, devatenáct Wiškovského fotografií včetně známého Praporu nebo záběru z restaurací Terasy na Barrandově – ale také snímků z tenisového utkání na Štvanici nebo z doktorské promoce v Karolinu – bylo zařazeno do knihy Josefa Ehma a V. V. Štecha s patetickým názvem Krásy plná, slávou i kletbou bohatá... Praho!, kterou v roce 1948 vydala Družstevní práce.

Záhy po nástupu komunistického režimu v Československu v roce 1948 začala být jednostranně preferována propagandistická a agitační role fotografie ve stylu socialistického realismu a pro tvůrčí experimenty ani pro hluboké teoretické stati vycházející z tvarové psychologie nebylo na oficiální fotografické scéně místo. V období nejtvrdšího stalinisticko-gottwaldovského režimu do roku 1953 se dokonce na stránkách fotografického tisku vedly diskuse, zda také krajinářské snímky bez traktorů nejsou buržoazním přežitkem. Wiškovský se tehdy stáhl do soukromí, odešel ze školství i z veřejného fotografického života. O jeho distanci i k umírněnějším projevům marxistické ideologie svědčí třeba ironické poznámky, které si tužkou vepisoval na okraj některých frází z textu Lubomíra Linharta v Sudkově monografii z roku 1956 nebo mnohých článků z tehdejšího časopisu Československá fotografie. Ve své fotografické tvorbě z 50. let se věnoval především práci na rozsáhlém cyklu imaginativních fotografií Ze Starého židovského hřbitova v Praze, kde vyhledával konfrontace rozpadávajících se náhrobků a bizarních tvarů okolních stromů a keřů, v nichž objevoval analogy a kontrasty uměle vytvořeného a přírodního světa. Sám o tom Anně Fárové v roce 1962 napsal: *„Na židovském hřbitově jsem se snažil zastihnout náhrobek v zajímavém osvětlení nebo spojit kámen* *s odumírající přírodou. Zastihl jsem hřbitov ještě v původní podobě – úplně zarostlý trávou, kapradím, keři, před pozdější jeho úpravou, která mnoho pěkných motivů odstranila.*“[22] Mnohdy se rovněž zaměřoval na detaily různých reliéfů a vytesaných nápisů, u nichž akcentoval jejich znakovost a symboličnost. Hřbitovní motivy přitahovaly řadu jiných českých fotografů, například Jindřicha Štyrského, Josefa Sudka, Jaromíra Funkeho, Viléma Kříže, Tibora Hontyho či Jindřicha Broka, ale žádný z nich se jim nevěnoval v takovém rozsahu jako Wiškovský. Přesto však nemají tyto jeho snímky vizuální sílu a objevnost fotografií z období nové věcnosti a konstruktivismu. Mnohé Wiškovského záběry ze Starého židovského hřbitova působí značně popisně a některé motivy se v nich opakují. Stále sice dokládají Wiškovského myšlenkovou hloubku i kompoziční mistrovství, ale současně naznačují autorův sestup z vrcholného období a ubývání jeho schopností objevovat nová zraková dobrodružství.

Eugen Wiškovský v té době fotografoval také historickou architekturu Prahy, květiny, které vyšly na několika pohlednicích, invenčnější abstrahující detaily fíkusových listů nebo citrónů ve vodě i žánrové záběry chodců v parku nebo dětí na vycházce. Vracel se však znovu i ke starým motivům konfrontace přírody a lidských zásahů do ní. V lomu u sv. Prokopa zachycoval kontrapunkty skal a kolejnic, v Hlubočepích konfrontoval romantickou krajinu s nedalekými továrnami a domy. Když mu nemoc (v roce 1958 byl operován pro hypertrofii prostaty a následně prošel těžkým stadiem anaerobní infekce) nedovolovala delší výpravy za krajinářskými motivy, dojížděl ze svého smíchovského bytu v Malátově ulici č. 17 tramvají na Petřín nebo na Karlovo náměstí a tam fotografoval. Na Karlově náměstí vzniklo i několik výtečných záběrů (například odvážná kompozice s fragmentem dvou starých mužů na lavičce nebo poetický snímek pomníku Elišky Krásnohorské pod mohutným akátem), které tvoří důstojné završení jeho fotografického díla. Byl v té době těžce nemocný, širší veřejností zapomenutý a stojící mimo ohniska tehdejšího fotografického života, dál se ale snažil být věrný svému přesvědčení, že *„moderní fotografie by měla spíše být zpodobením nějaké myšlenky nebo nějakého citu pomocí specificky fotografického zobrazení zvolených předmětů, nežli pouhým zachycením těchto předmětů jako takových.“*[23] Jediným výraznějším připomenutím jeho osobnosti, fotografií i teoretických prací byl článek fotografa a publicisty Jiřího Jeníčka v dubnovém čísle Československé fotografie z roku 1957, doprovázený třemi Wiškovského snímky.[24]

V 80. letech jsem intenzivně spolupracoval s oběma dcerami Eugena Wiškovského na přípravě dvou publikací o jejich otci, ale ani jedna z nich nevyšla, protože shodou okolností jak edice bromografických portfolií Mezinárodní fotografie v Pressfotu, tak edice velkých monografií Fotografie – Osobnosti v nakladatelství Panorama zanikly těsně před tím, než v nich uvedené publikace měly vyjít. Jsem rád, že shromážděné materiály našly po tolika letech uplatnění v této malé monografii. Ta by měla být další drobnou splátkou dluhu, kterou historiografie české fotografie vůči Eugenu Wiškovskému má. Jeho dílo dnes už není zapomenuto a v dějinách české fotografie je neopominutelné, na své zasloužené zařazení do mezinárodního kontextu však stále ještě čeká.

Poznámky

1 Opasek, Anastáz: *Dvanáct zastavení*, Praha, Torst 1992, s. 20–21.
2 Dopis Eugena Wiškovského Anně Fárové z října 1962, uložený v archivu Anny Fárové, s. 5.
3 Anděl, Jaroslav: *Josef Sudek o sobě*, Praha, Torst 2001, s. 41.
4 Wiškovský, Eugen: O obrazové fotografii, *Foto*, 1929, č. 12, s. 184.
5 tamtéž, s. 185.
6 Wiškovský, Eugen: Zobrazení, projev, sdělení, *Fotografický obzor*, 1941, č. 1, s. 2.
7 *Eugen Wiškovský o fotografii*. Zápisky v archivu Anny Fárové, kolem roku 1962, s. 2.
8 Rozhovor autora s Josefem Ehmem, Praha 28. 8. 1983.
9 Janda, Jiří: *Kamery obskury. Fotografické přístroje z let 1840–1940*, Praha, Nakladatelství dopravy a spojů 1983, s. 198.
10 Wiškovský, Eugen: *Je fotografie uměním?* Rukopis v archivu Anny Fárové, asi 1962, s. 15.
11 Dopis Eugena Wiškovského Anně Fárové z října 1962, archiv Anny Fárové.
12 Wiškovský, Eugen: Tvar a motiv, *Fotografický obzor*, 1940, č. 10, s. 113.
13 Fuchs, Bohuslav: *Masarykův studentský domov*, Brno, vlastním nákladem 1930.
14 Viz Birgus, Vladimír (ed.): *Česká fotografická avantgarda 1918–1948*, Praha, KANT 1999, s. 128–129, a Anděl, Jaroslav: *Nová vize. Avantgardní architektura v avantgardní fotografii 1918–1938*, Praha, Slovart 2005, s. 182–185.
15 Rozhovor autora s Josefem Ehmem, Praha 28. 8. 1983.
16 Wiškovský, Eugen: Proč fotografujeme krajiny, *Československá fotografie*, 1947, č. 6, s. 81.
17 Viz např.: Anděl, Jaroslav: Teoretické přístupy a interpretace – Eugen Wiškovský, *Československá fotografie*, 1974, č. 1, s. 6–8, č. 2, s. 56–57. – Sobek, Evžen: *Teoretické práce Eugena Wiškovského*, bakalářská diplomová práce, Opava, Institut tvůrčí fotografie FPF Slezské univerzity 1998. – Sobek, Evžen: *Teoretické práce české fotografické avantgardy*, Opava, Slezská univerzita 2004.
18 Wiškovský, Eugen: Tvar a motiv, *Fotografický obzor*, 1940, č. 10. s. 109.
19 tamtéž, s. 111.
20 Hermann, Karel: Učme se dívat fotograficky, *Fotografie*, 1940, č. 22, s. 348.

21 Wiškovský, Eugen: Desorientace názorů na fotografii, *Fotografický obzor*, 1940, č. 12, s. 125–126.

22 Dopis Eugena Wiškovského Anně Fárové z října 1962, uložený v archivu Anny Fárové, s. 12.

23 Fárová, Anna: Imaginární rozhovor s Eugenem Wiškovským, *Československá fotografie*, 1964, č. 5, s. 150.

24 Jeníček, Jiří: Eugen Wiškovský, *Československá fotografie*, 1957, č. 4, s. 41–42.

25 „zázračný rybolov" (Lukáš 5.4–11).

26 Dopis Eugena Wiškovského Anně Fárové z 8. 12. 1963, uložený v archivu Anny Fárové v Praze, s. 2–3.

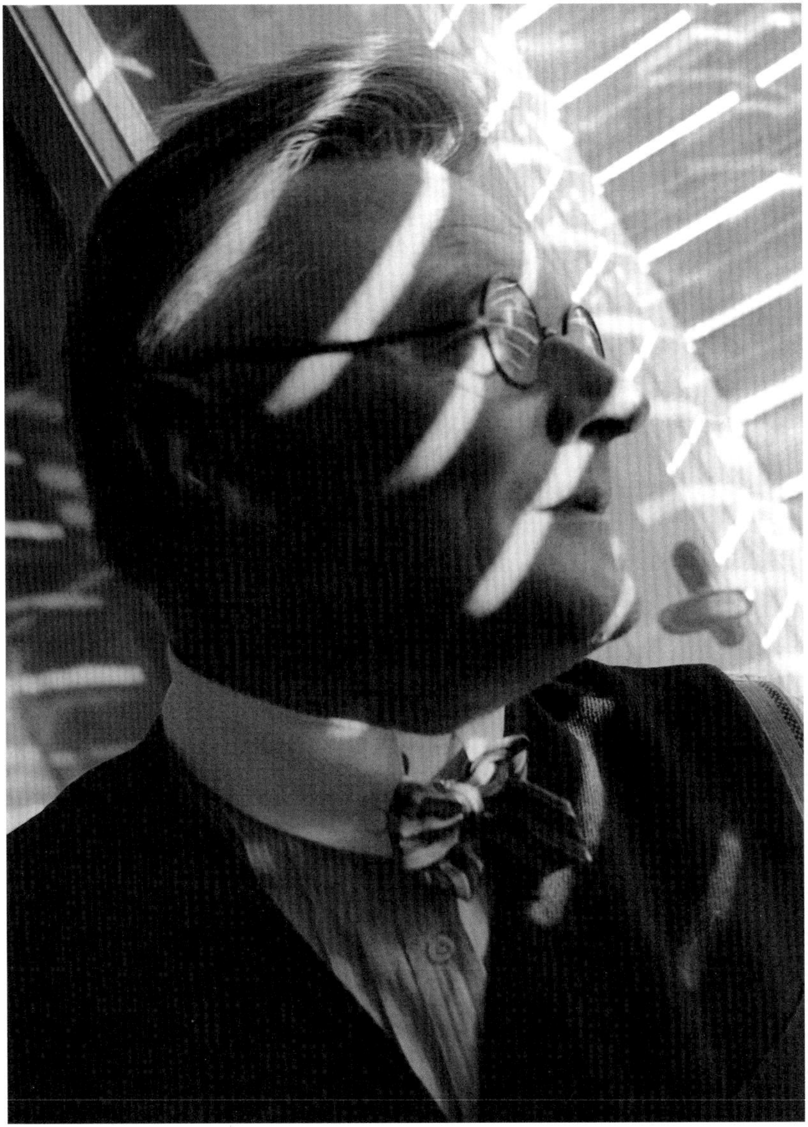

1 **Portrait of a Composer / Portrét komponisty** 1930

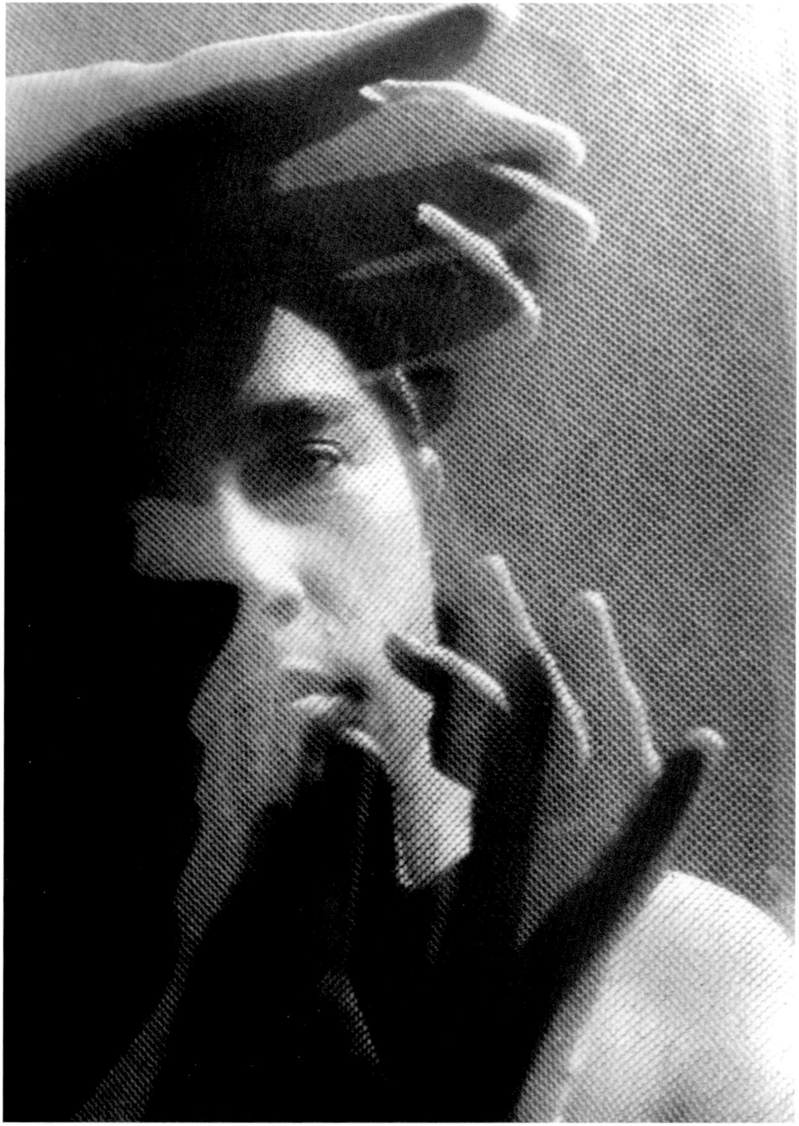

2 **Portrait / Portrét** 1928

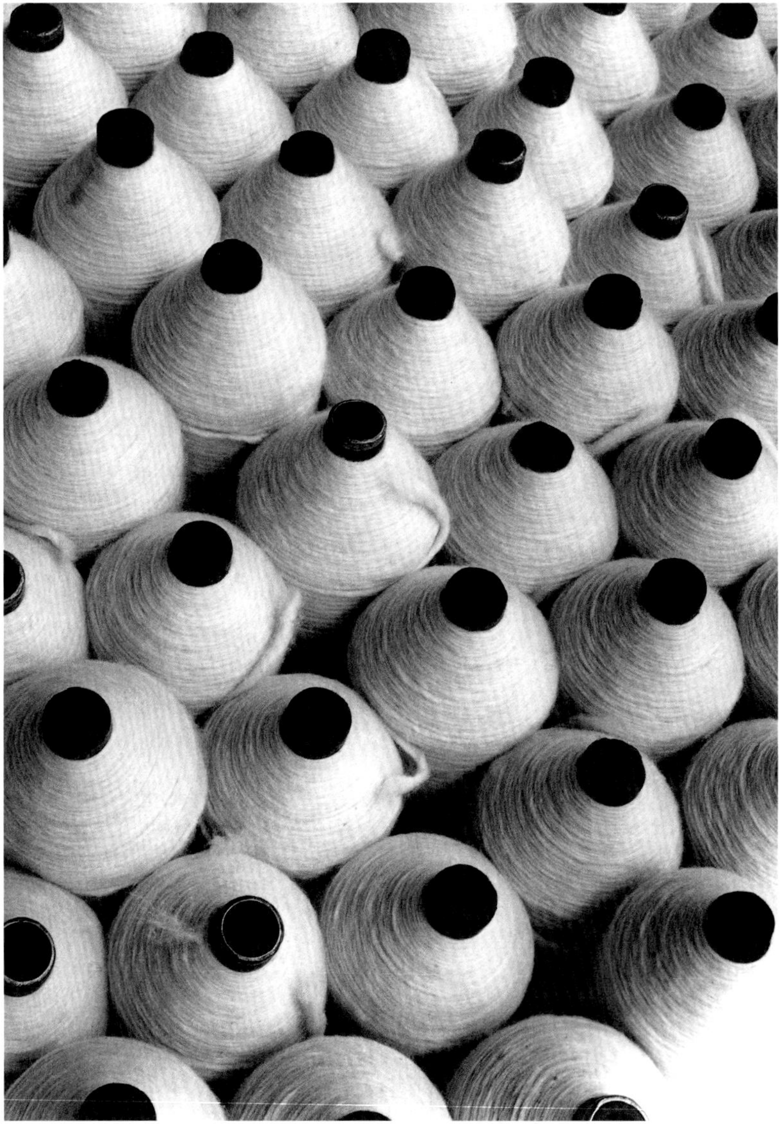

3 **Coils / Cívky** 1928

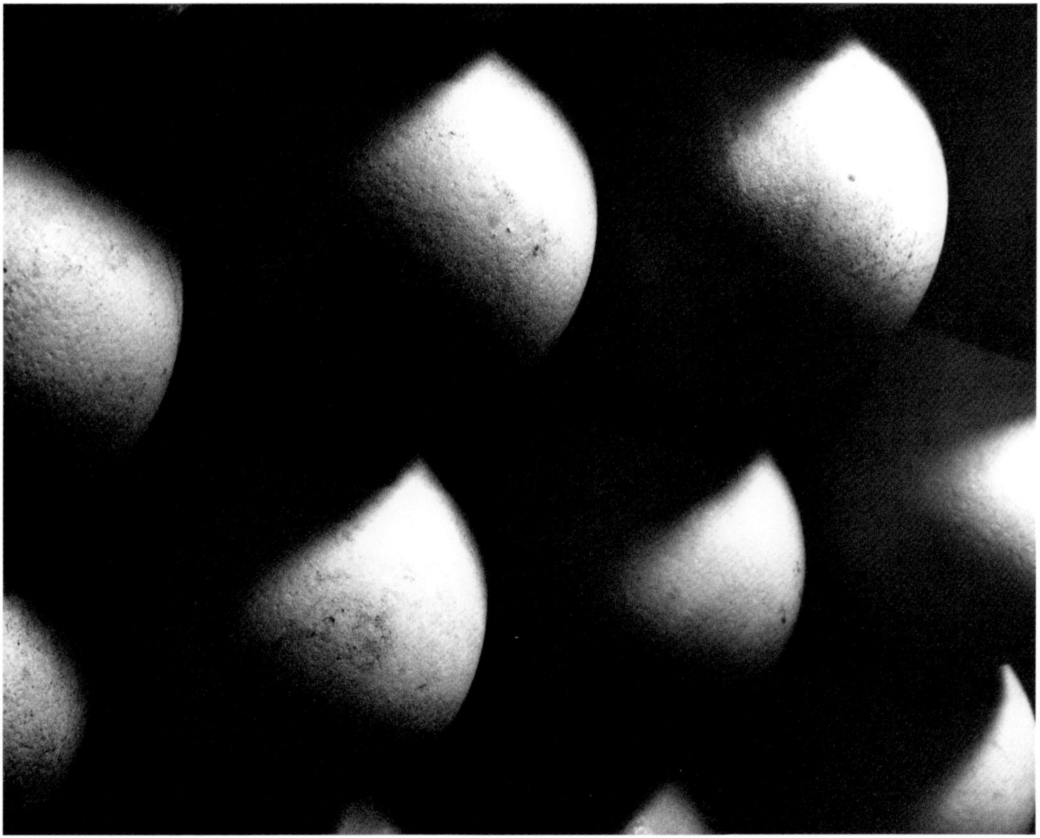

4 **Eggs / Vejce** 1929

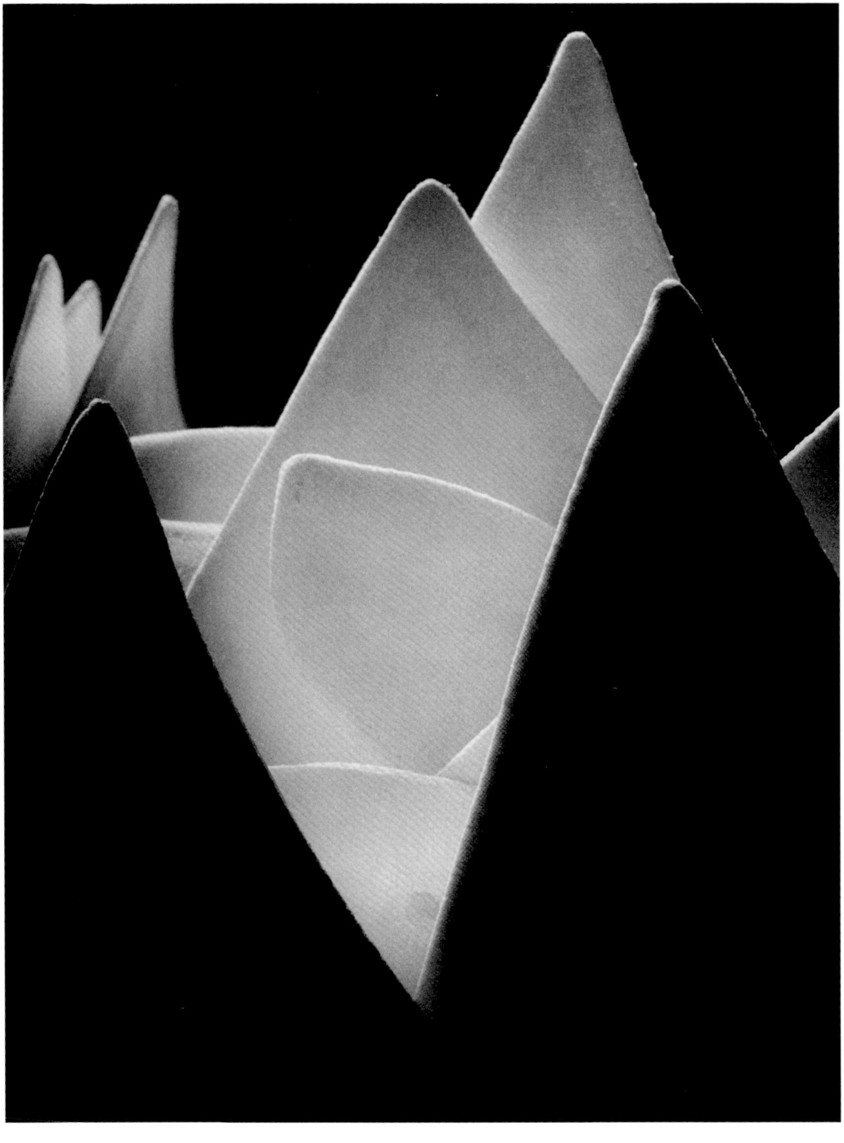

5 **Lunar Landscape I (Collars I) / Měsíční krajina I (Límce I)** 1929

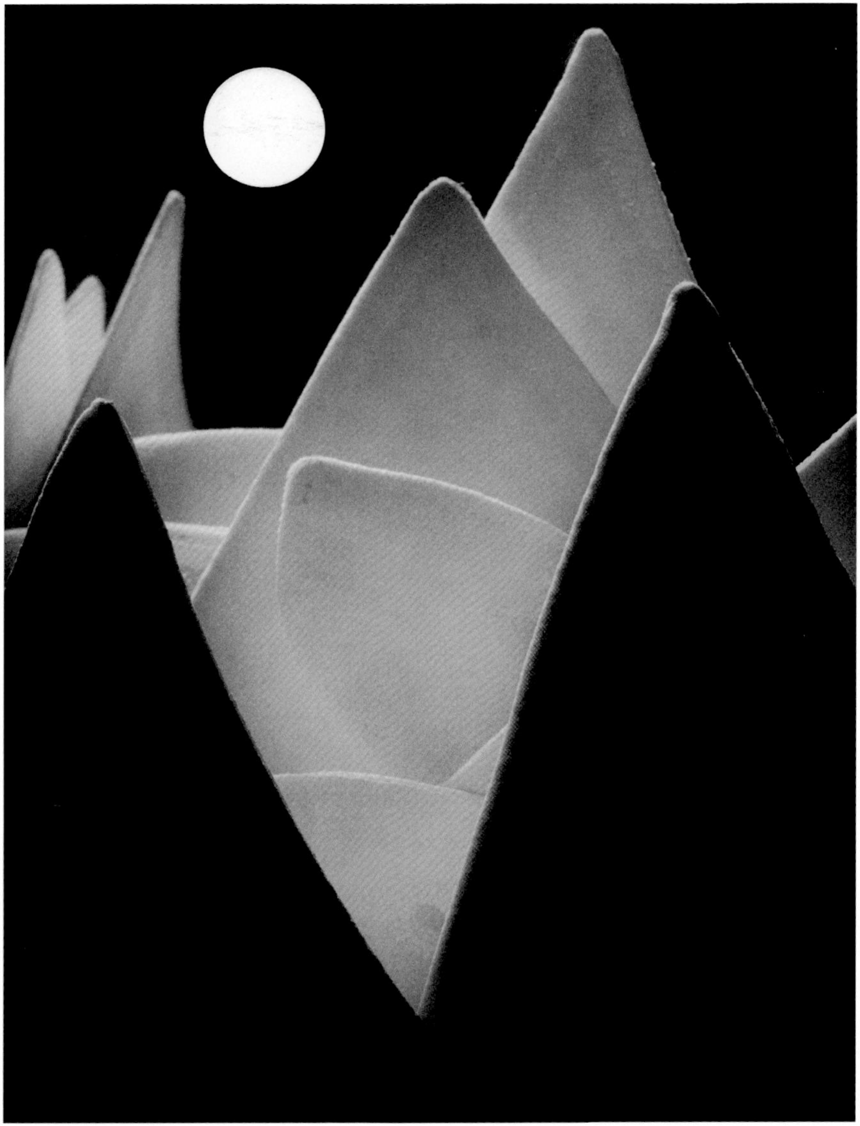

6 **Lunar Landscape II (Collars II) / Měsíční krajina II (Límce II)** 1929

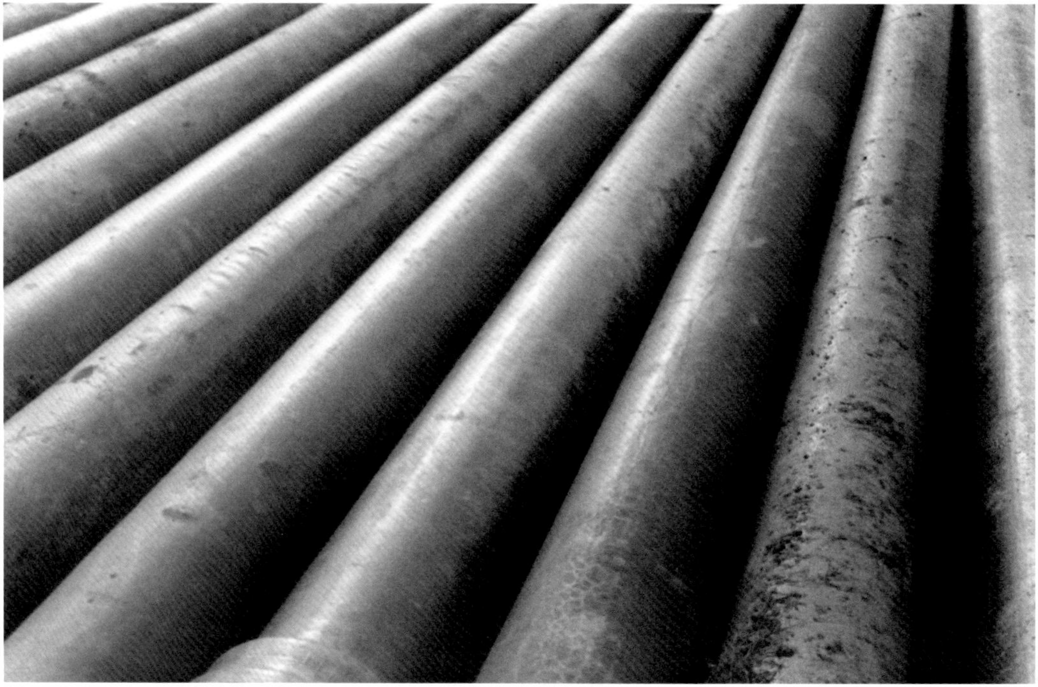

7 **Pipes / Roury** 1930

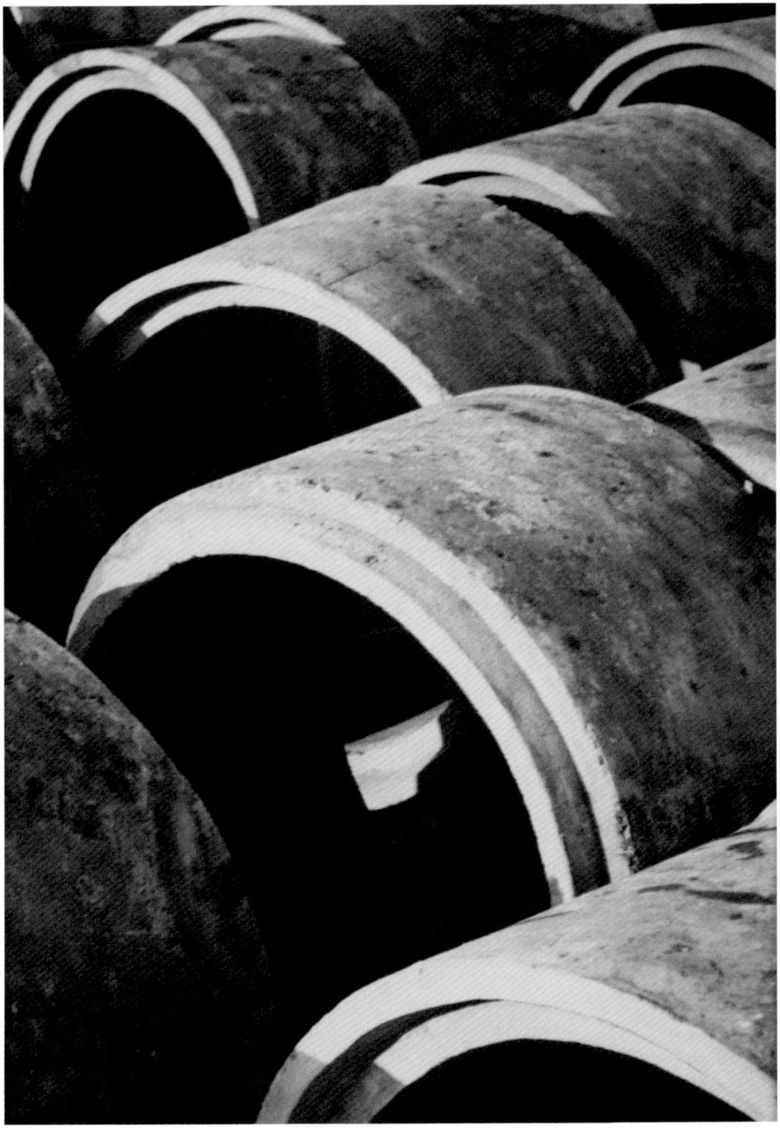

8 **Concrete Rings / Cementové skruže** 1928–29

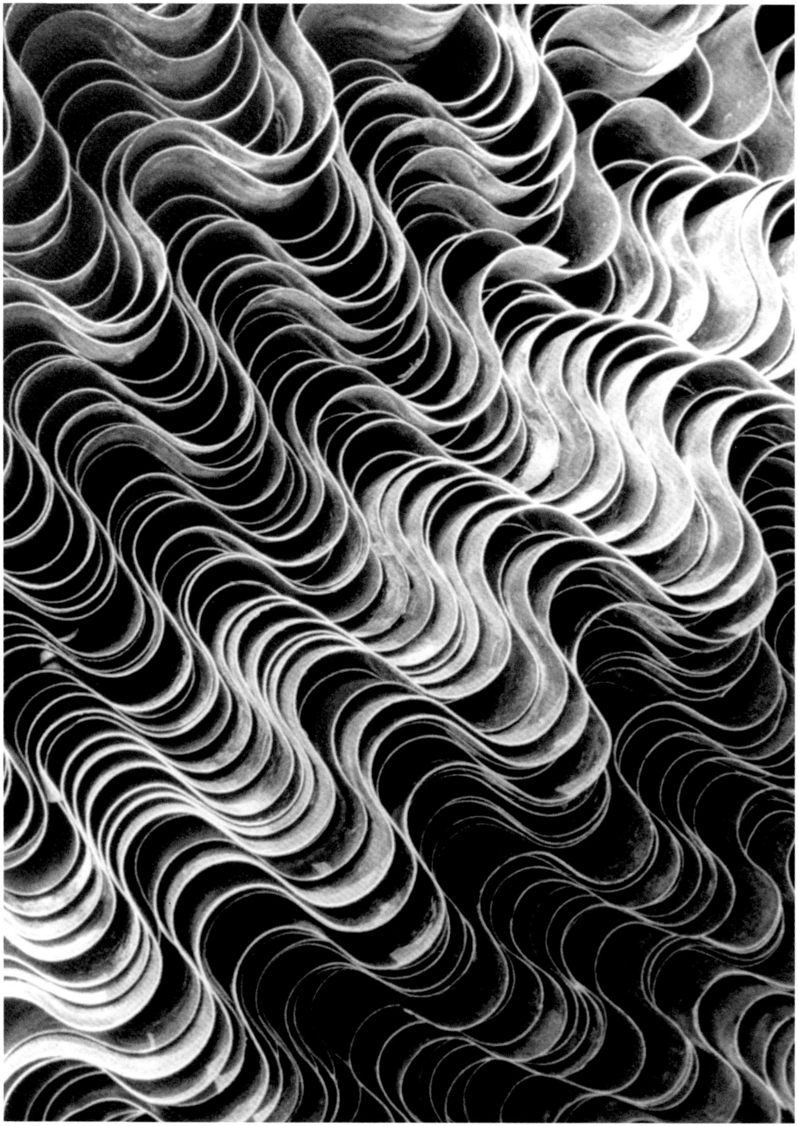

9 **Corrugated Metal / Vlnitý plech** 1934

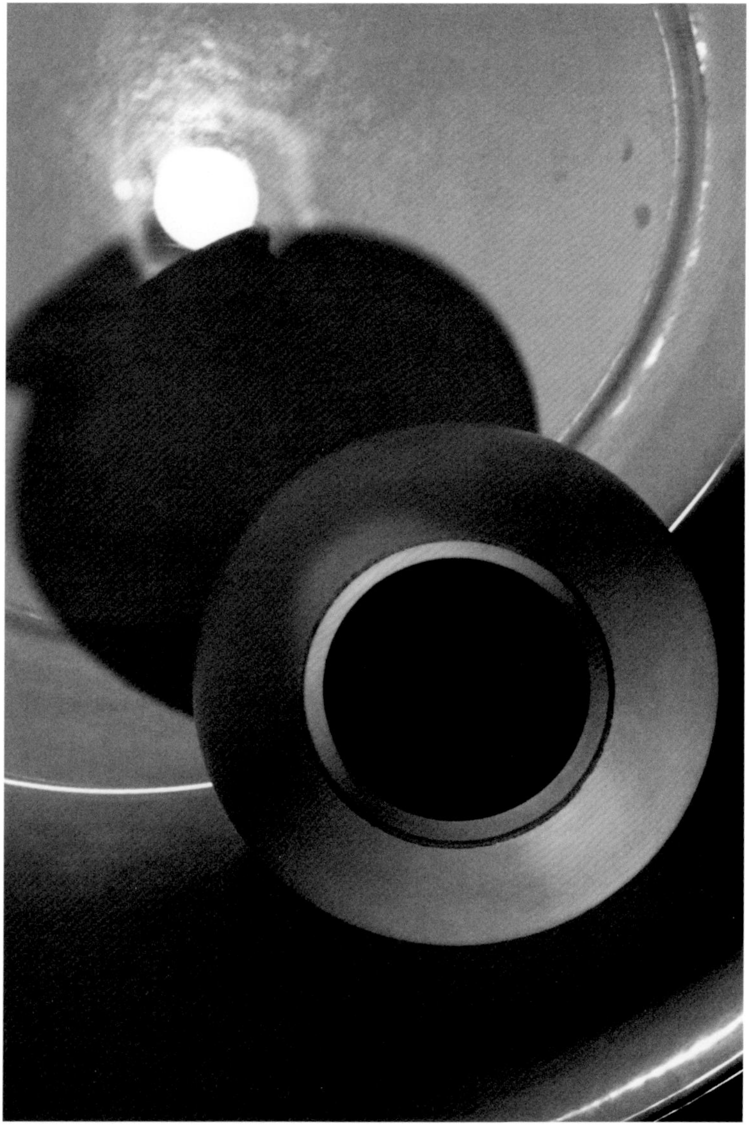

10 **Still Life / Zátiší** 1929

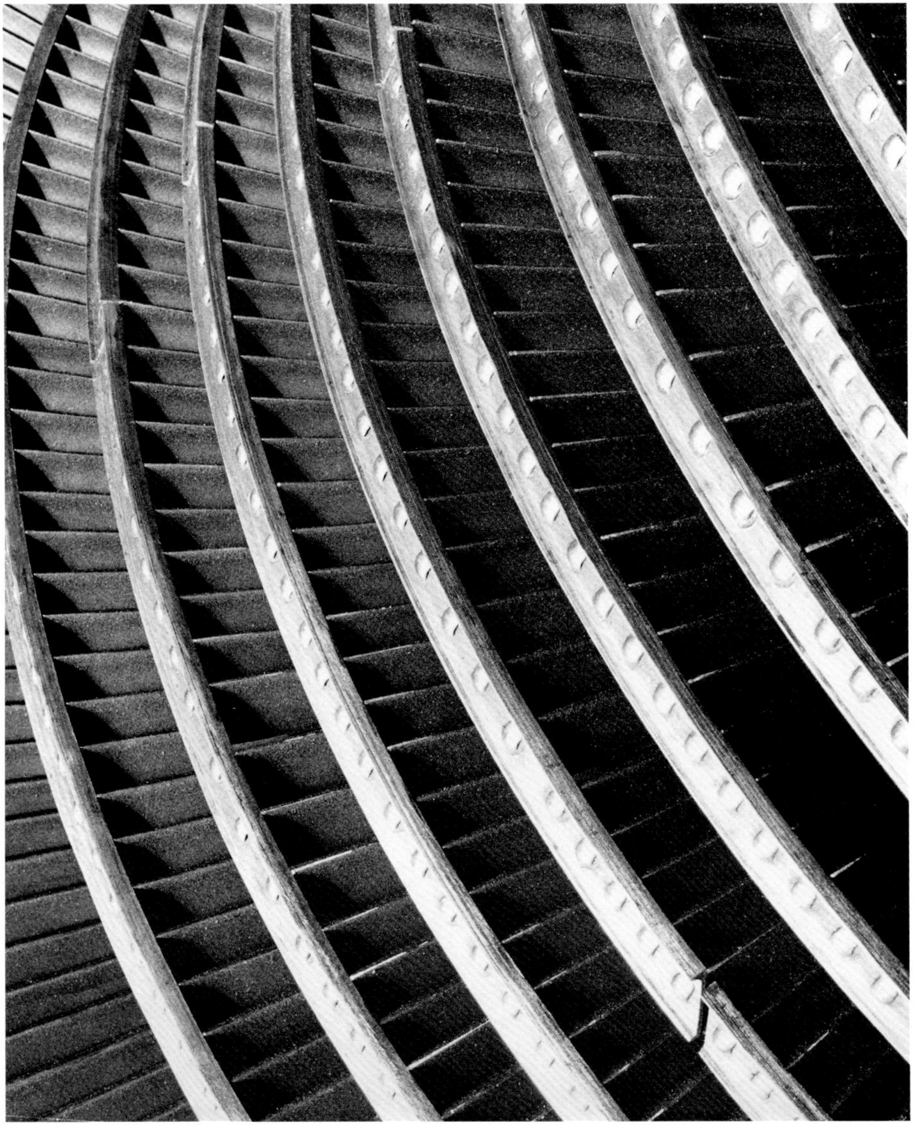

11 **Turbine Detail / Detail turbíny** 1932

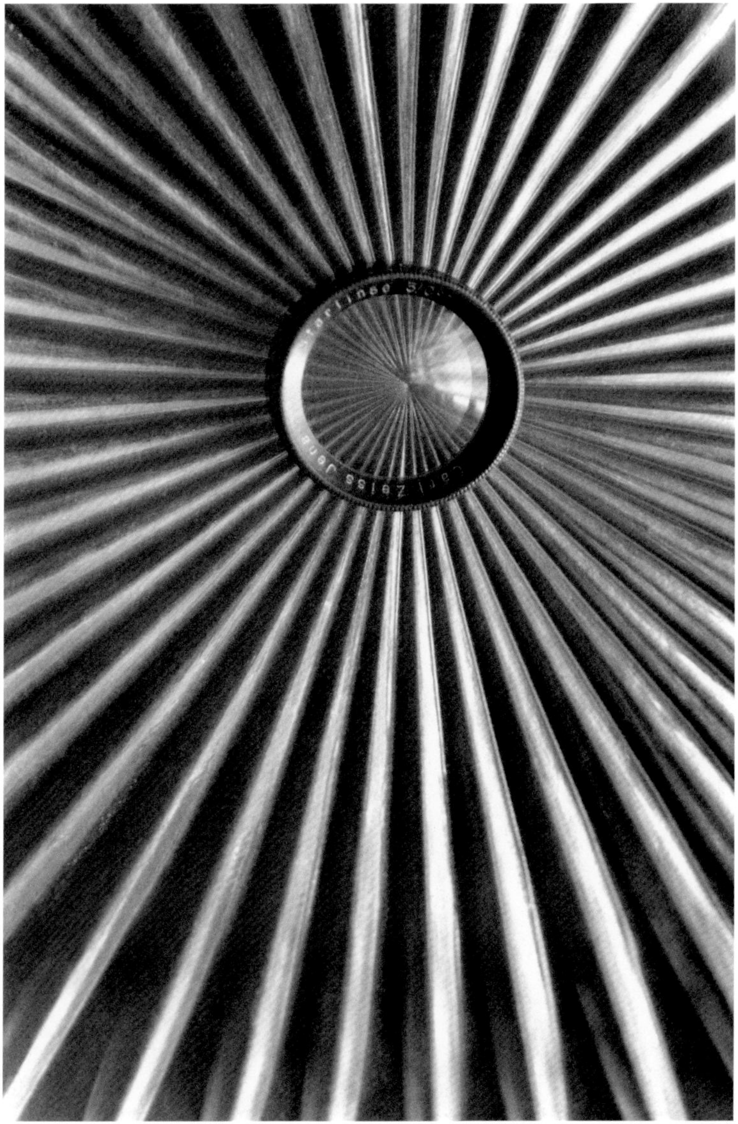

12 **Rays / Paprsky** 1930

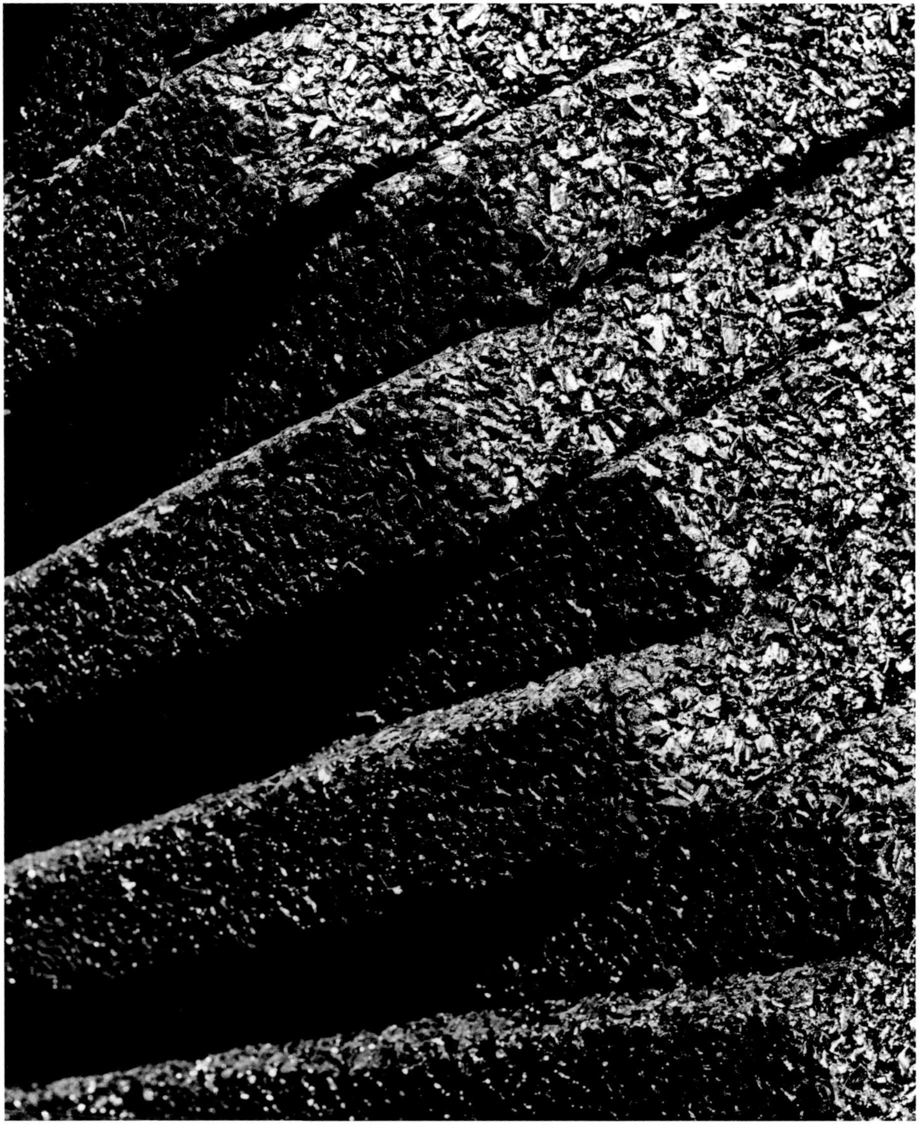

13 **Insulation / Izolace** 1929

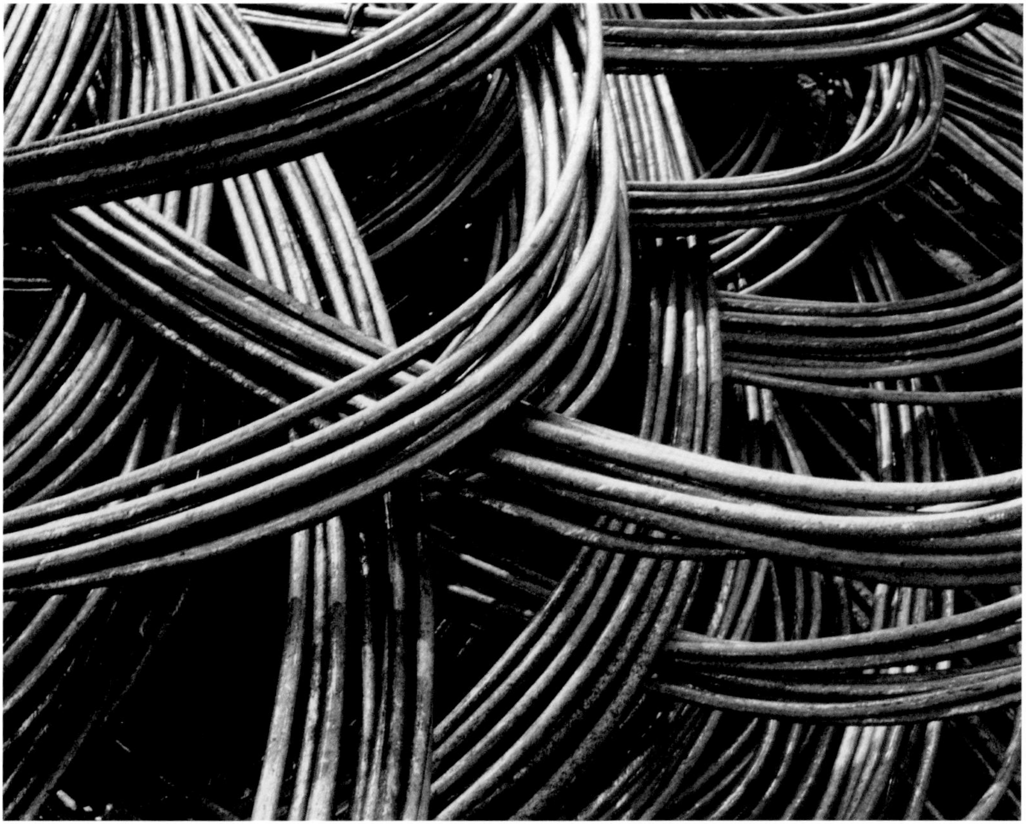

14 **Iron Rods / Železné pruty** 1928

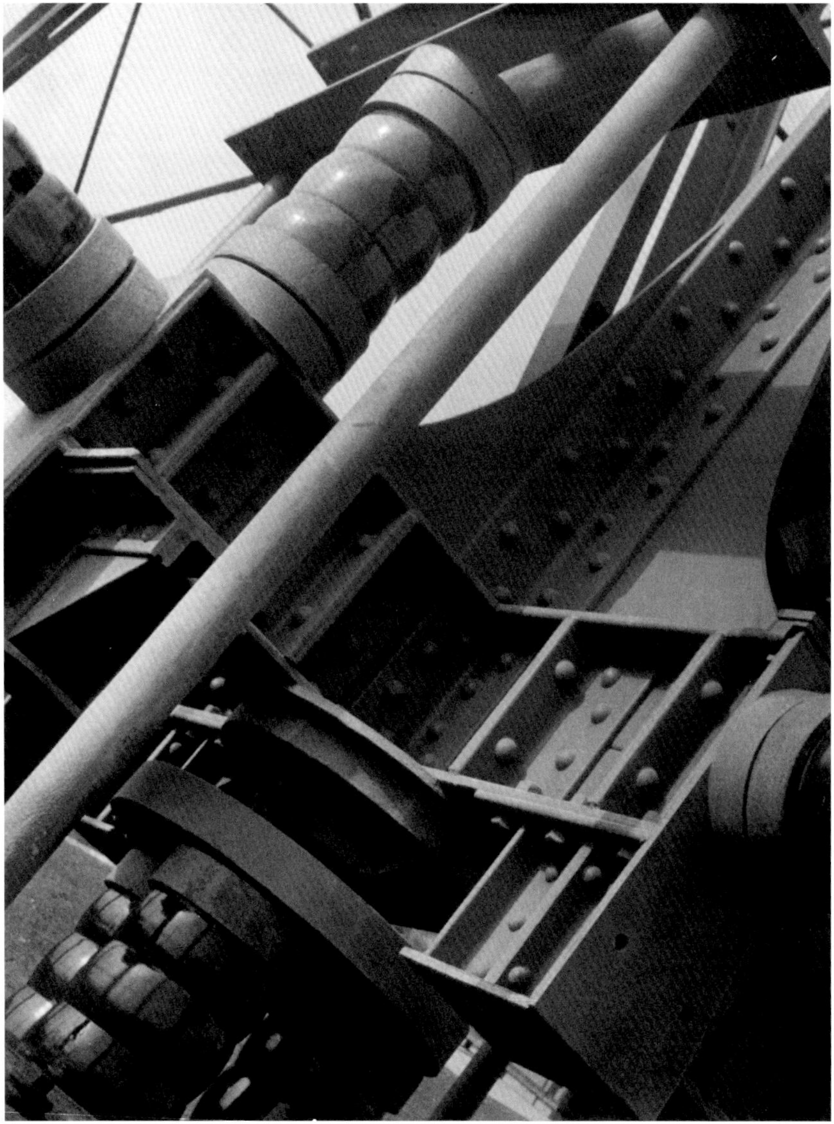

15 **Bottom of the Antenna in Libice / Spodek antény v Libicích** 1930s / 30. léta

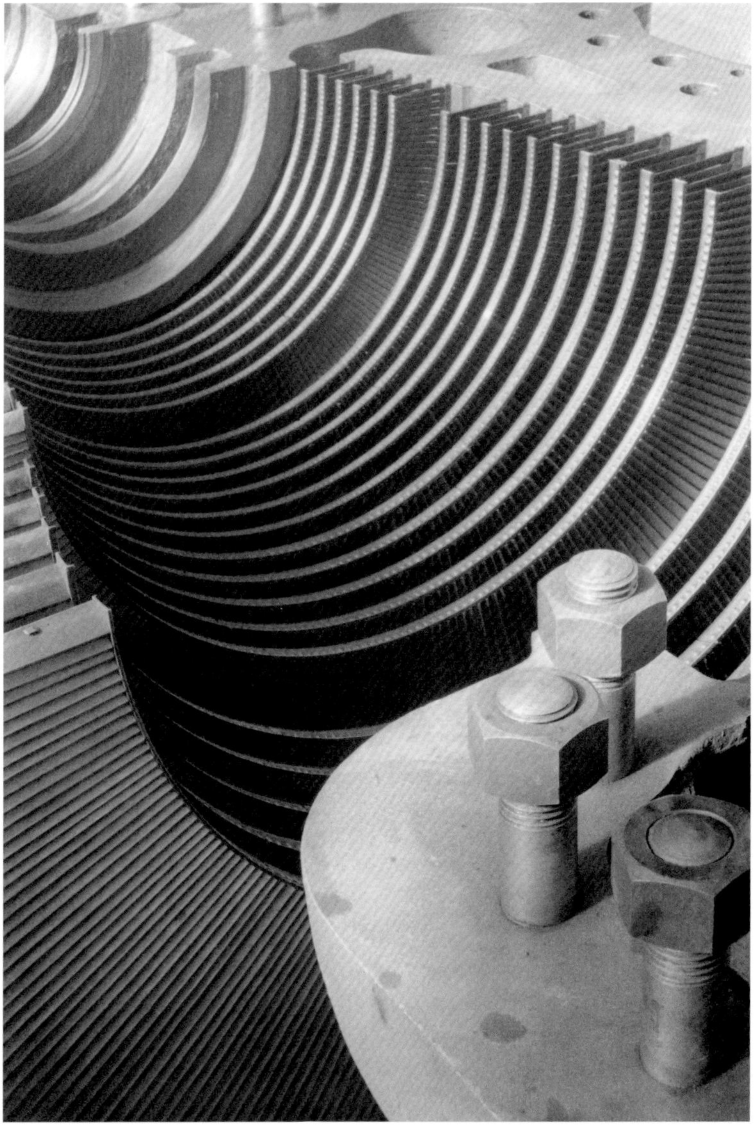

16 **Bolts / Šrouby** 1933–34

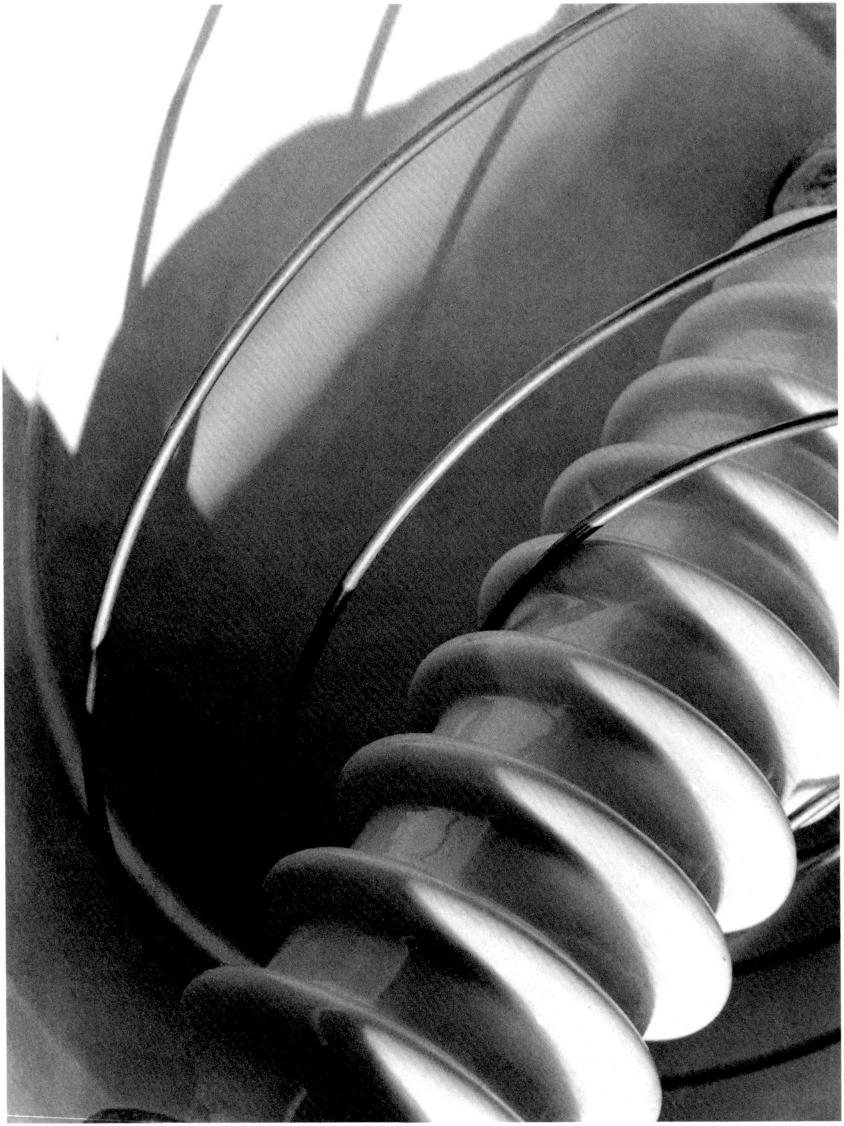

17 **Insulator / Izolátor** 1933

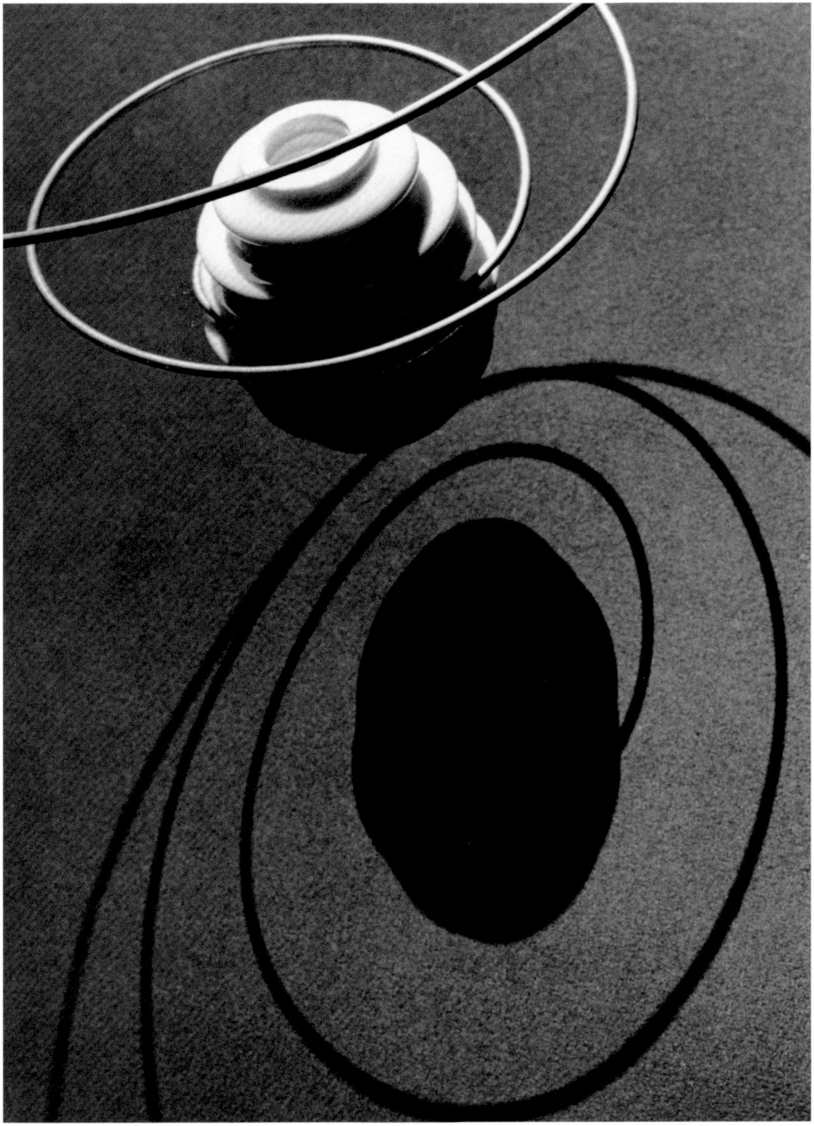

18 **Insulator with Spring / Izolátor s pružinou** 1933–35

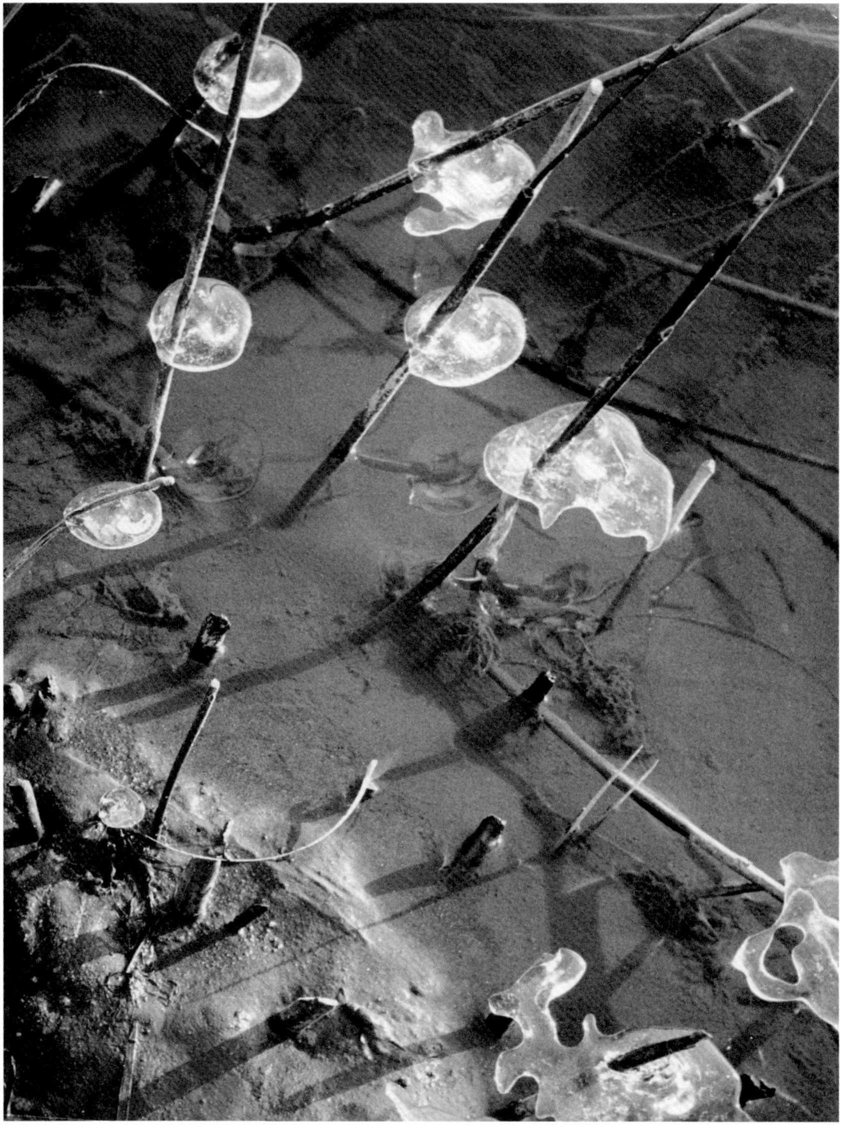

19 **Leftover Ice / Zmrazky** 1930

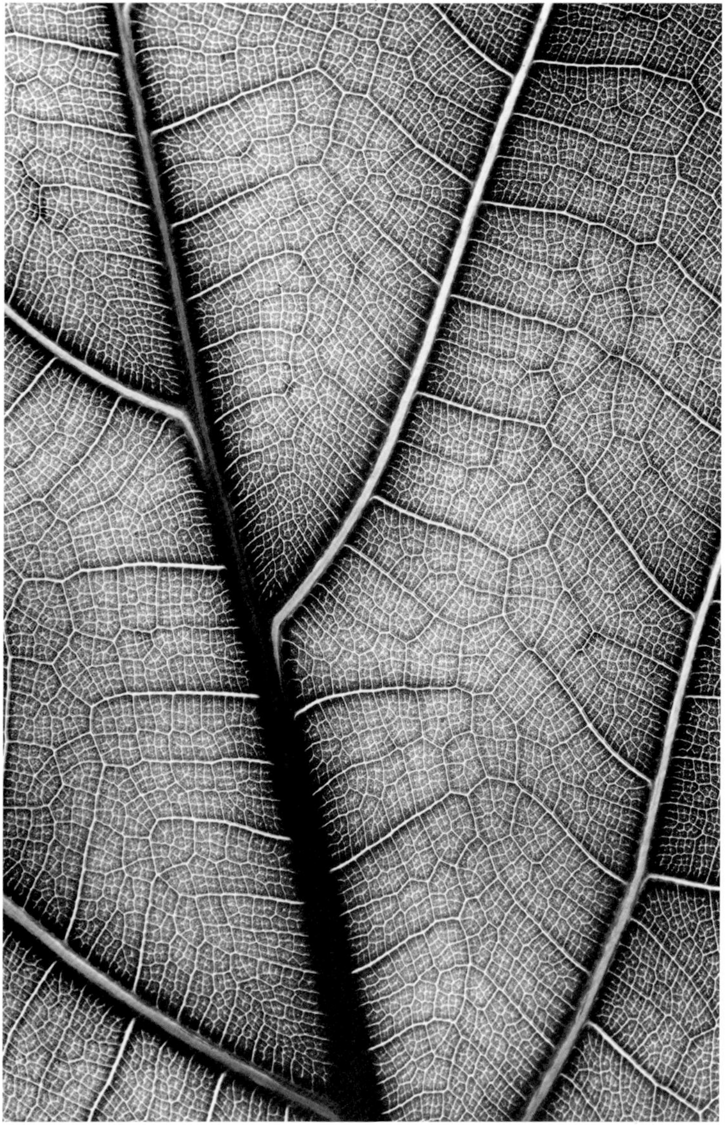

20 **Leaf Venation / Nervatura listu** 1939

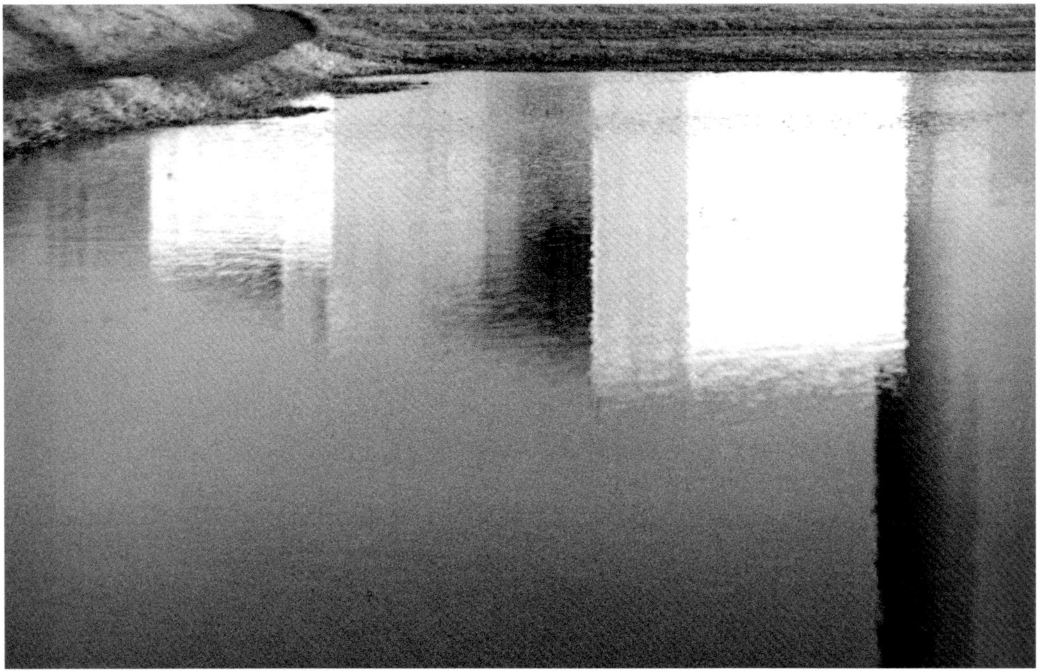

21 **Reflection / Odraz** 1935

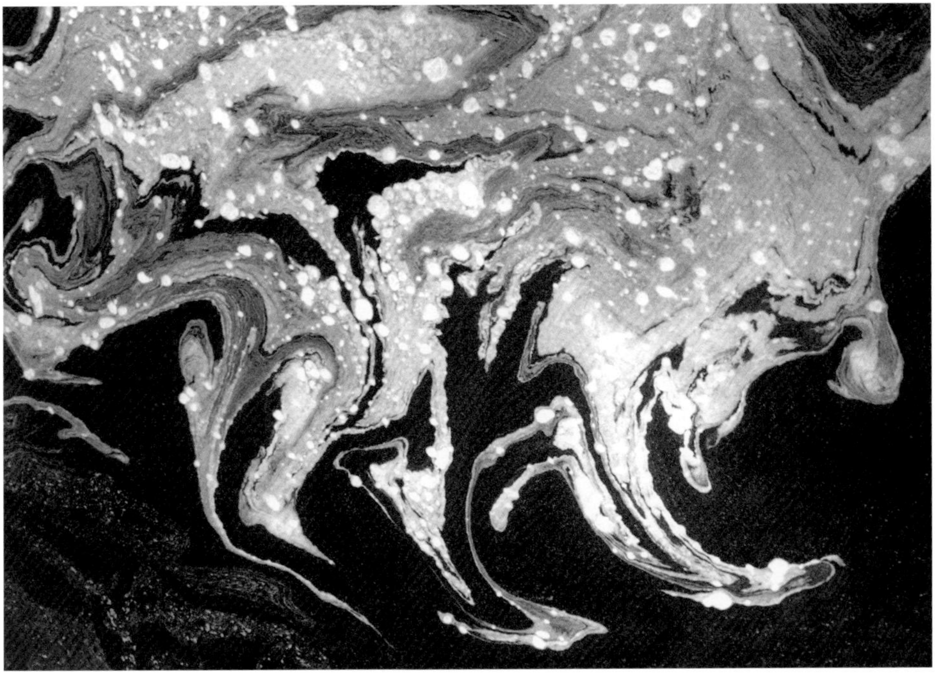

22 **Arabesque / Arabeska** 1931

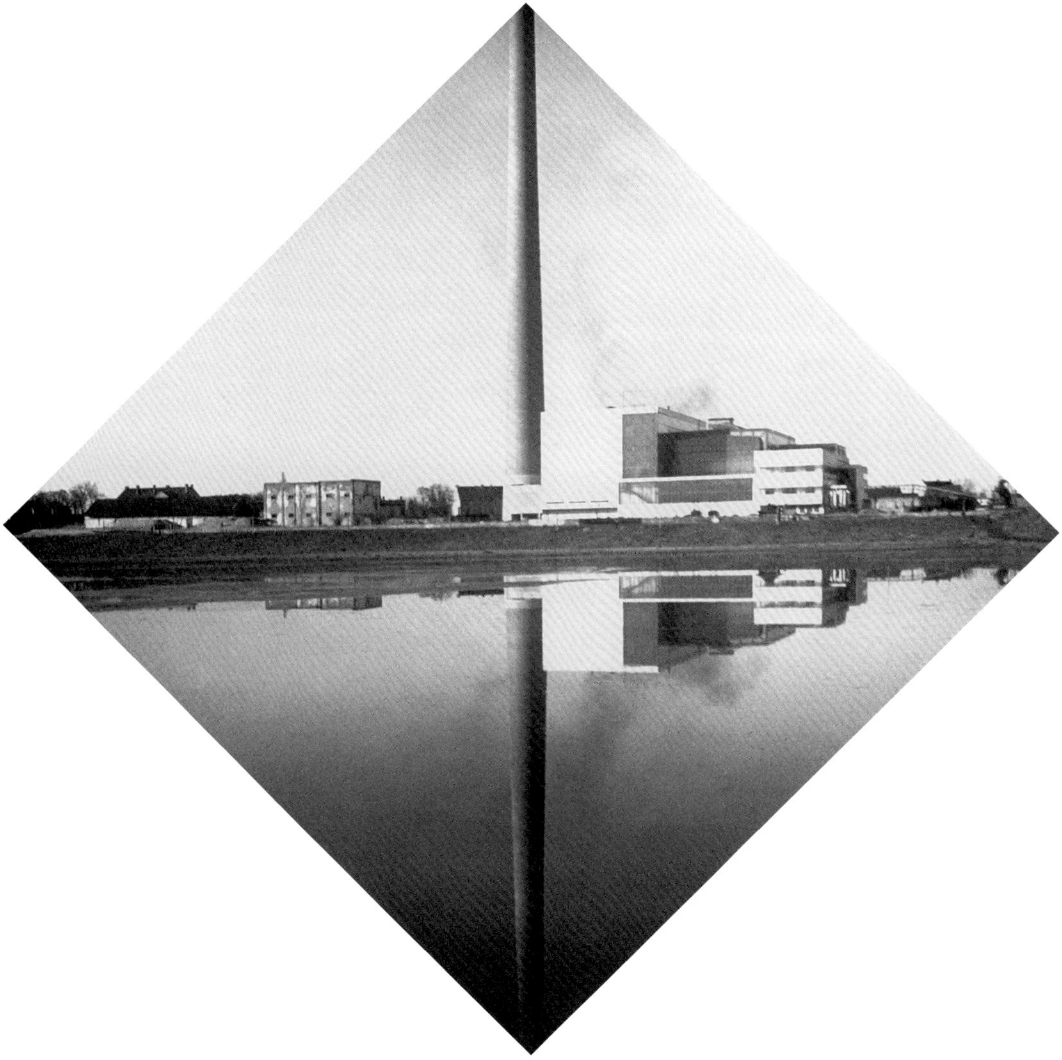

23 **Power Plant II / Elektrárna II** 1934

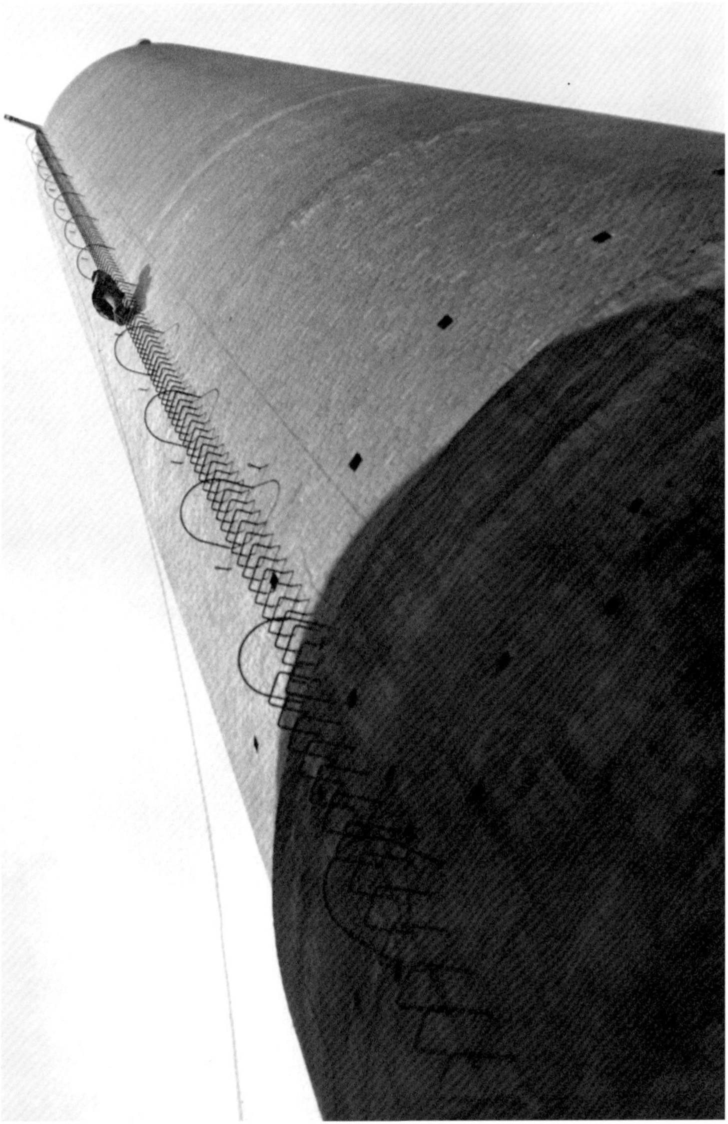

24 **Smokestack / Komín** 1932

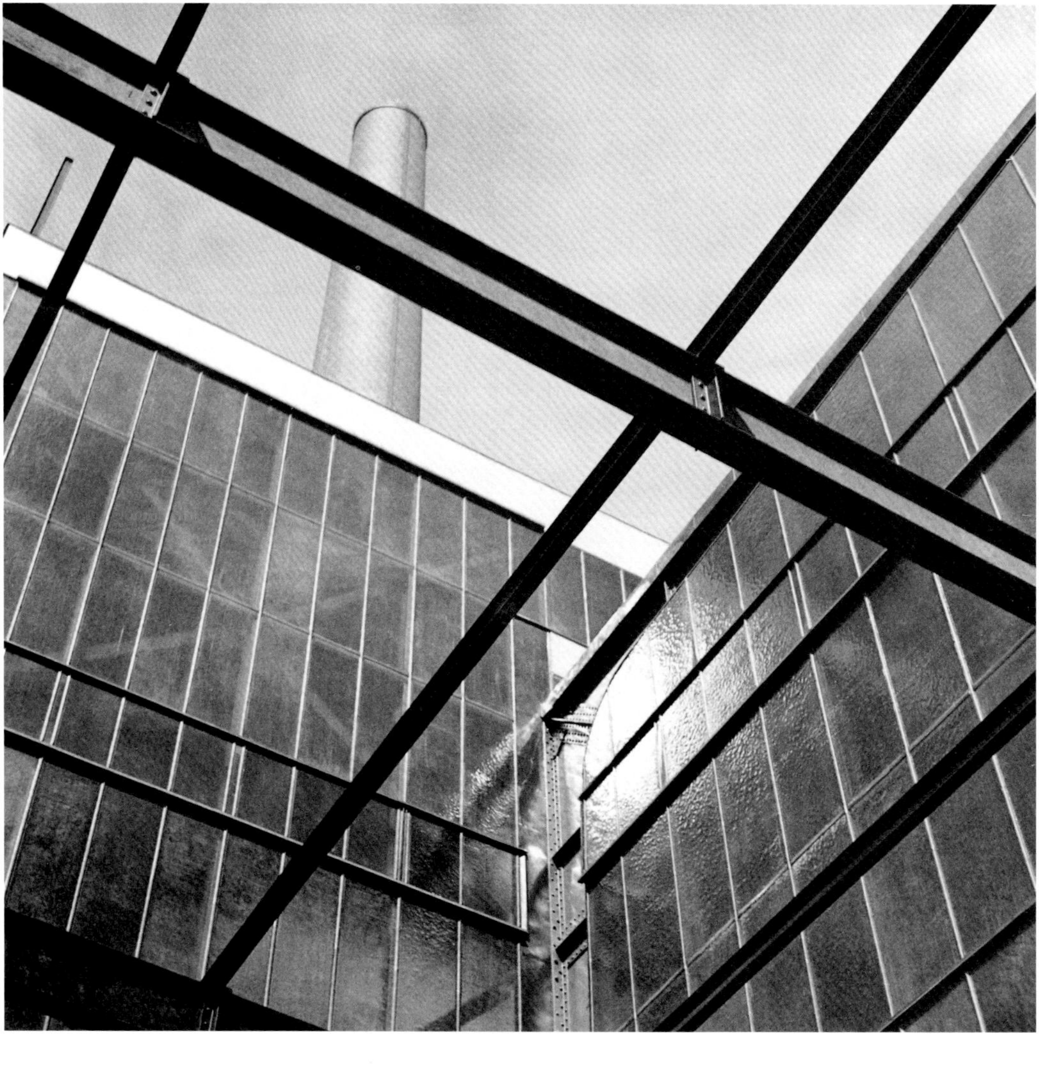

25 **Power Plant in Kolín / Elektrárna v Kolíně** 1932

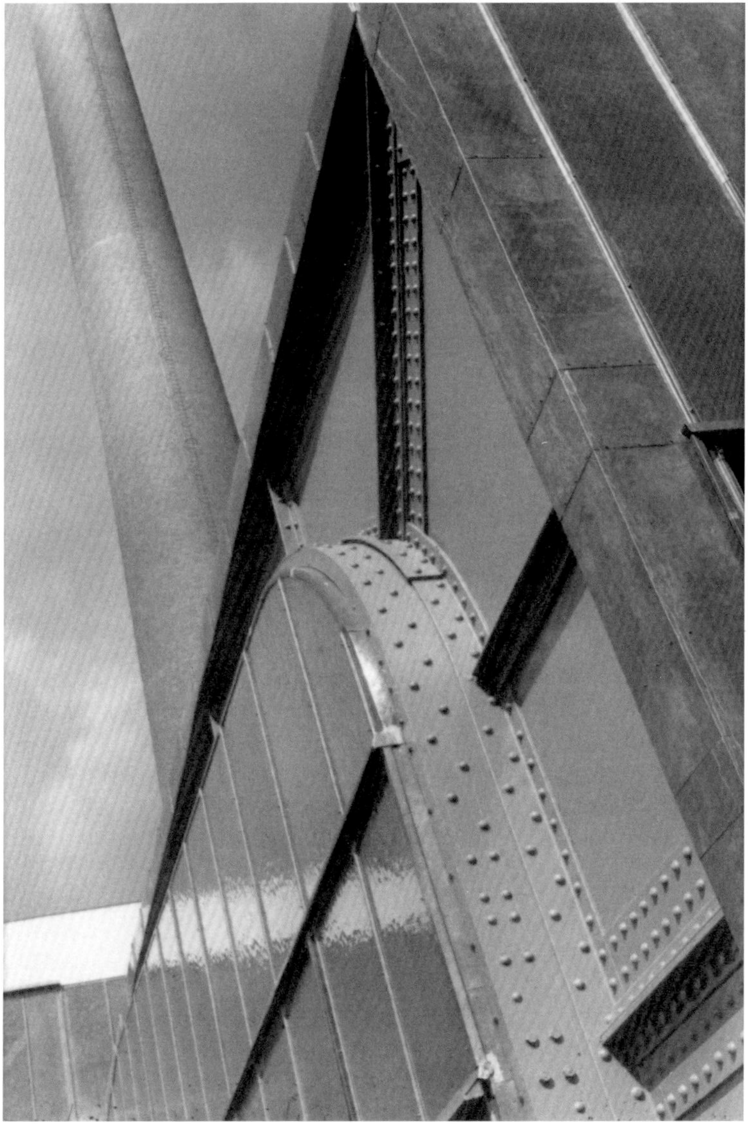

26 **Power Plant, Detail / Detail elektrárny** 1932–33

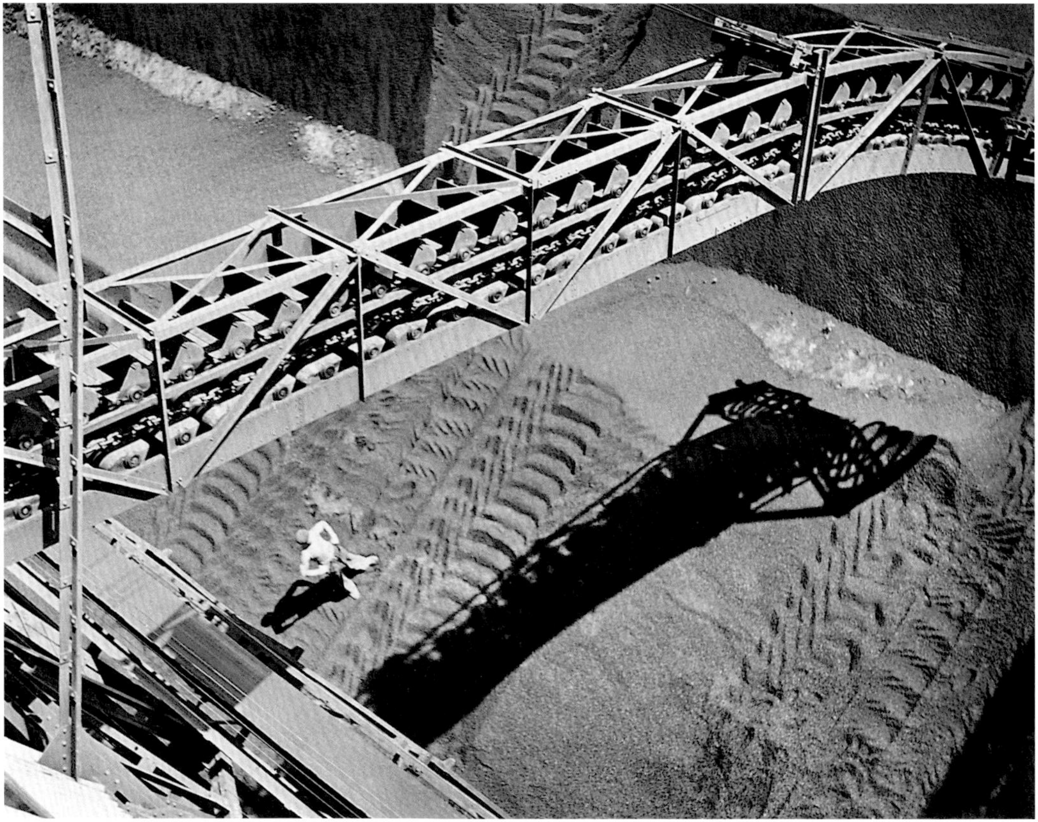

27 **Building the Power Plant in Kolín / Stavba elektrárny v Kolíně** 1929–32

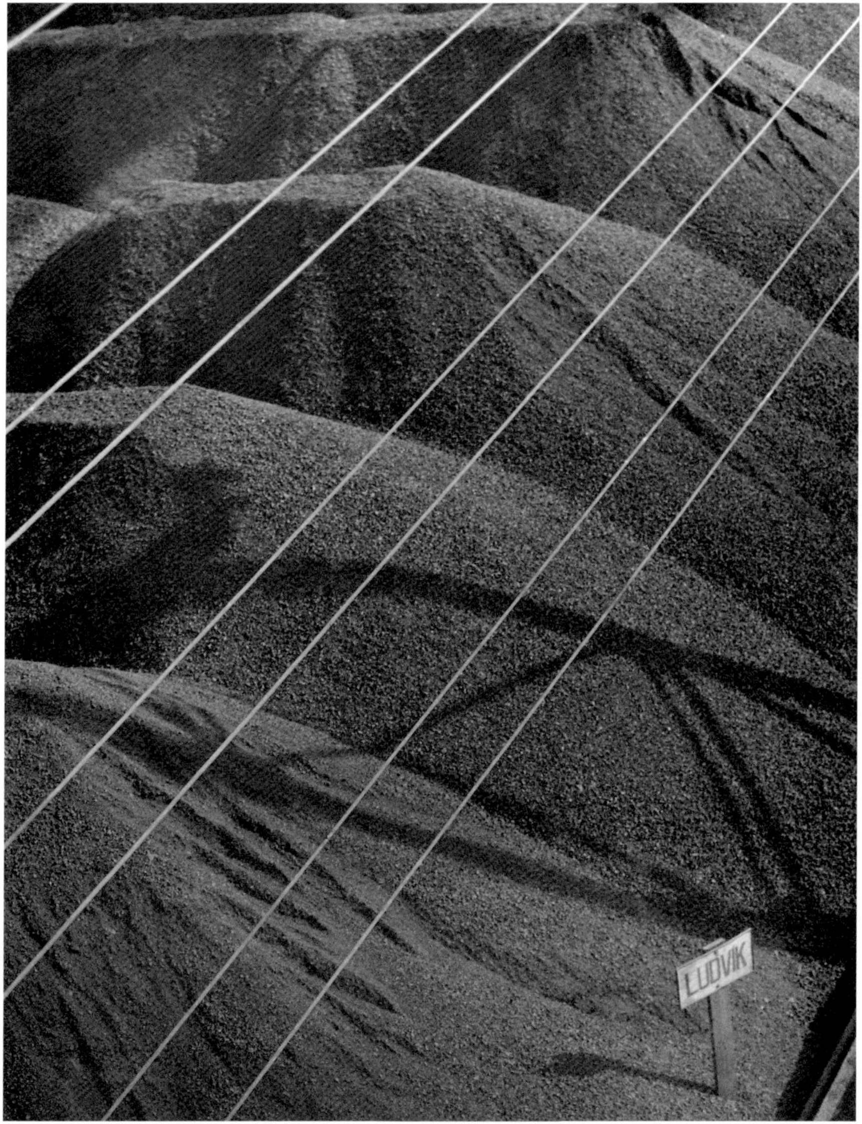

28 **Slag Heaps (Coal) / Haldy (Uhlí)** 1932

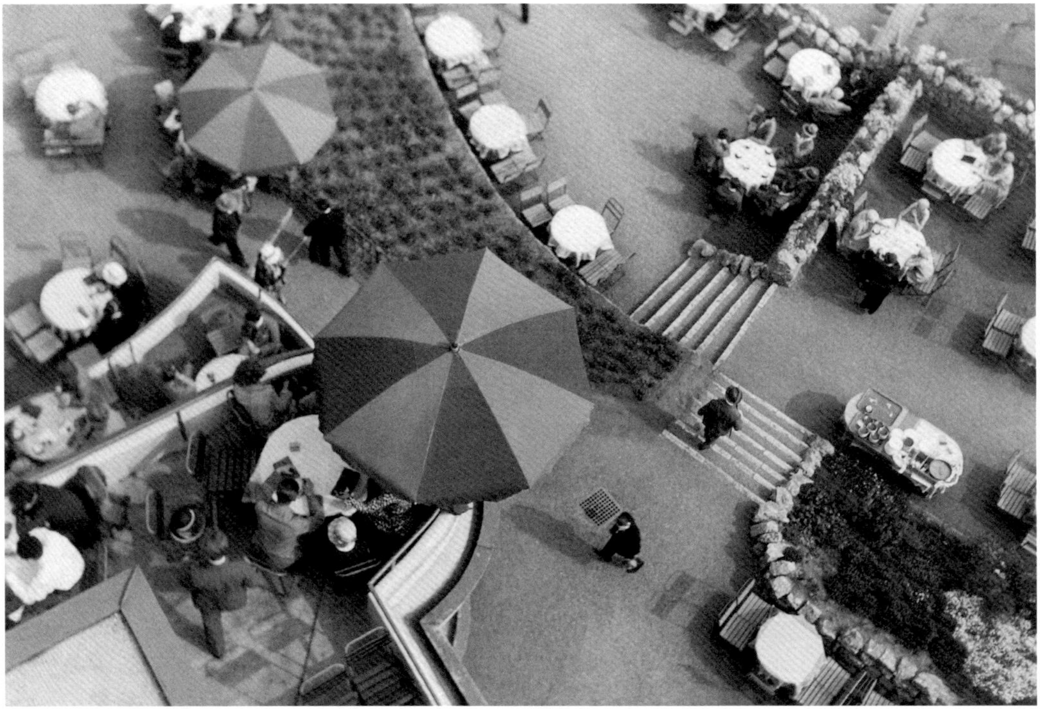

29 **Barrandov Terraces I / Terasy Barrandov I** 1930s / 30. léta

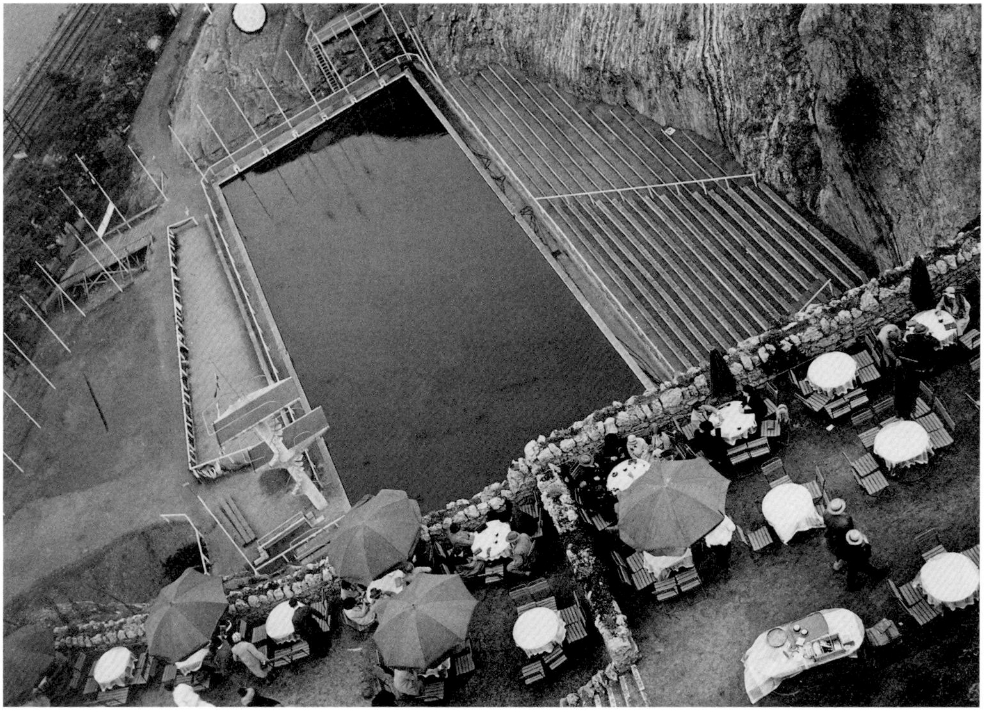

30 **Barrandov Terraces II / Terasy Barrandov II** 1930s / 30. léta

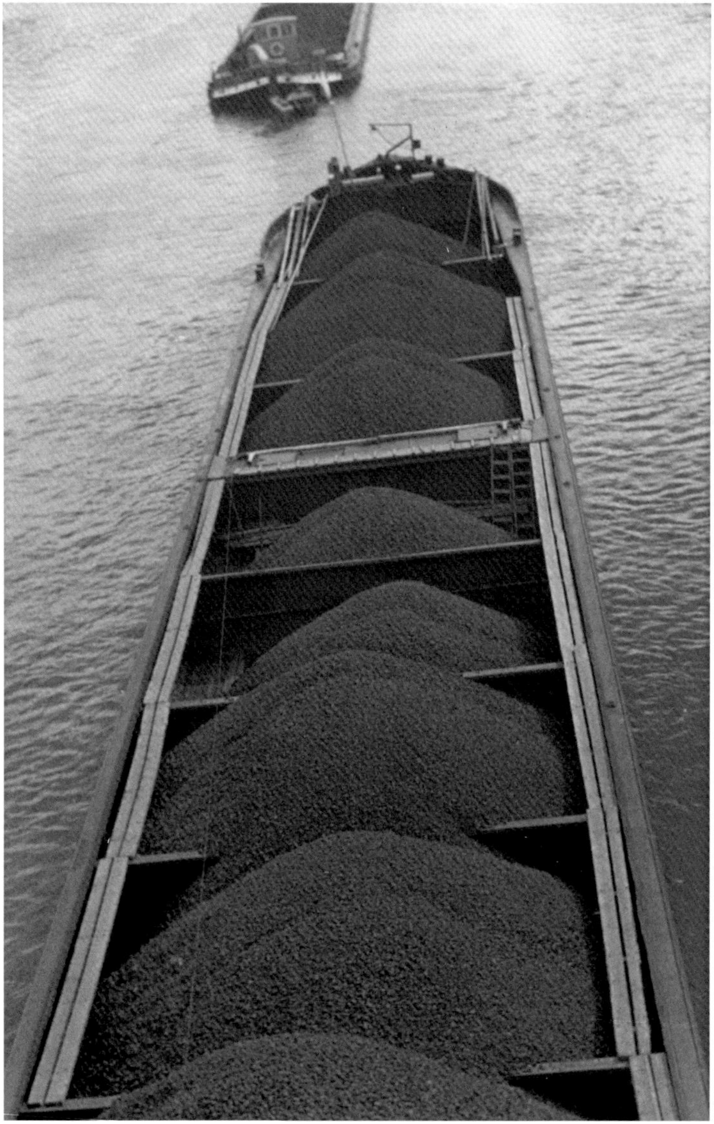

31 **Ship on a River / Lodě na řece** first half of the 1930s / první polovina 30. let

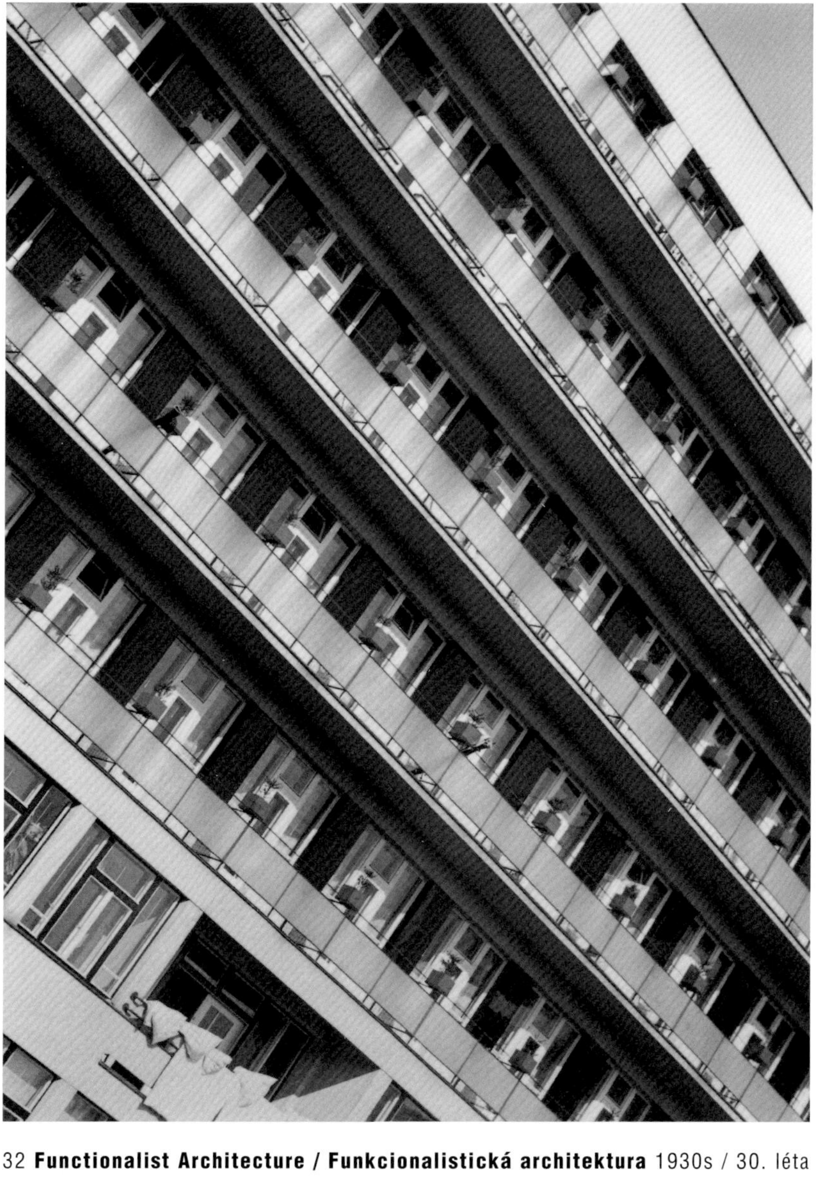

32 **Functionalist Architecture / Funkcionalistická architektura** 1930s / 30. léta

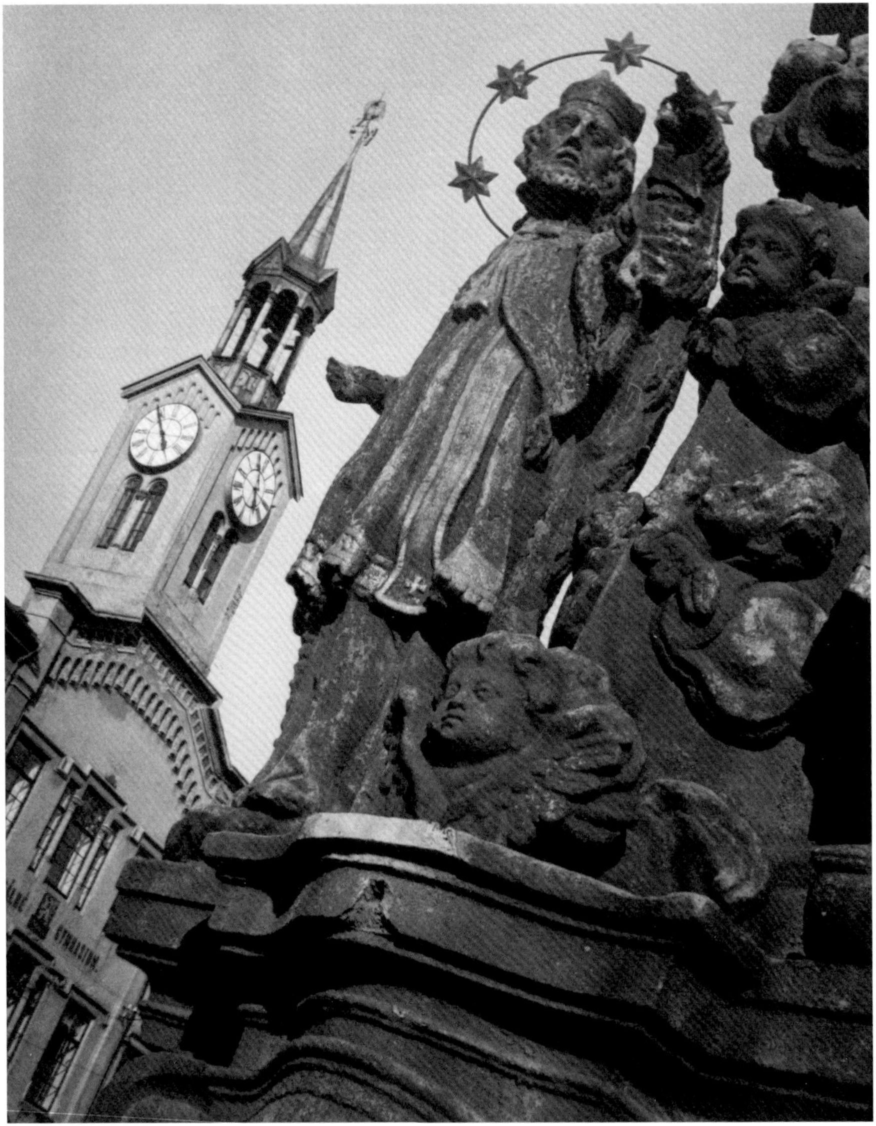

33 **Kolín** 1932–36

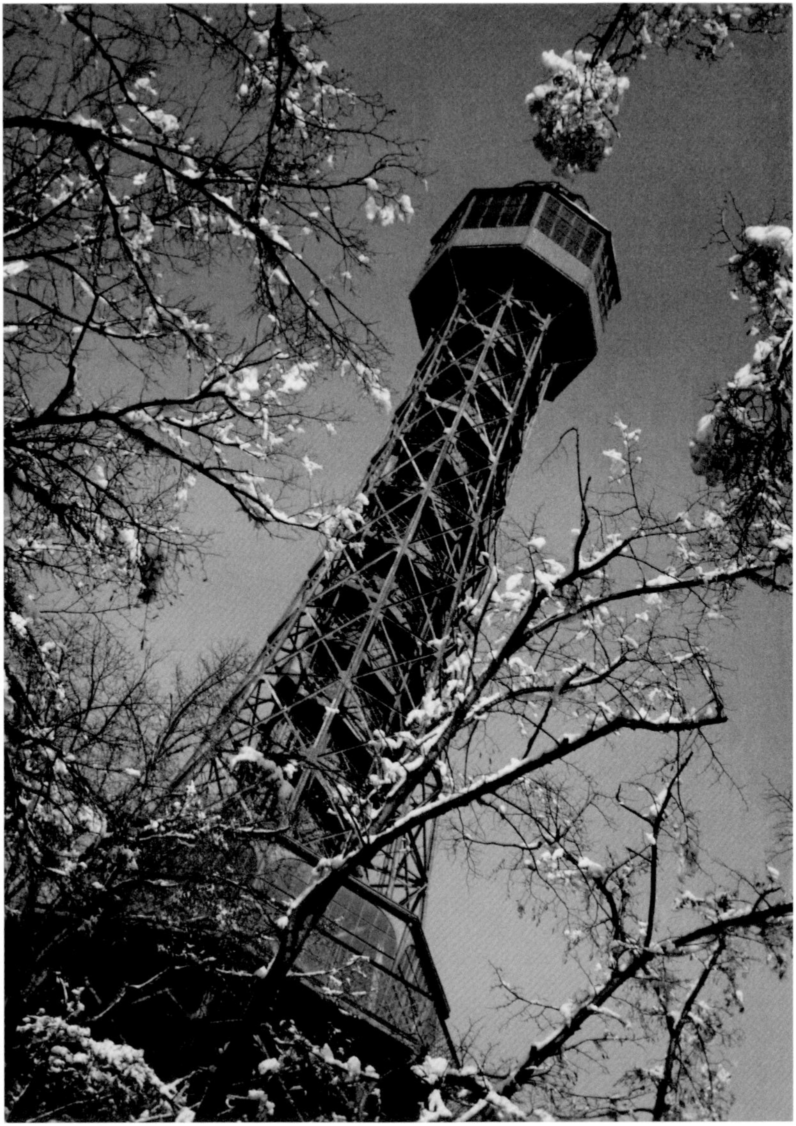

34 **Petřín Lookout Tower, Prague / Petřínská rozhledna v Praze** 1937

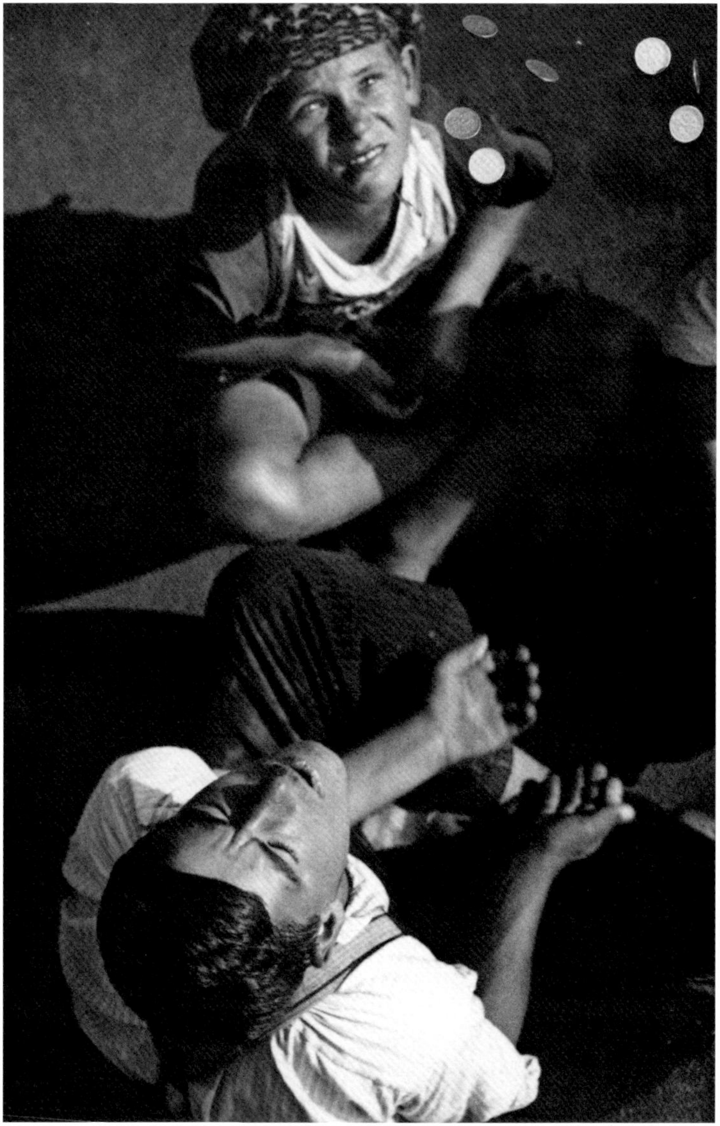

35 **Untitled / Bez názvu** 1928 – 29

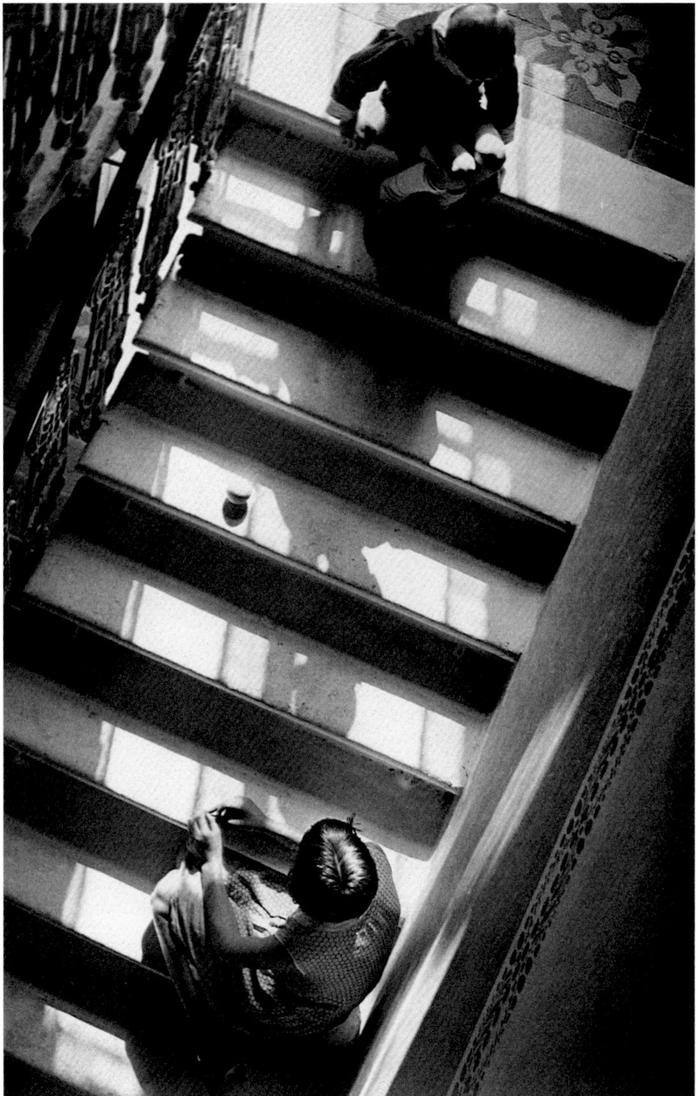

36 **Game / Hra** 1929

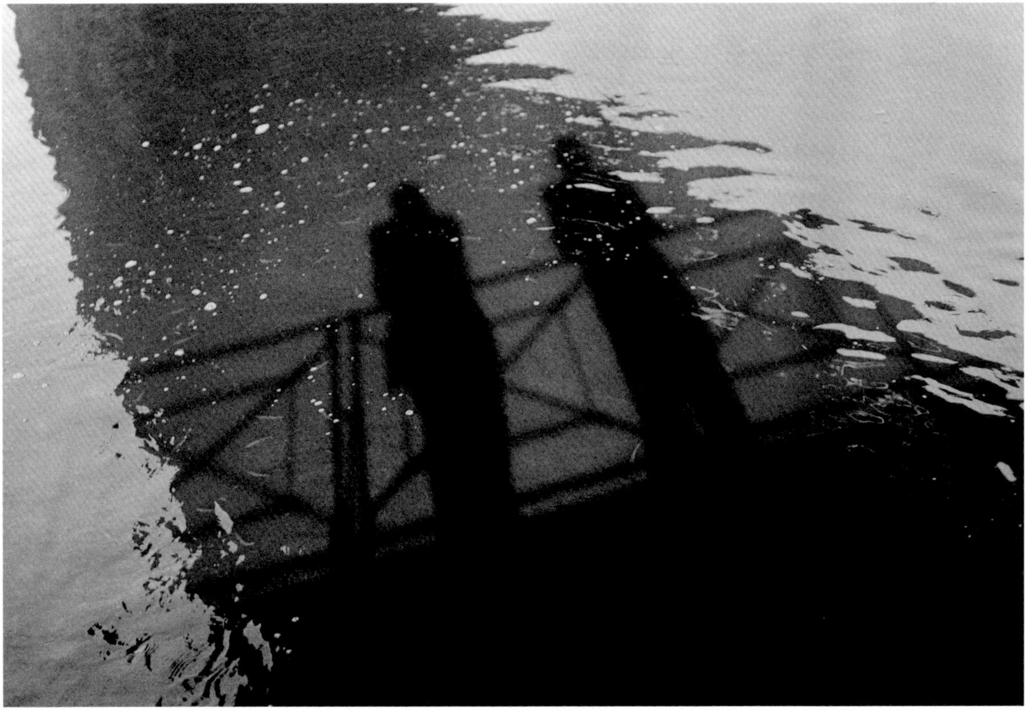

37 **Shadows / Stíny** 1930s / 30. léta

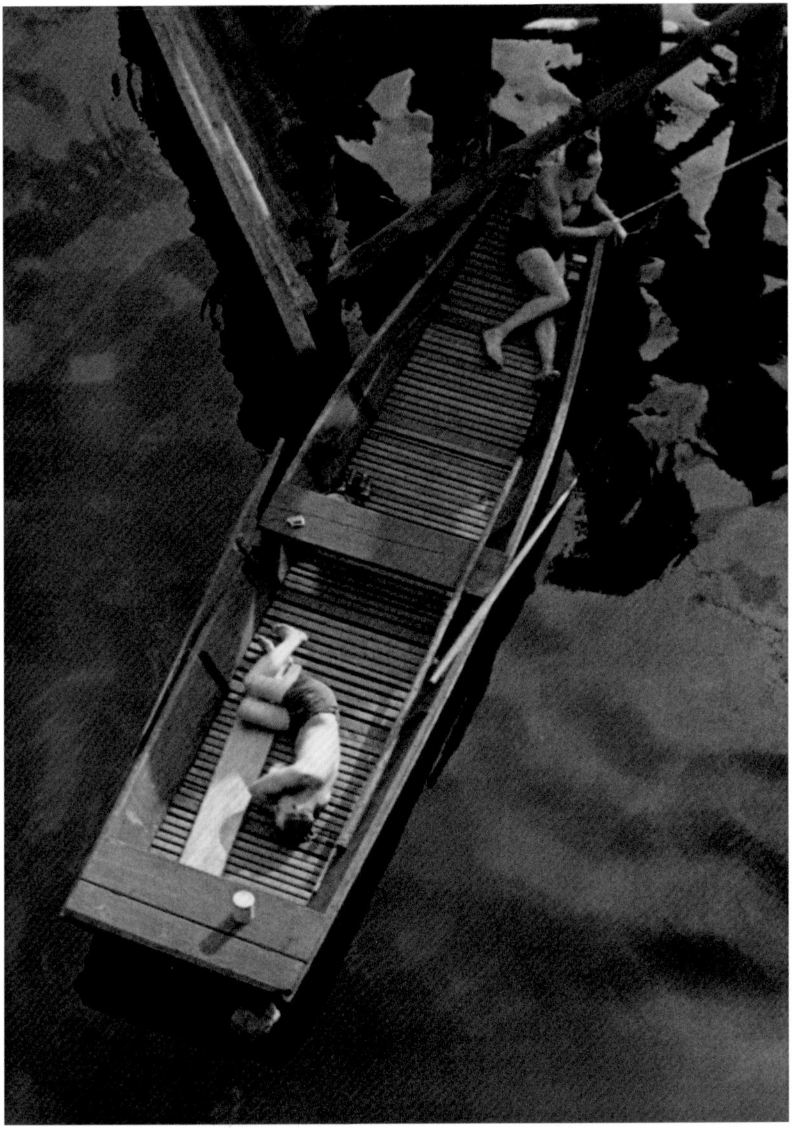

38 **Little Boat / Lodička** 1930s / 30. léta

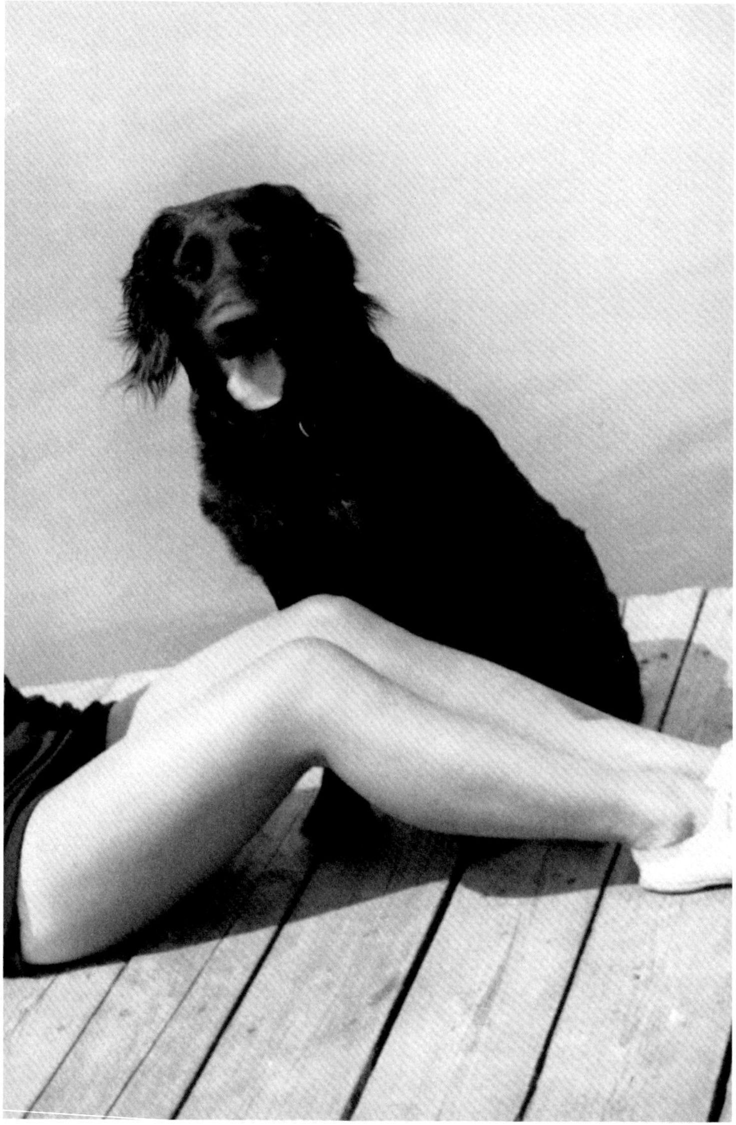

39 **Untitled / Bez názvu** 1930s / 30. léta

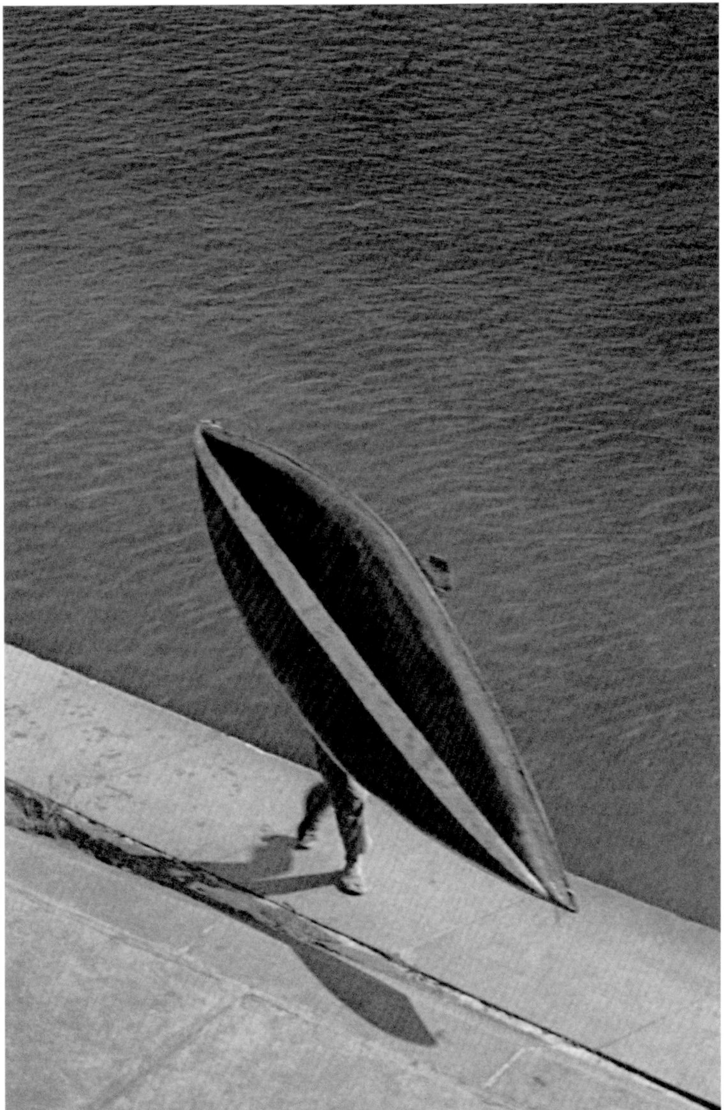

40 **Canoe / Kánoe** 1930s / 30. léta

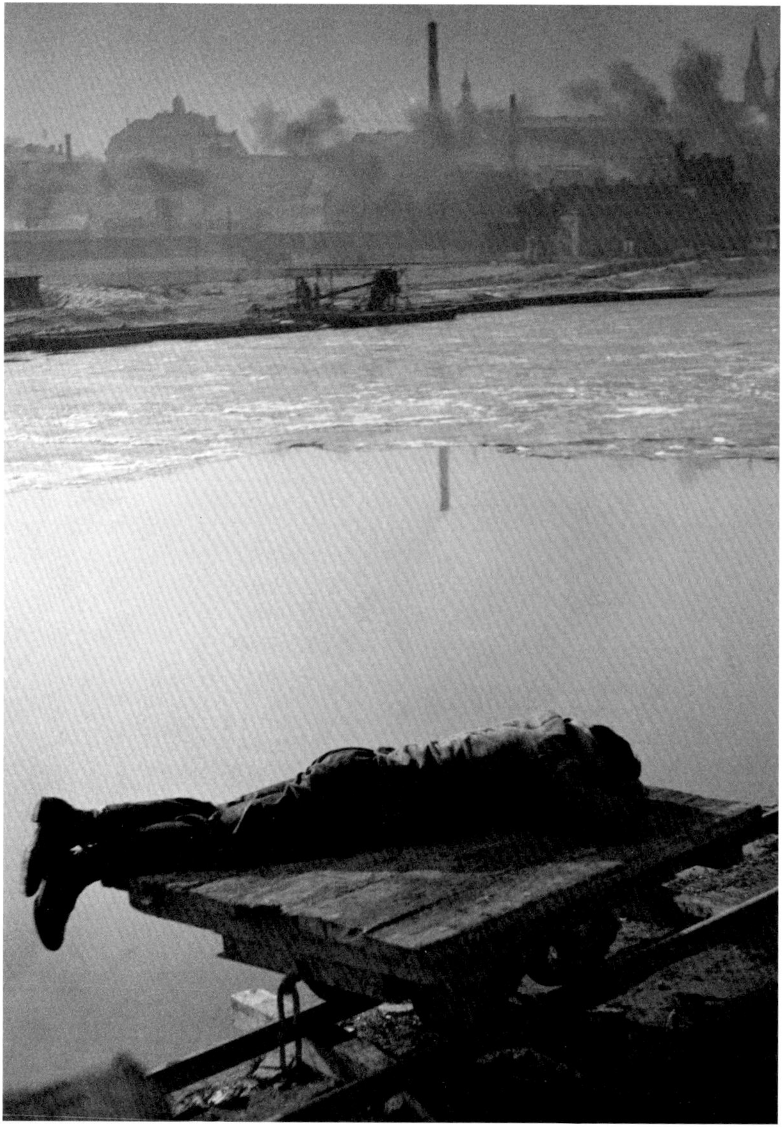

41 **On the Embankment / Na nábřeží** 1930s / 30. léta

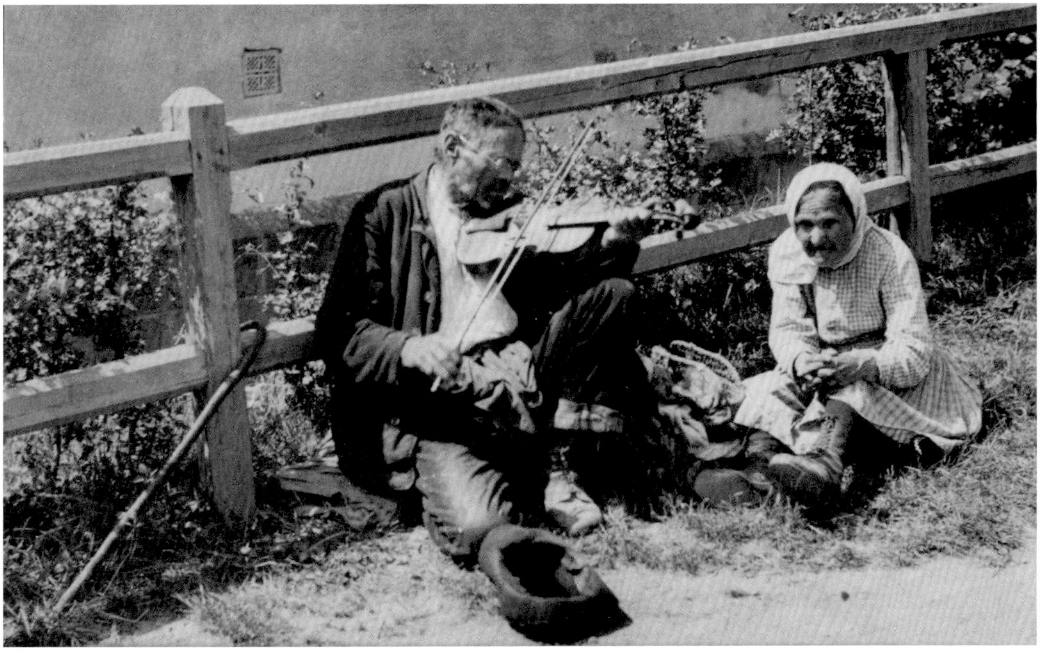

42 **Beggars / Žebráci** 1930s / 30. léta

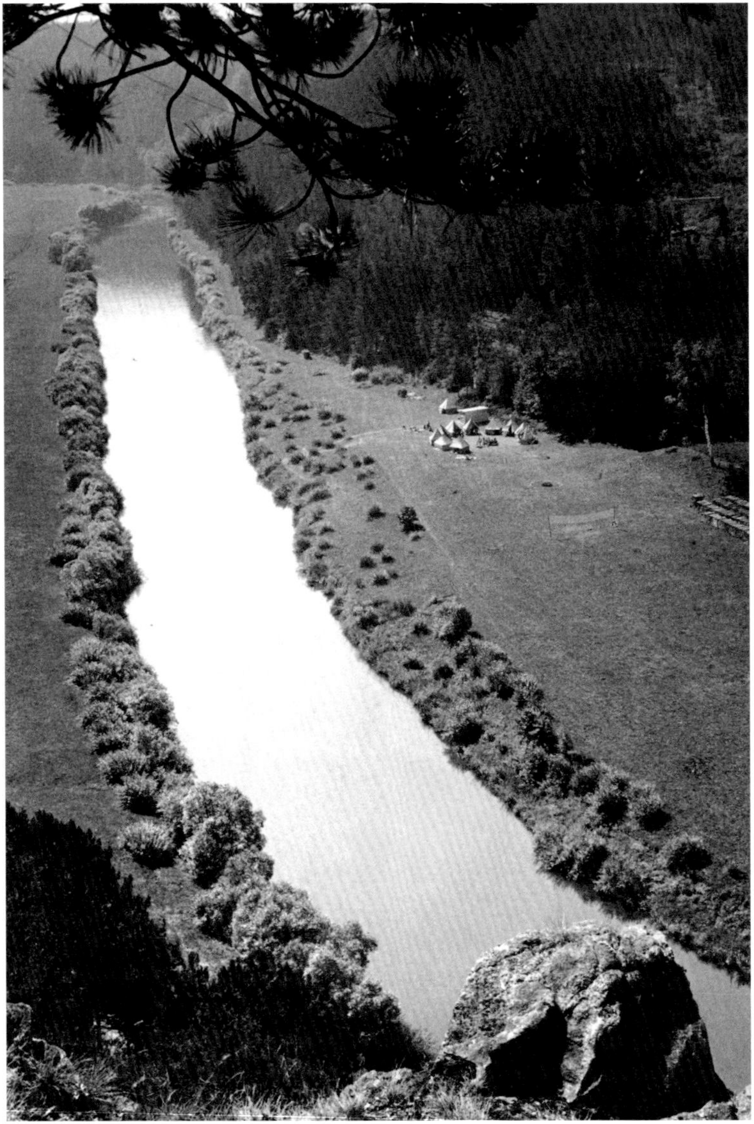

43 **Sázava** 1934

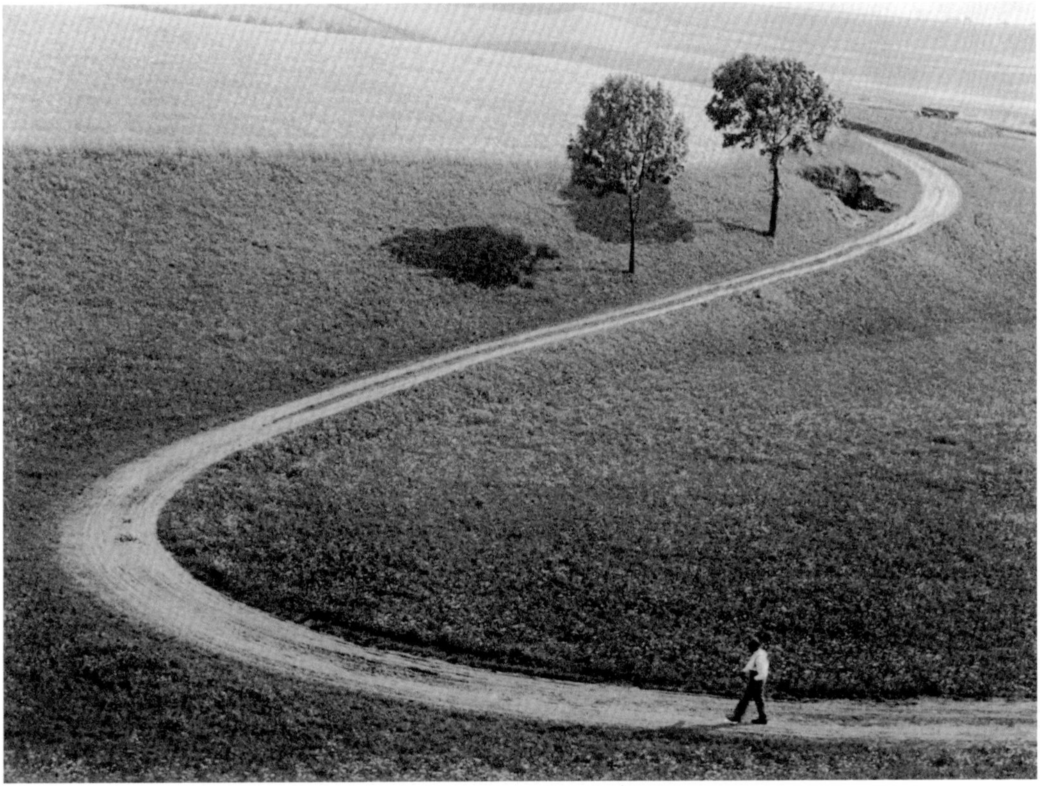

44 **Way near Police nad Metují / Cesta u Police nad Metují** before 1933 / před 1933

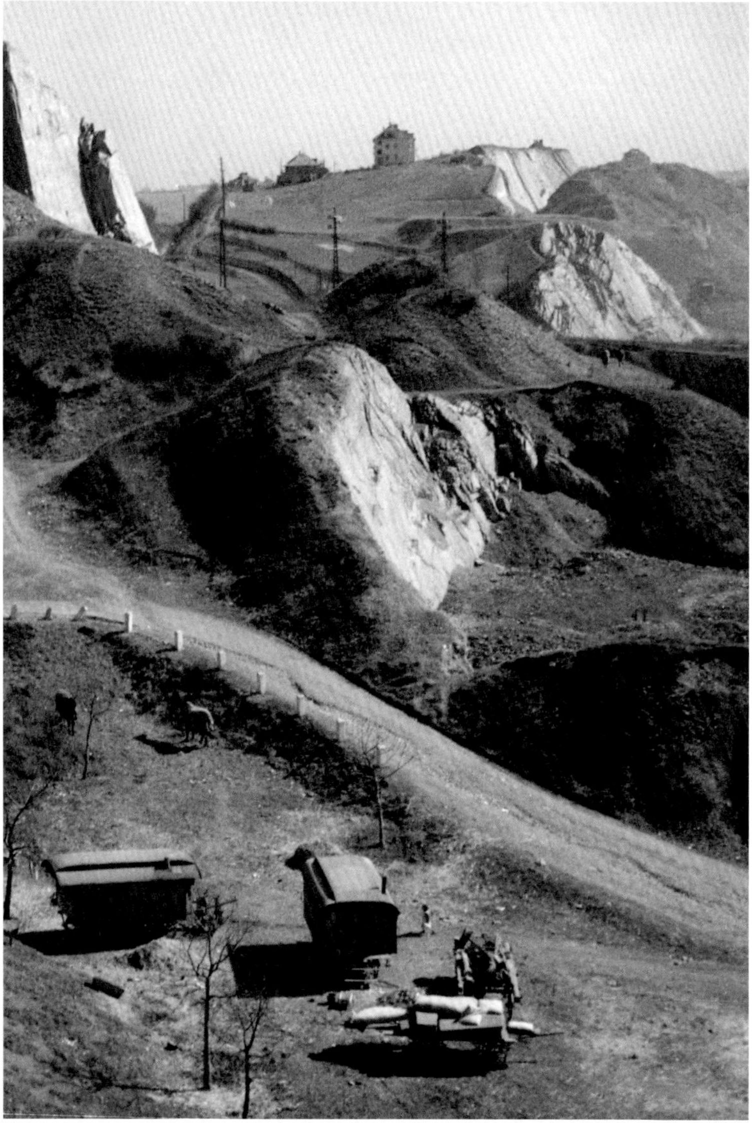

45 **Hlubočepy** c.1940

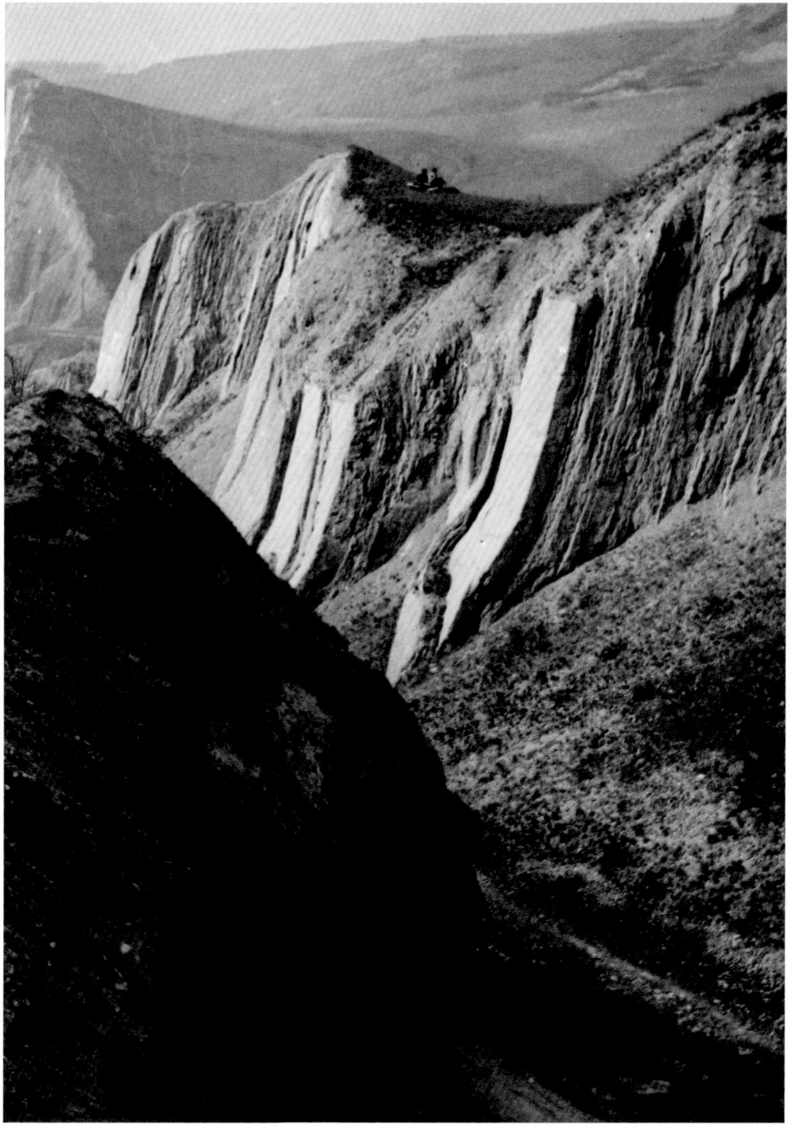

46 **Hlubočepy Cliffs / Hlubočepské skály** 1940

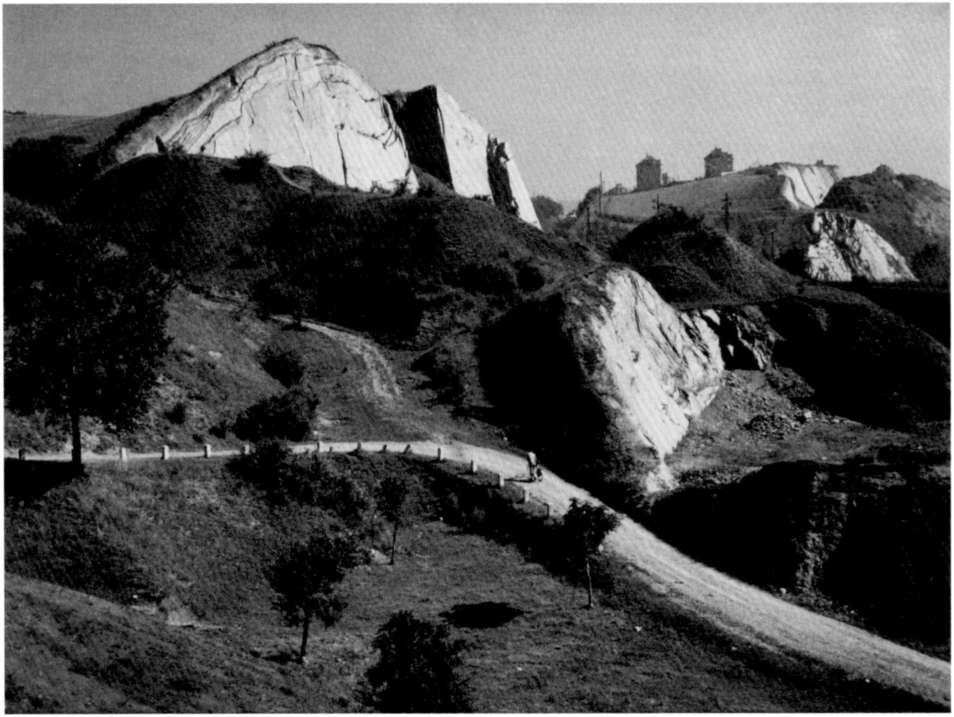

47 **Hlubočepy** 1943–44

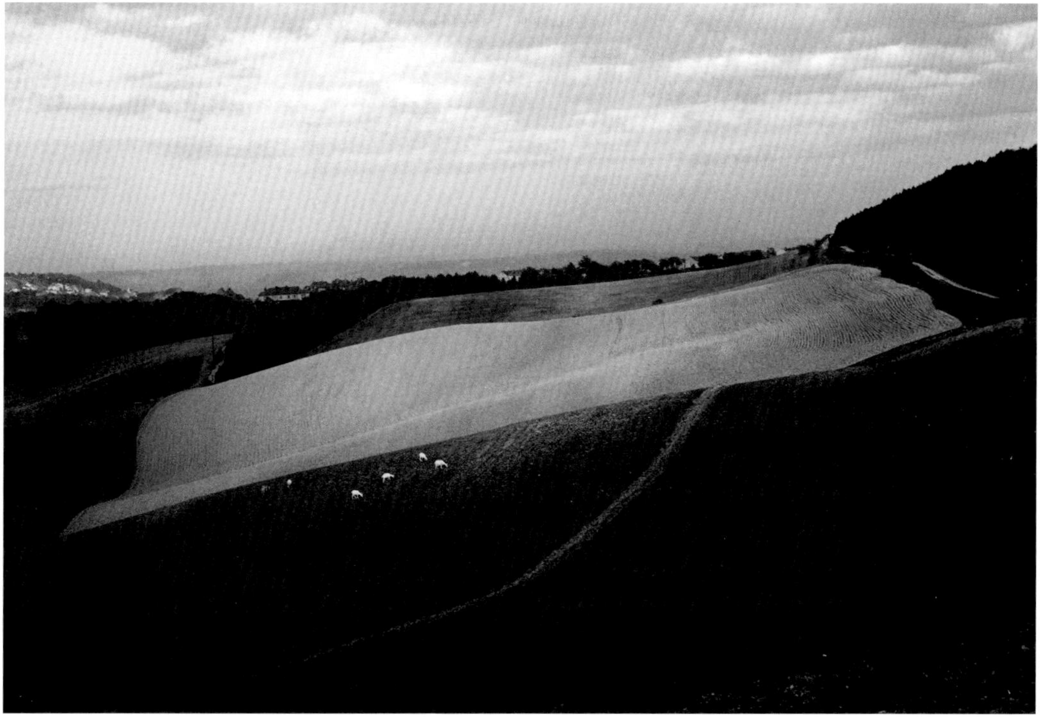

48 **Undulating Terrain II (Slapy) / Zvlněný terén II (Slapy)** 1946

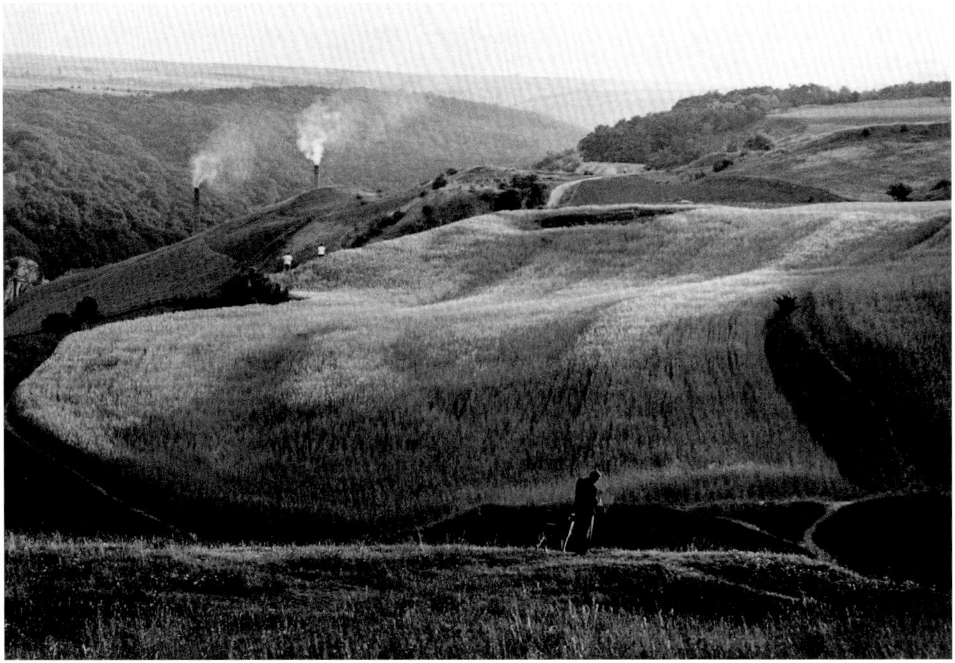

49 **Impressions / Imprese** 1942

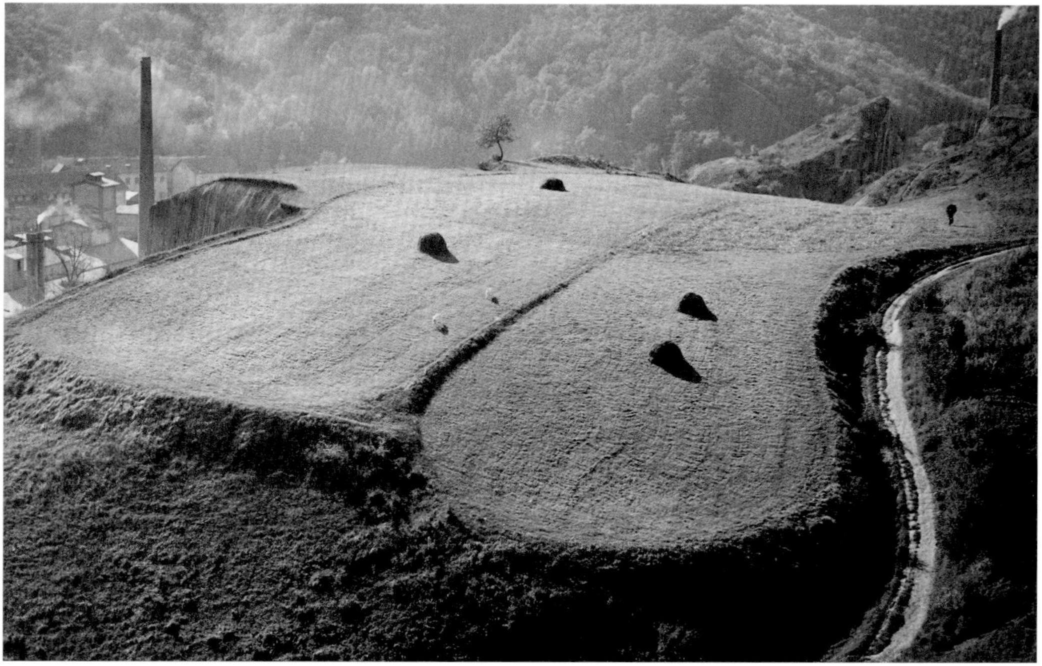

50 **Landscape near Prague (Hlubočepy) / Krajina u Prahy (Hlubočepy)** 1939

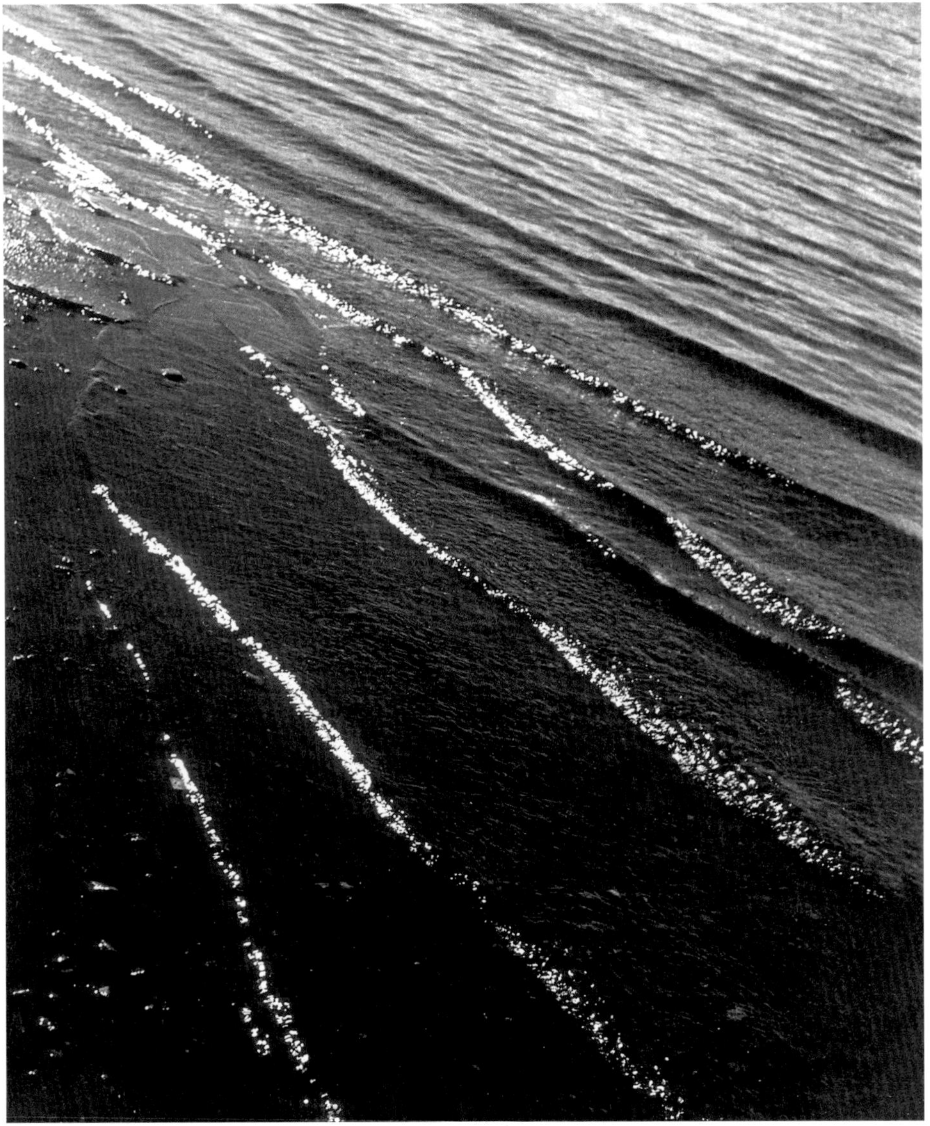

51 **Water / Voda** 1938

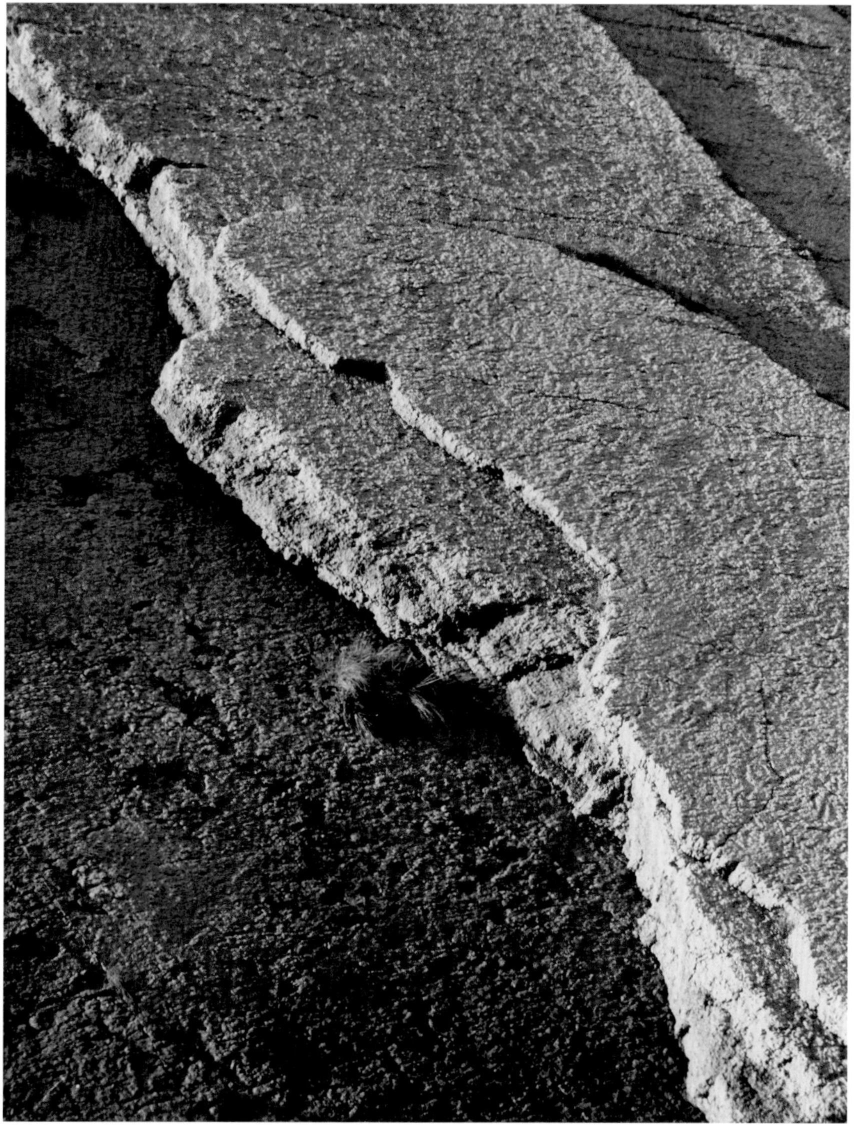

52 **Texture / Struktura** 1944

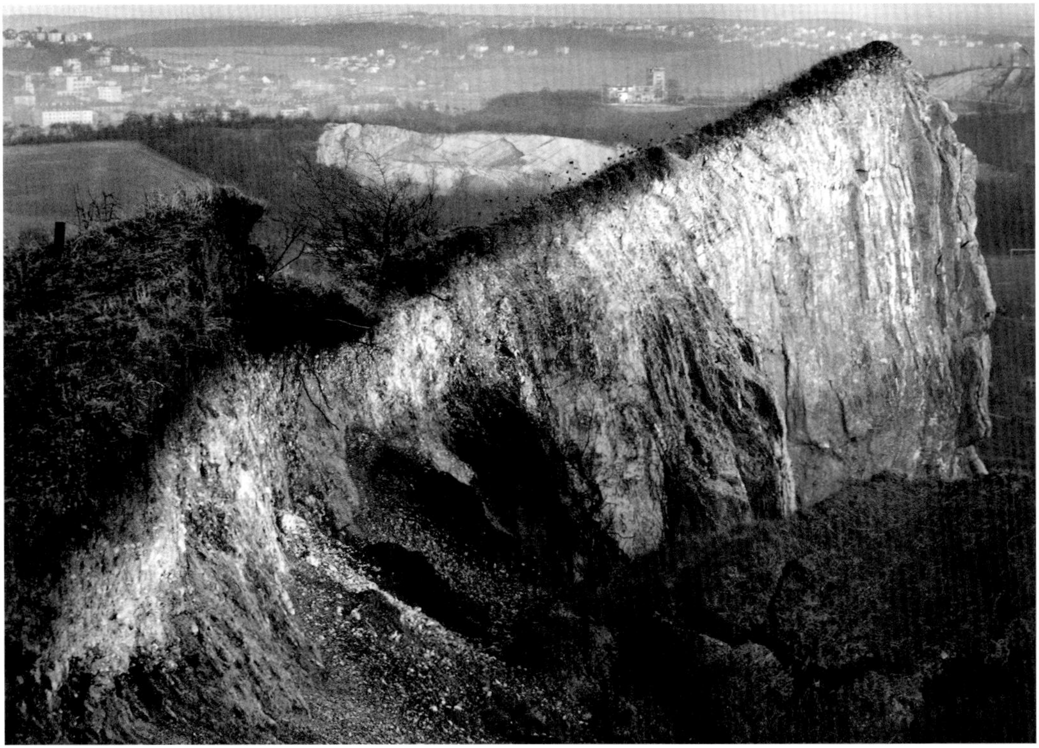

53 **Cliffs / Skála** 1946

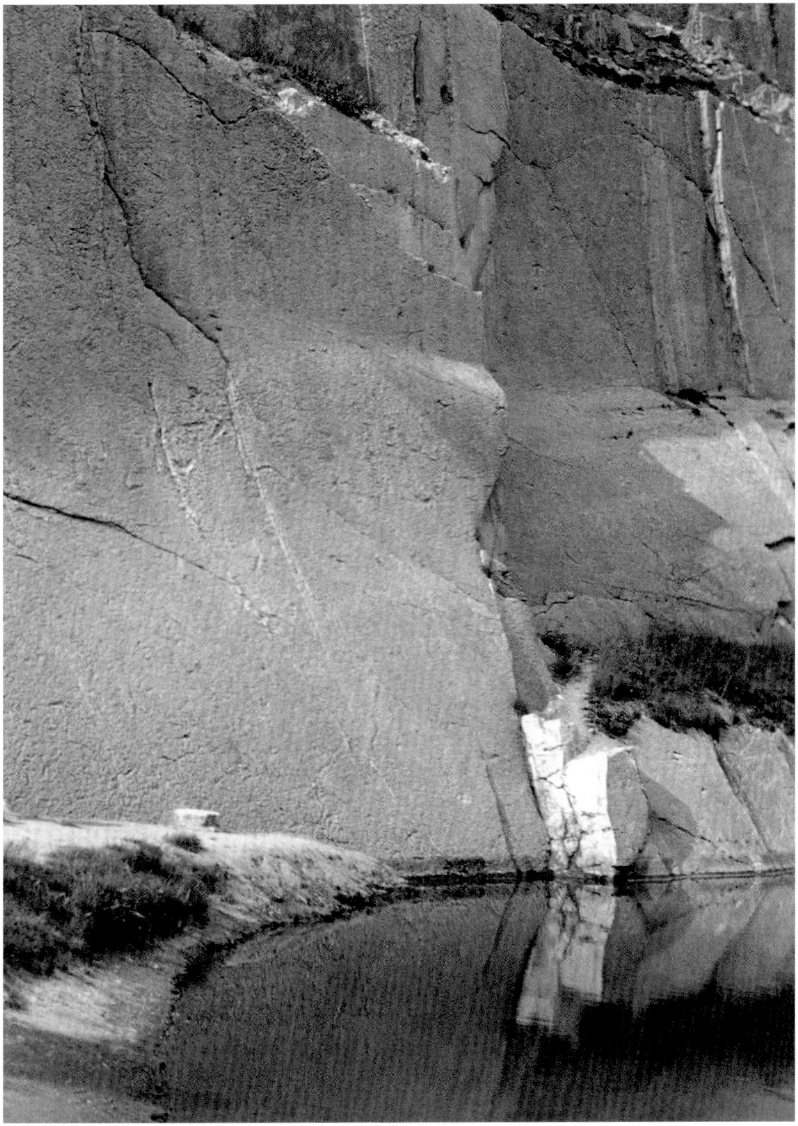

54 **Little Lake / Jezírko** 1940s / 40. léta

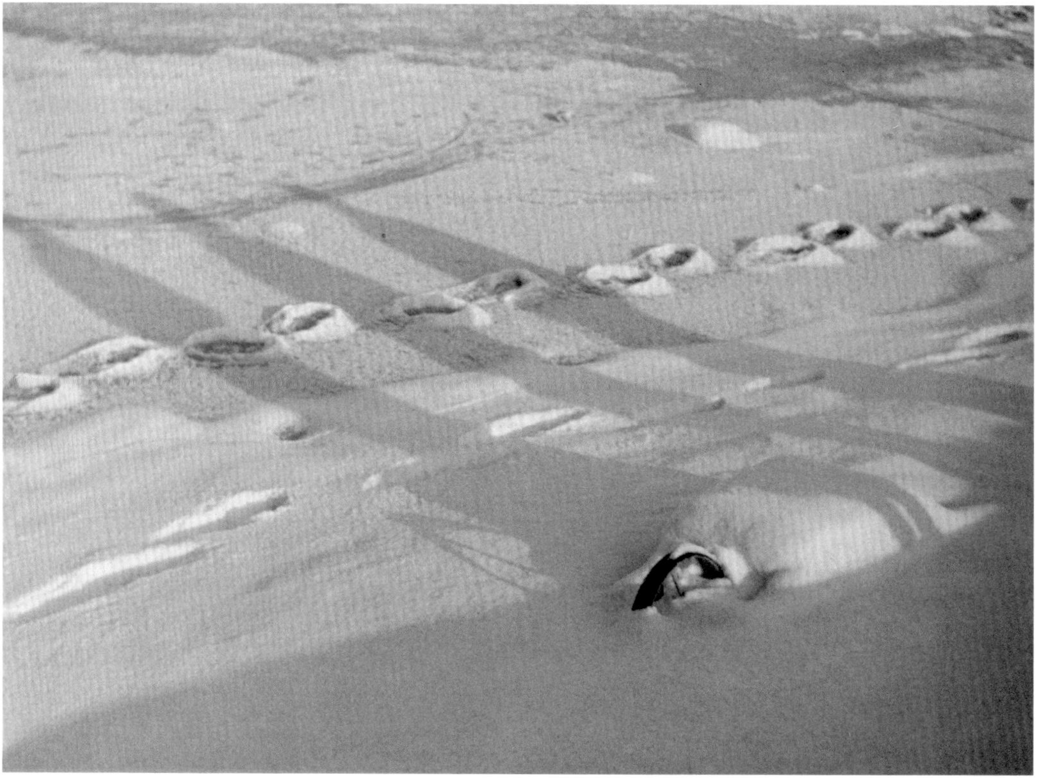

55 **Untitled / Bez názvu** 1929

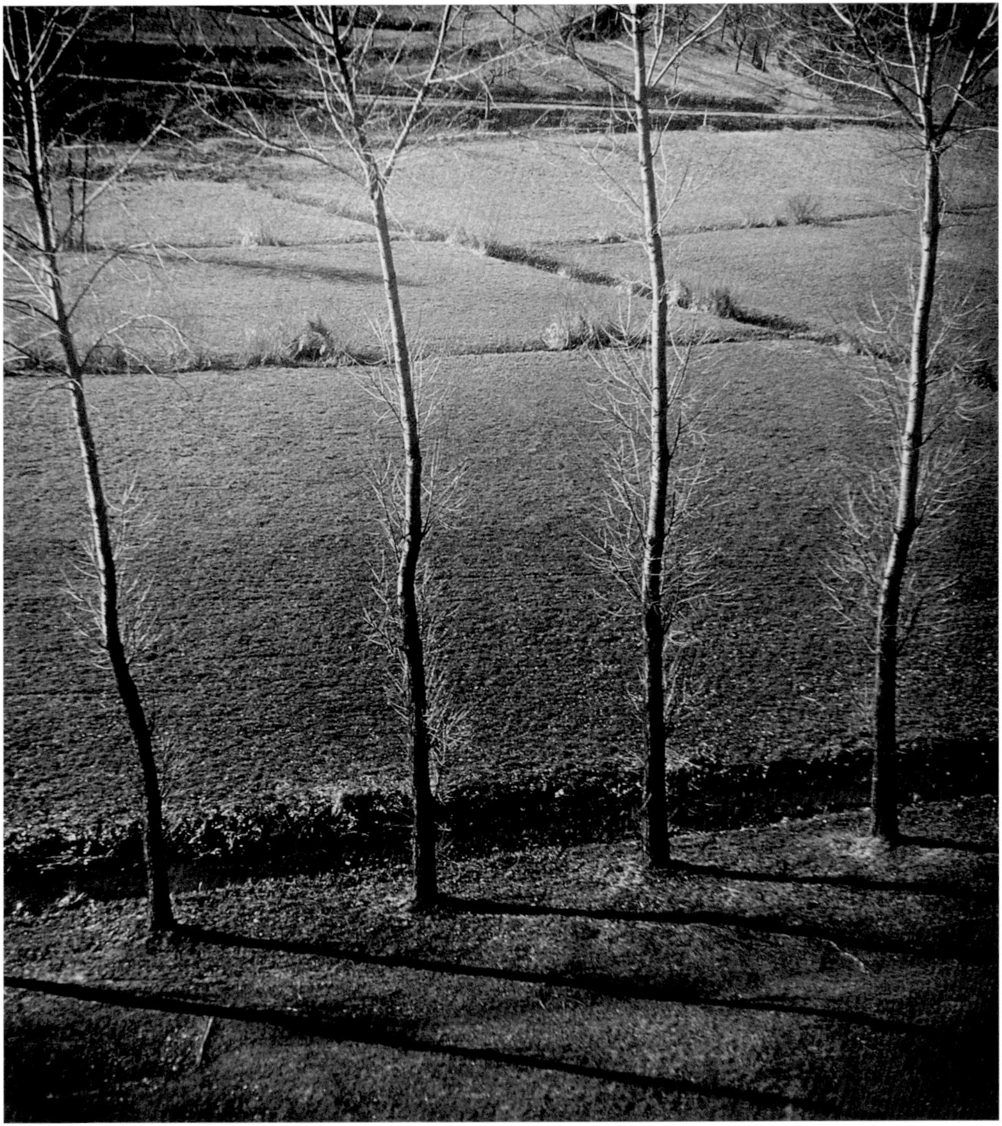

56 **Landscape near Kolín / Krajina u Kolína** 1933

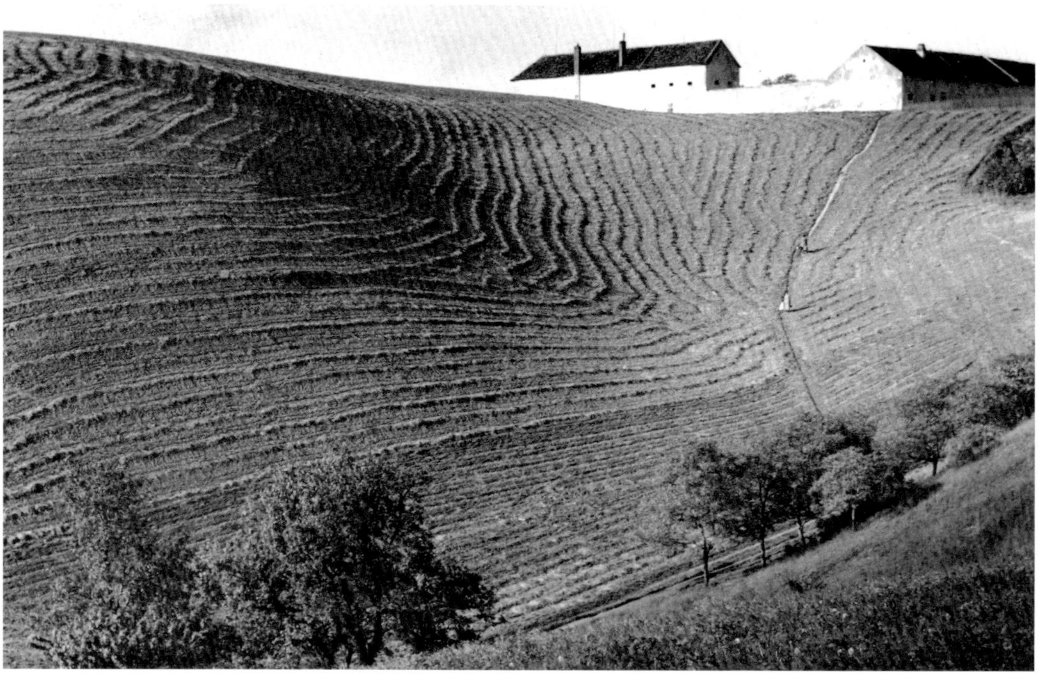

57 **Contour Lines / Vrstevnice** 1940–41

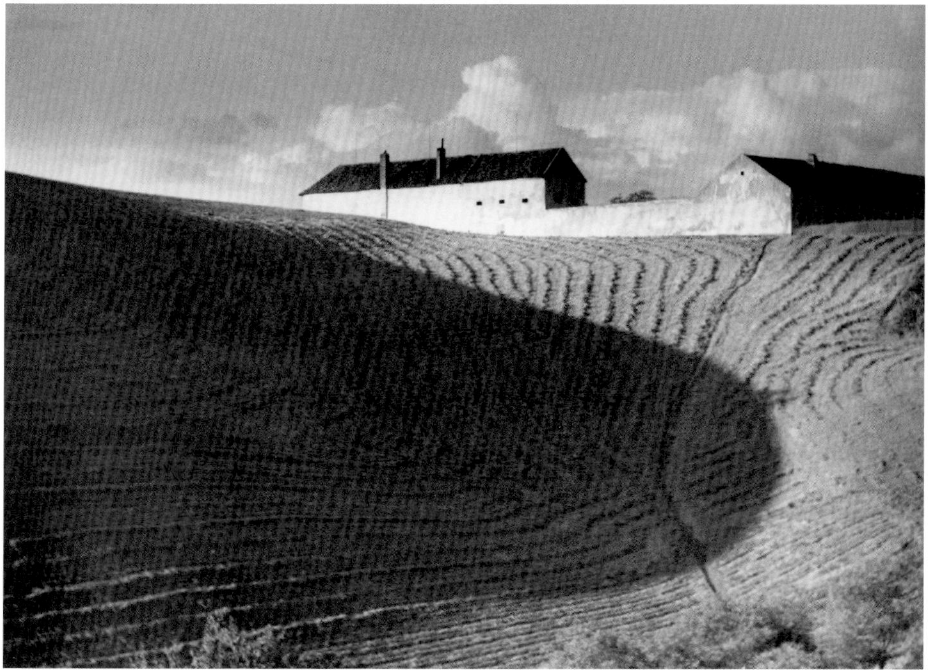

58 **Shadow / Stín** 1940

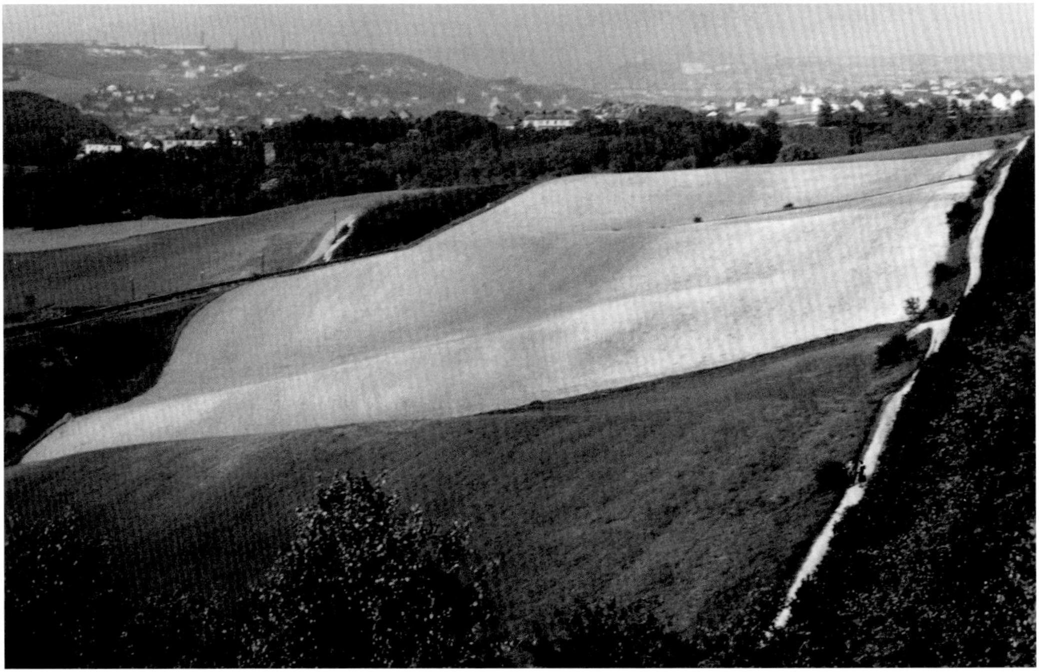

59 **Banner / Prapor** 1944

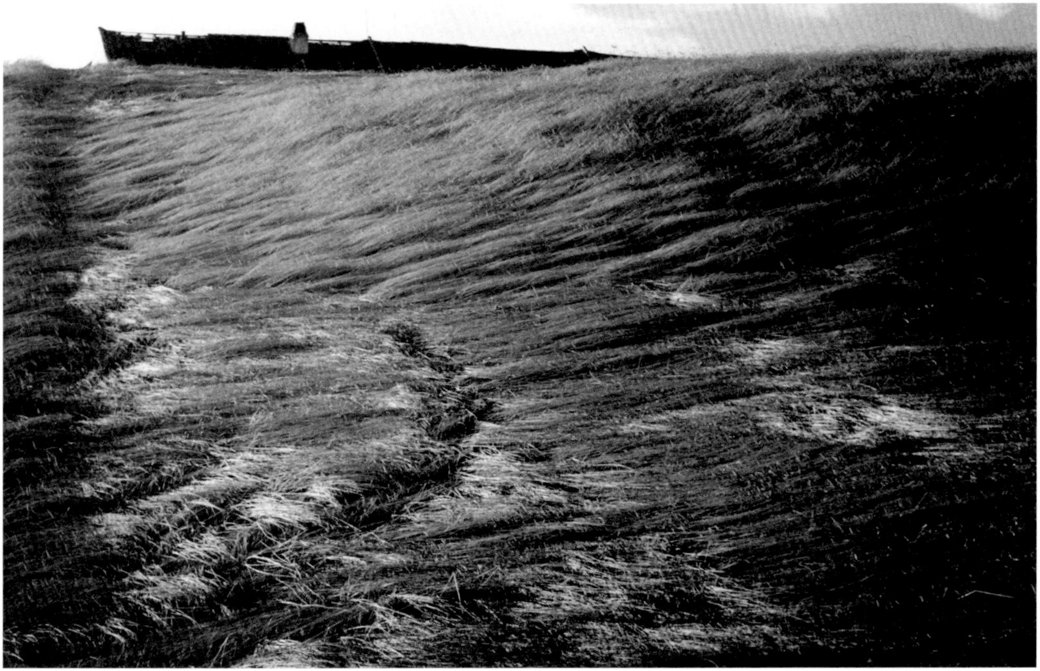

60 **Disaster (Wheat) / Katastrofa (Obilí)** 1939

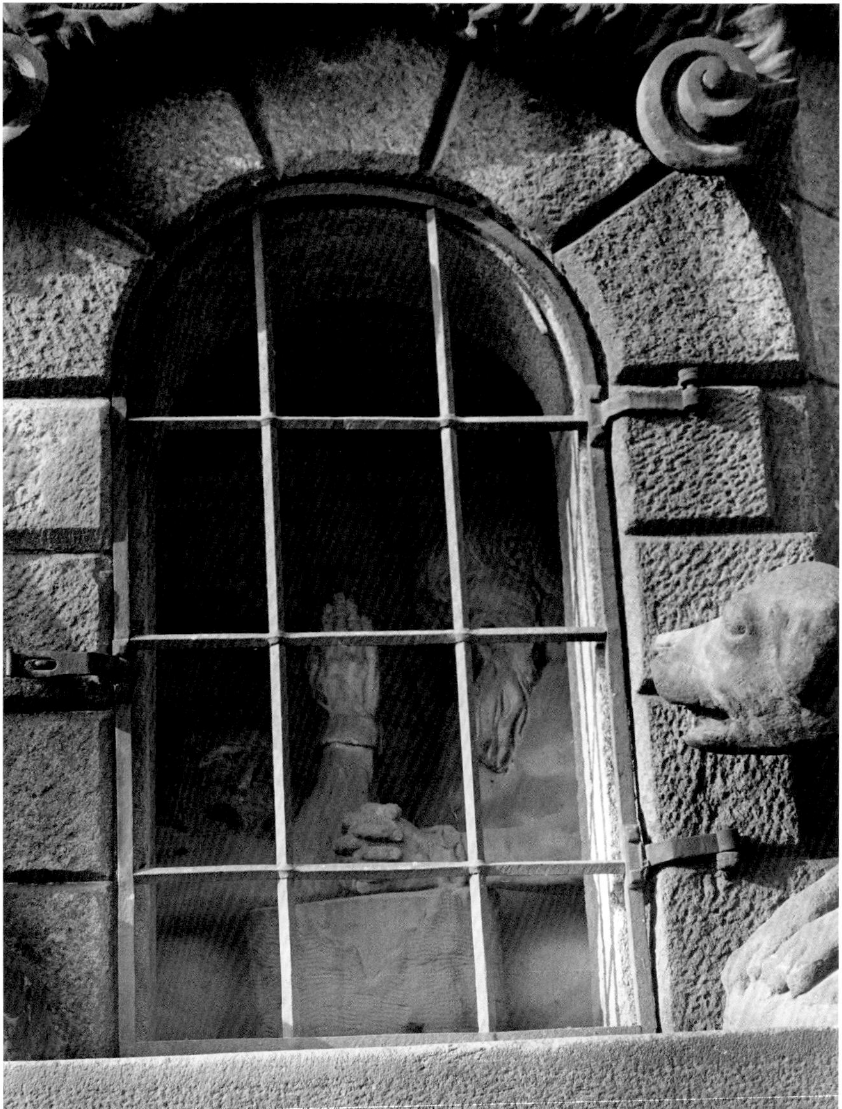

61 **Untitled / Bez názvu** undated / nedatováno

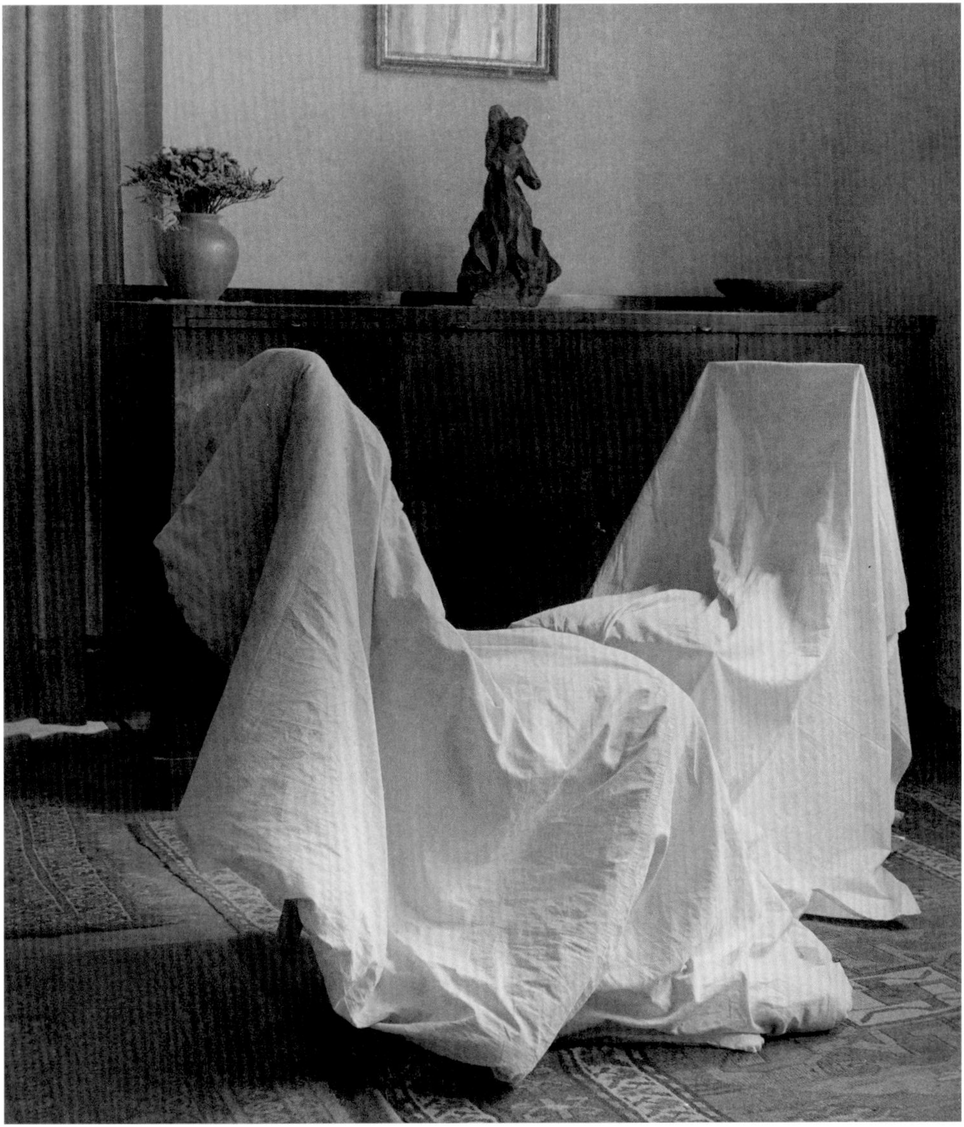

62 **Specters / Přízraky** 1939

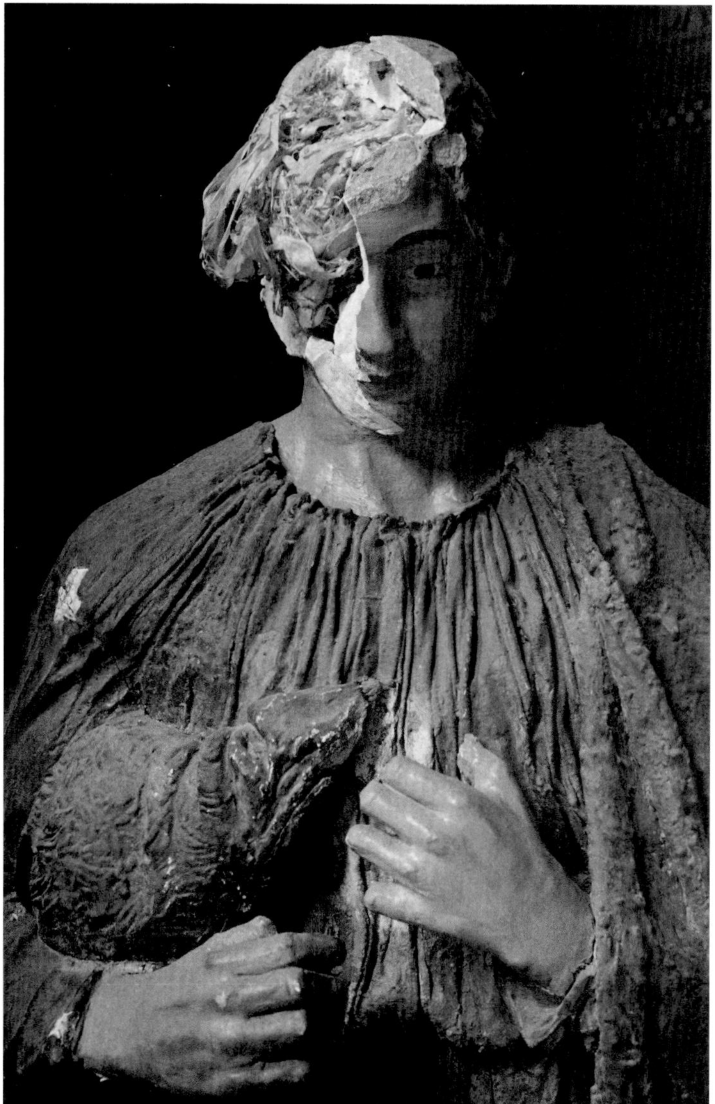

63 **Untitled / Bez názvu** undated / nedatováno

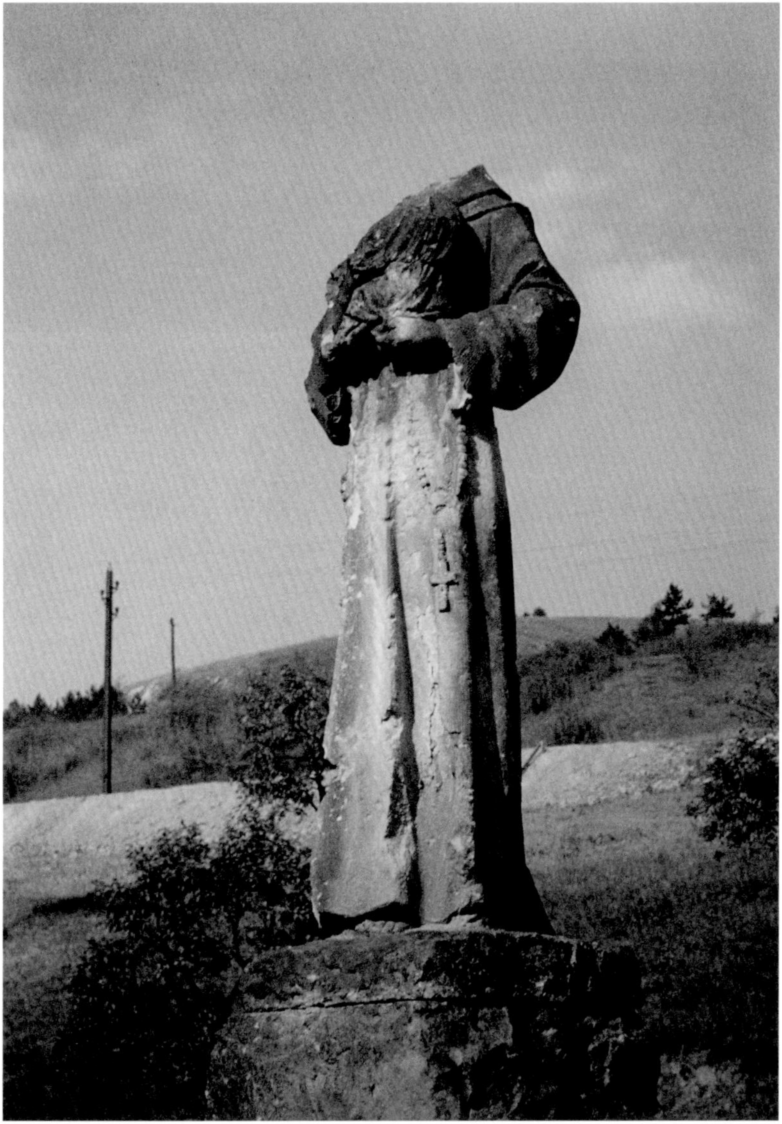

64 **Wounded Statue / Zraněná socha** undated / nedatováno

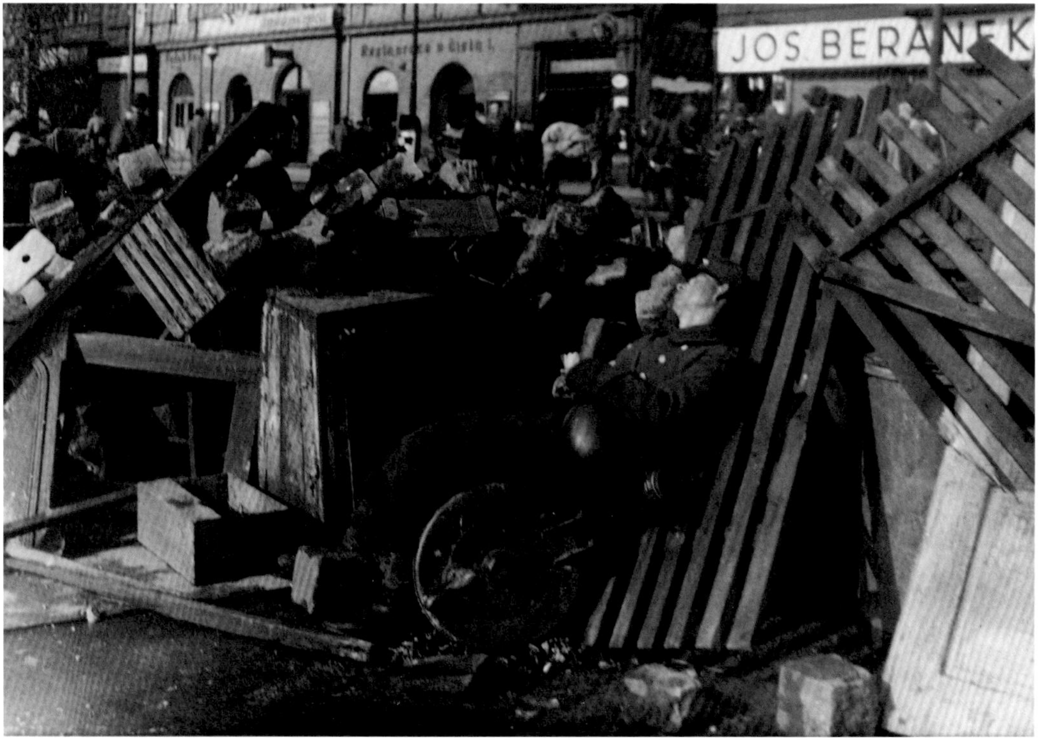

65 **Barricade, Prague Uprising / Barikáda, Pražské povstání** 1945

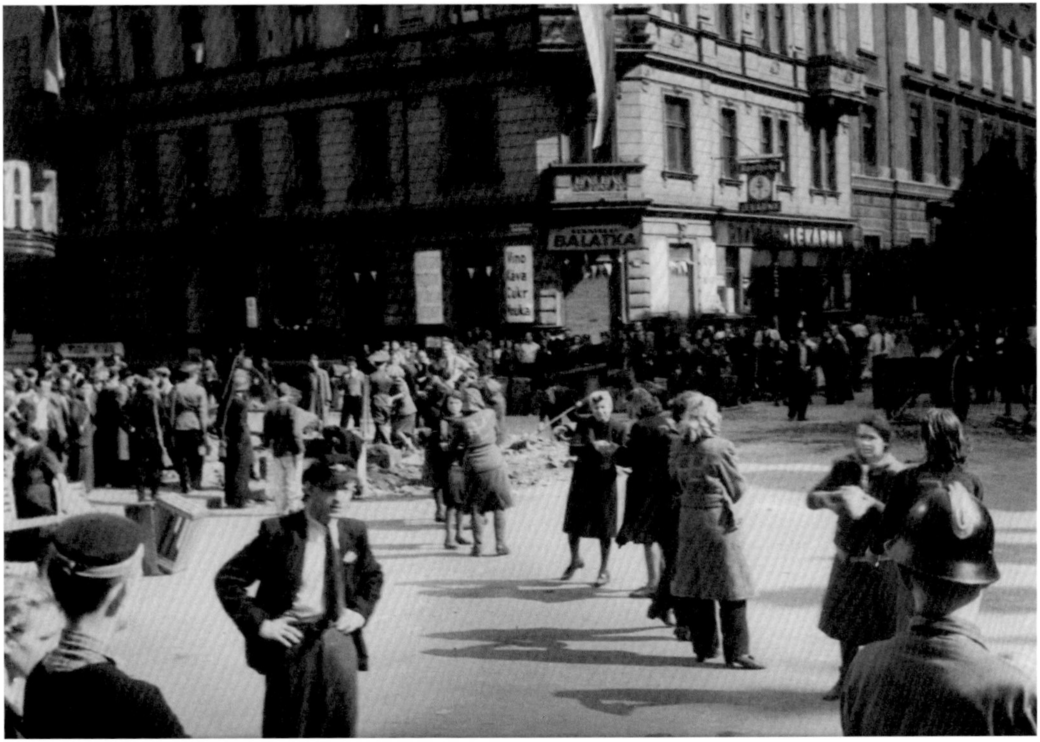

66 **German Women and Czech Collaborators Removing Barricades, Prague / Německé ženy a české kolaborantky při uklízení barikád v Praze** 1945

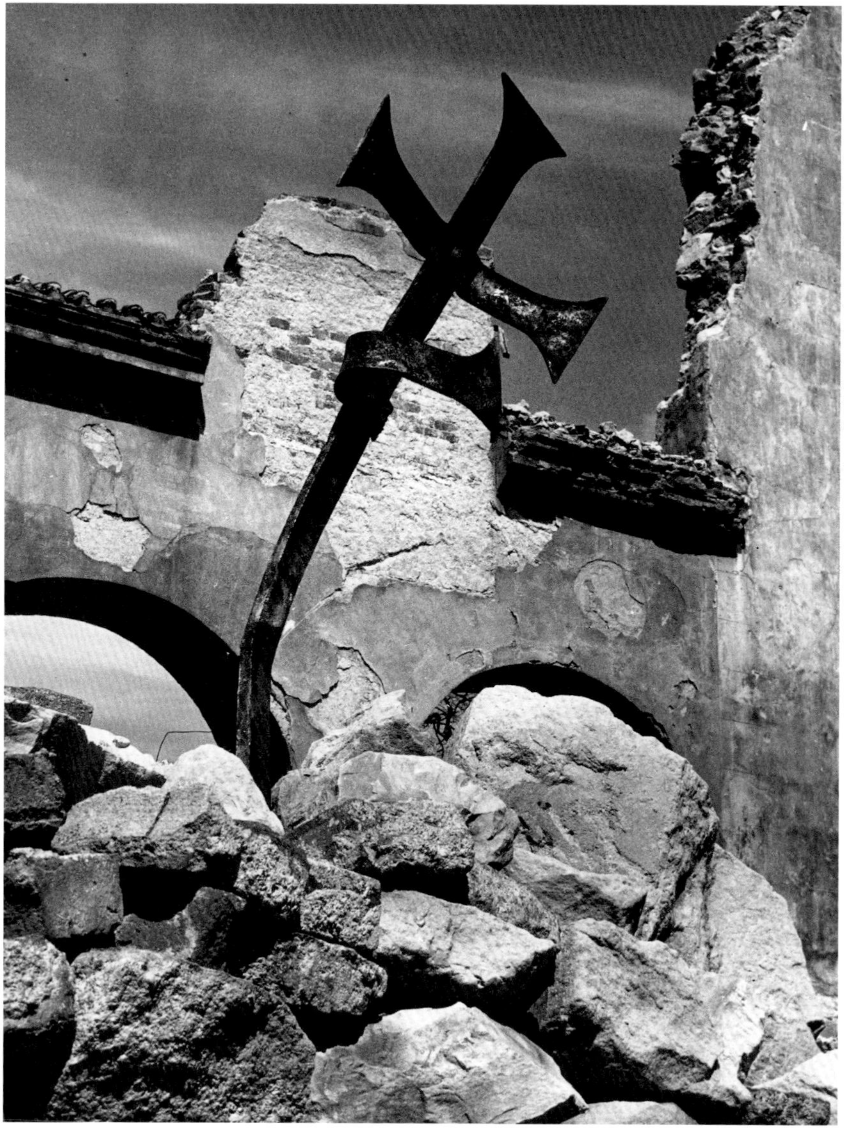

67 **After an Air Raid / Po náletu** 1945

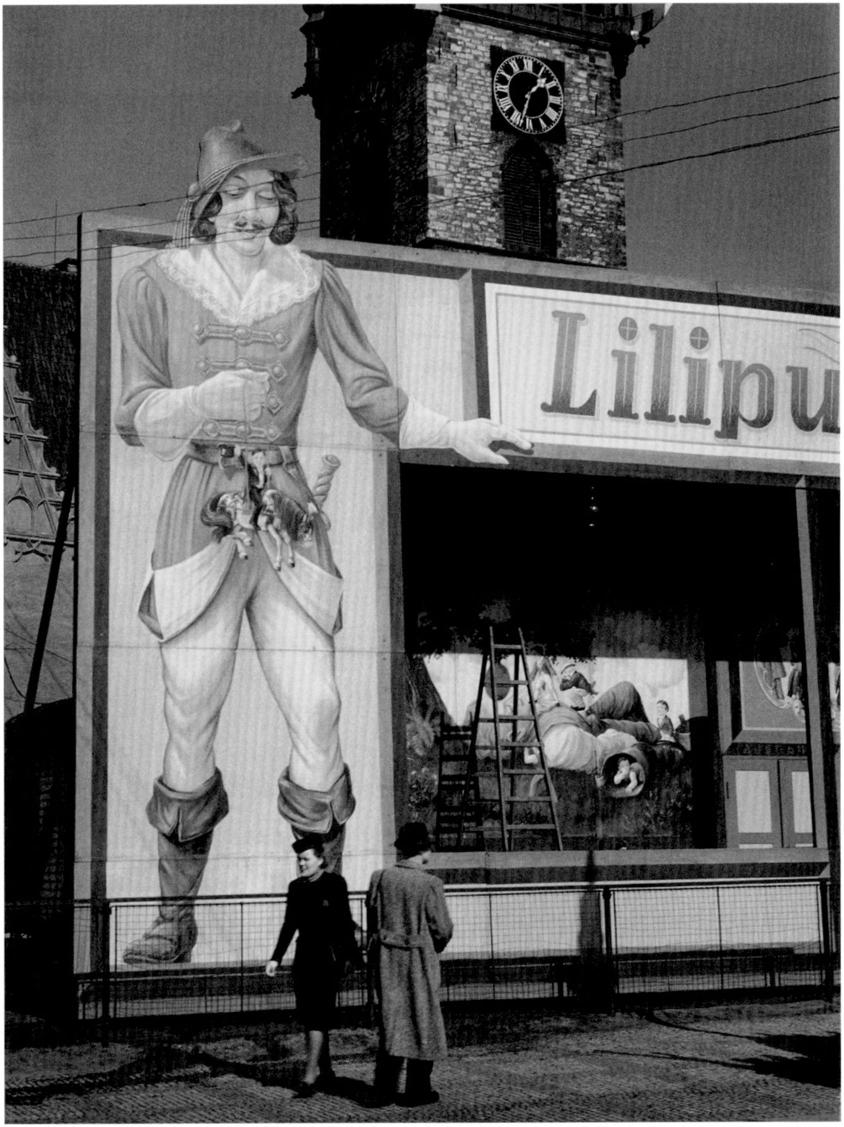

68 **At the New Town City Hall / U Novoměstské radnice** undated / nedatováno

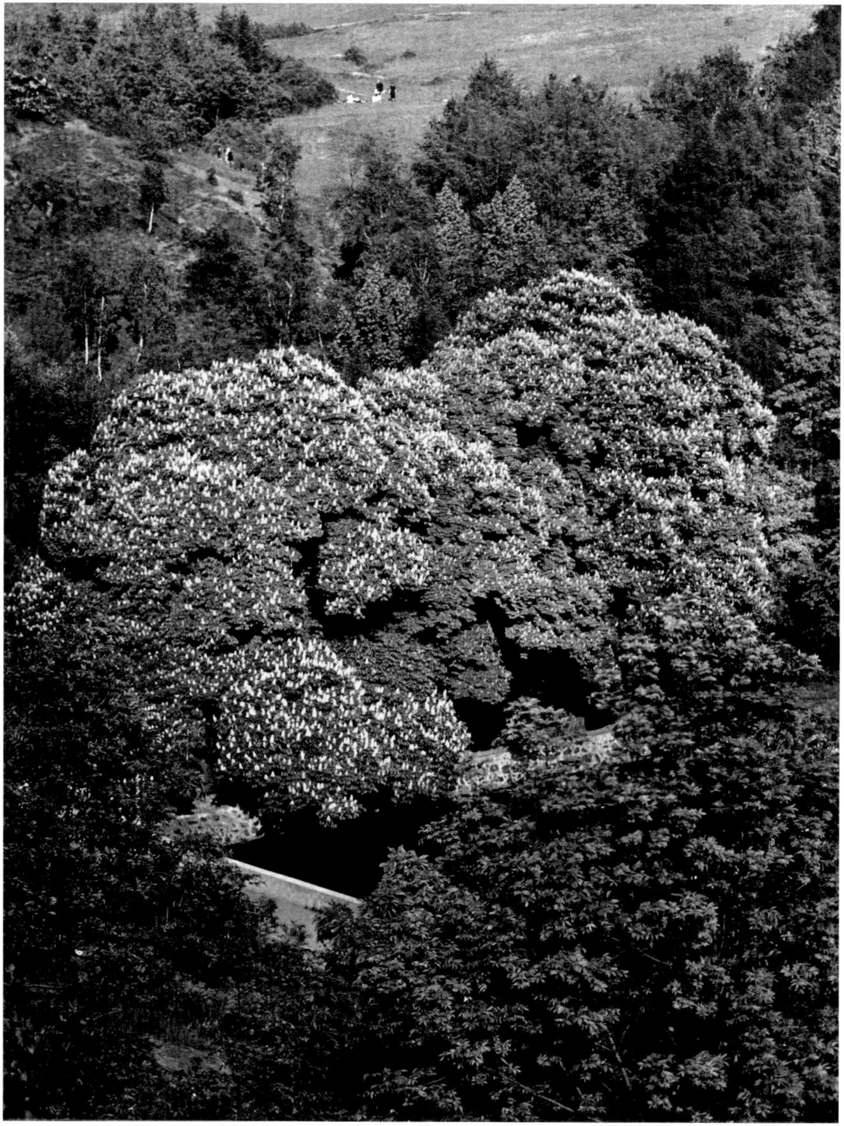

69 **Chestnuts / Kaštany** 1948

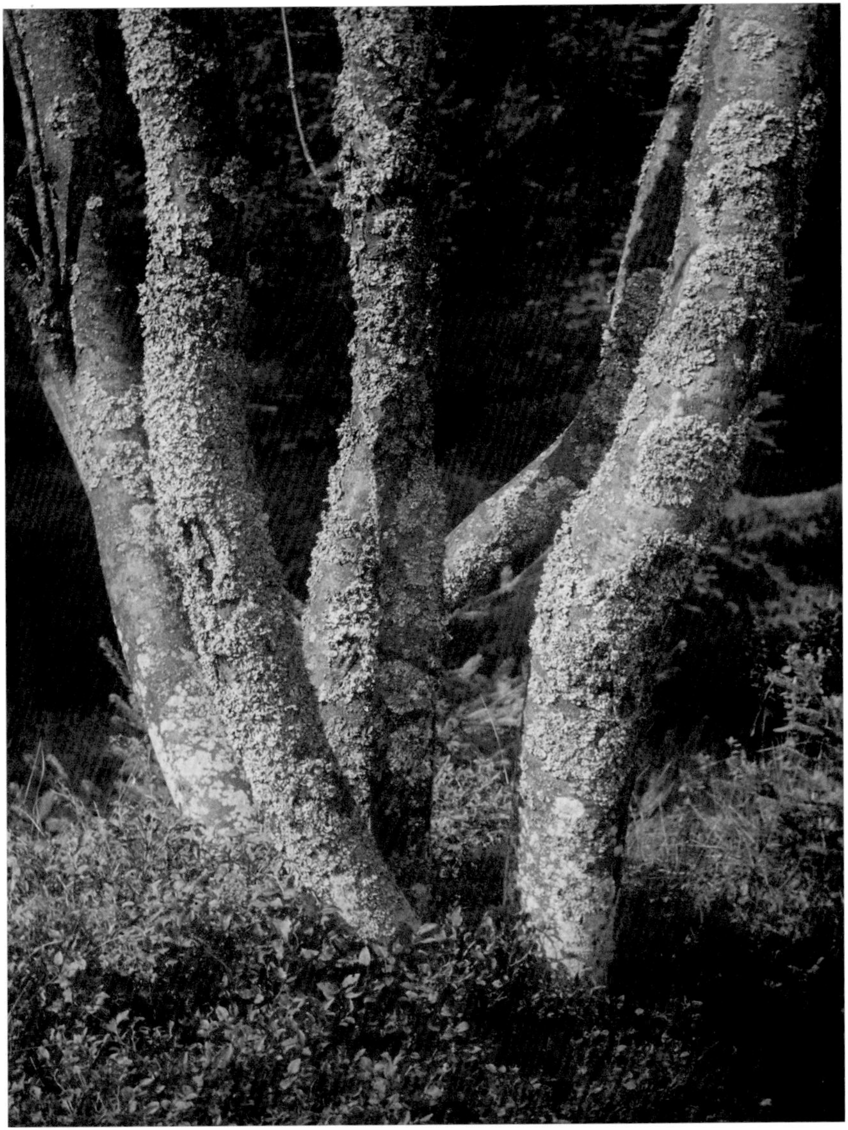

70 **Lichens / Lišejníky** 1954

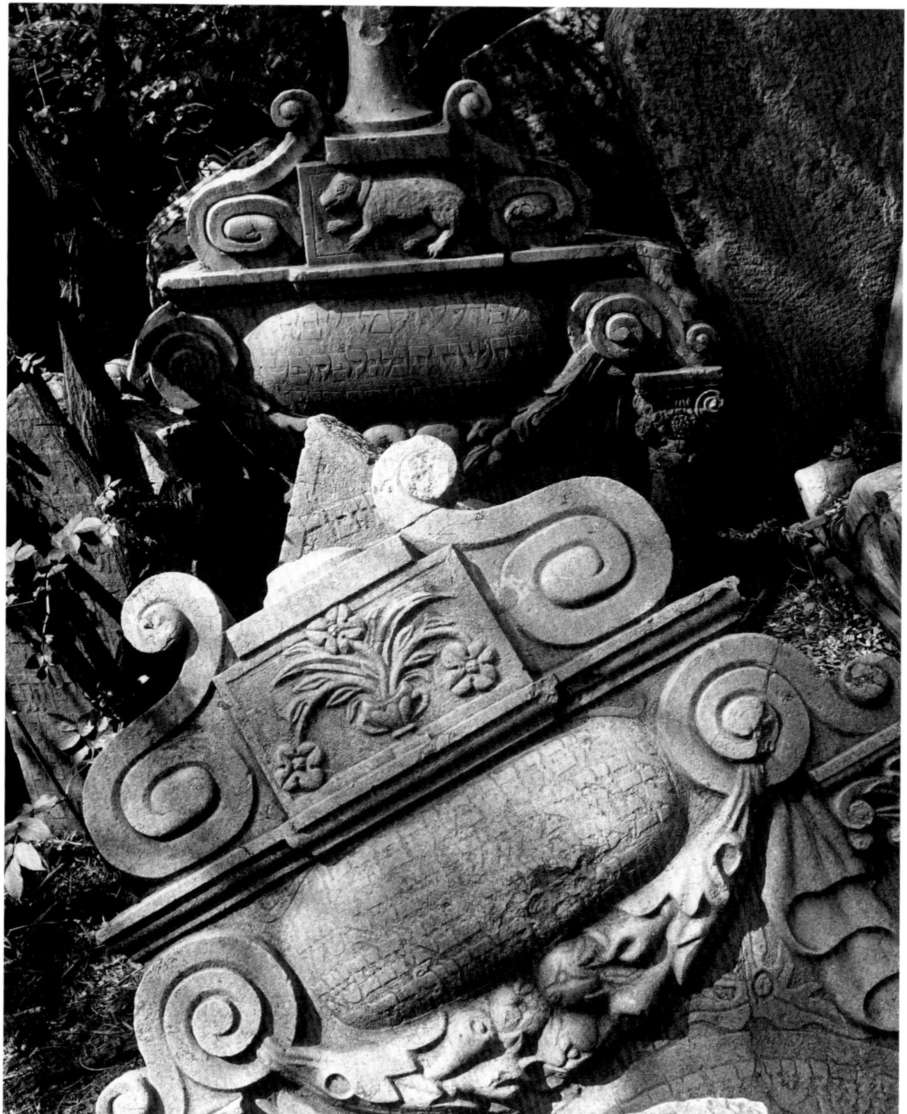

71 **The Old Jewish Cemetery / Ze Starého židovského hřbitova** 1953

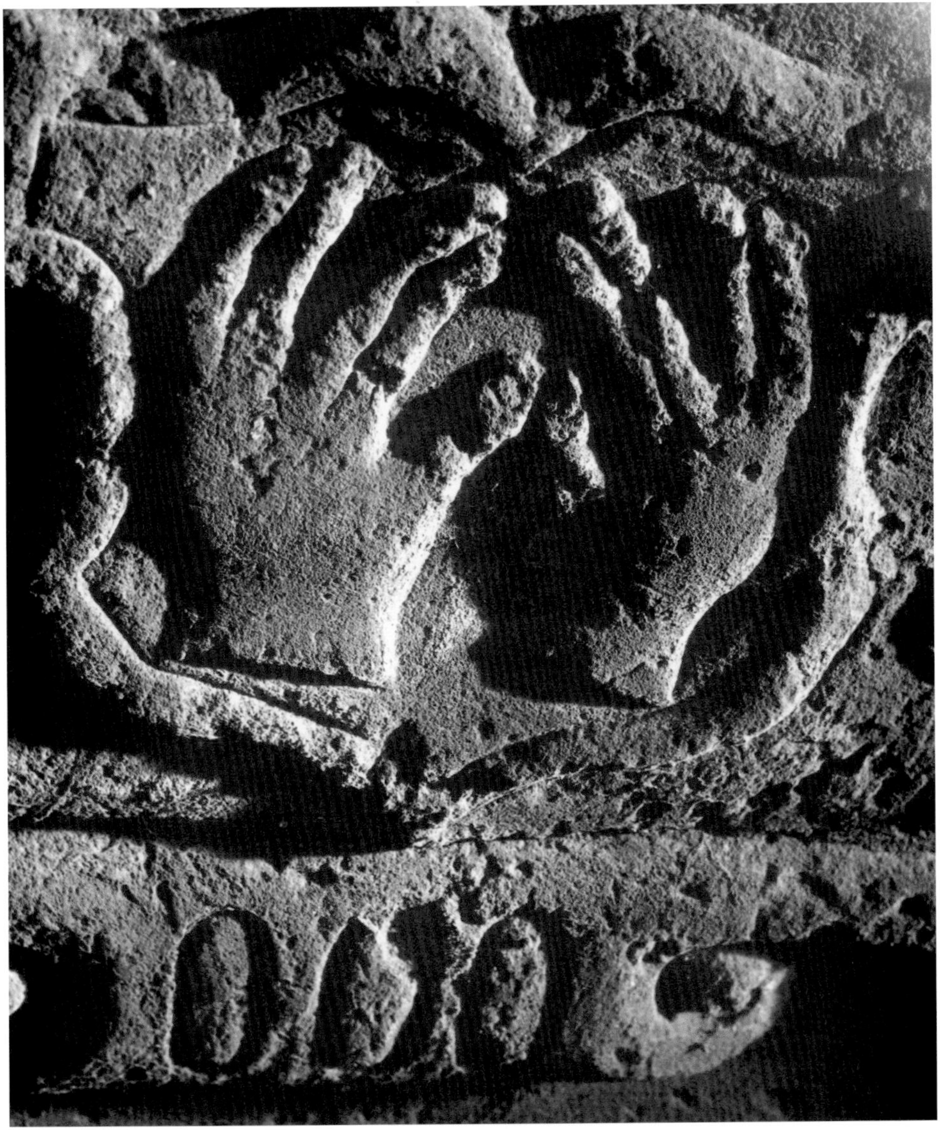

72 **The Old Jewish Cemetery (Sign) / Ze Starého židovského hřbitova (Znak)** 1952

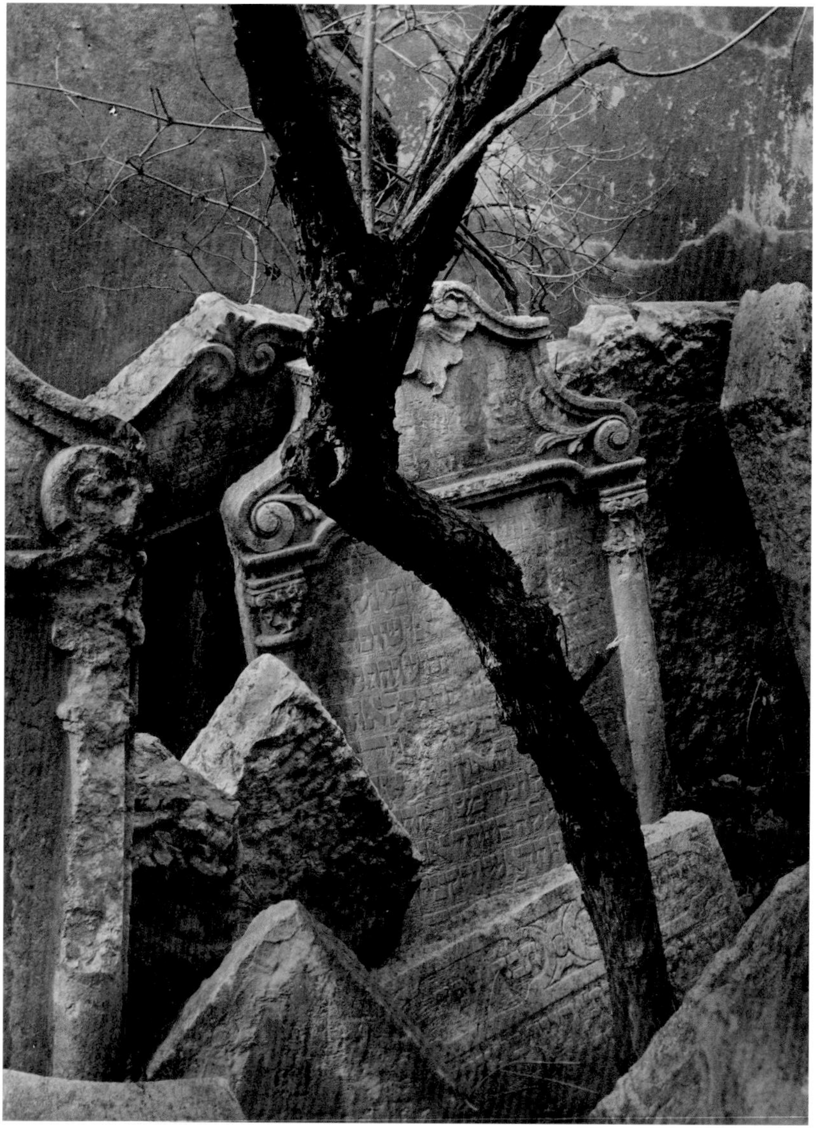

73 **The Old Jewish Cemetery / Ze Starého židovského hřbitova** 1950–51

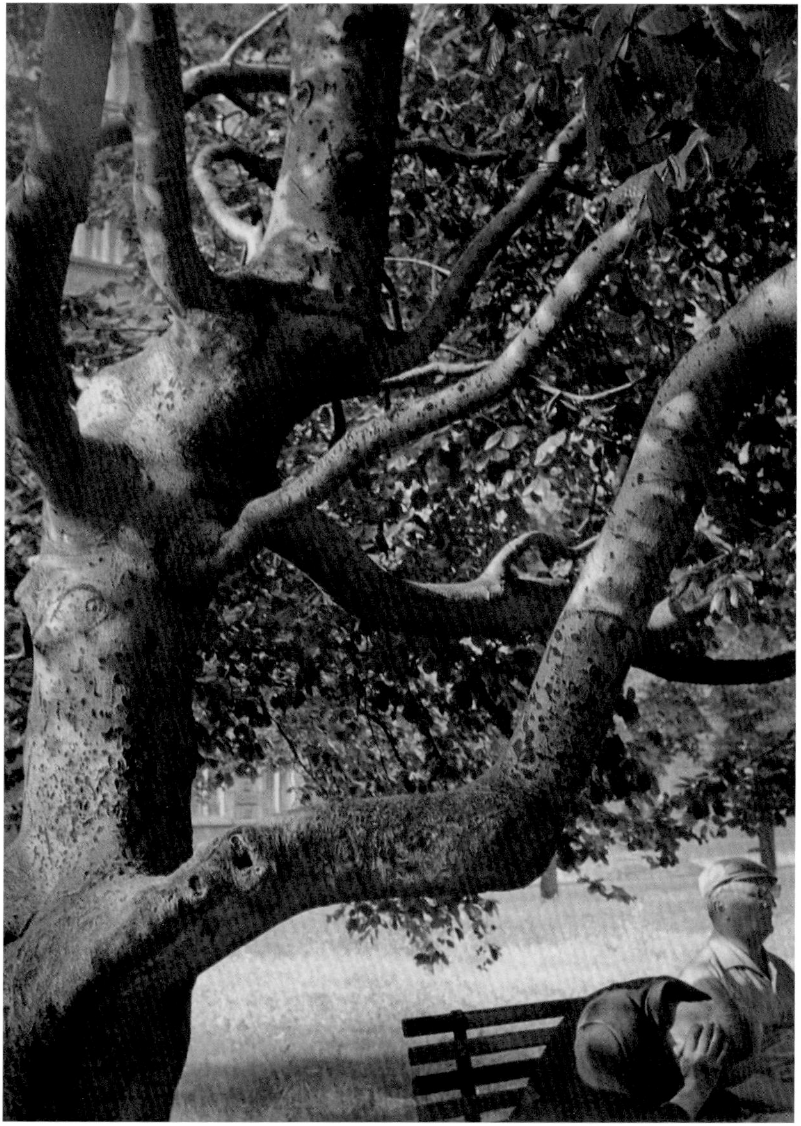

74 **On Charles Square / Na Karlově náměstí** 1950s / 50. léta

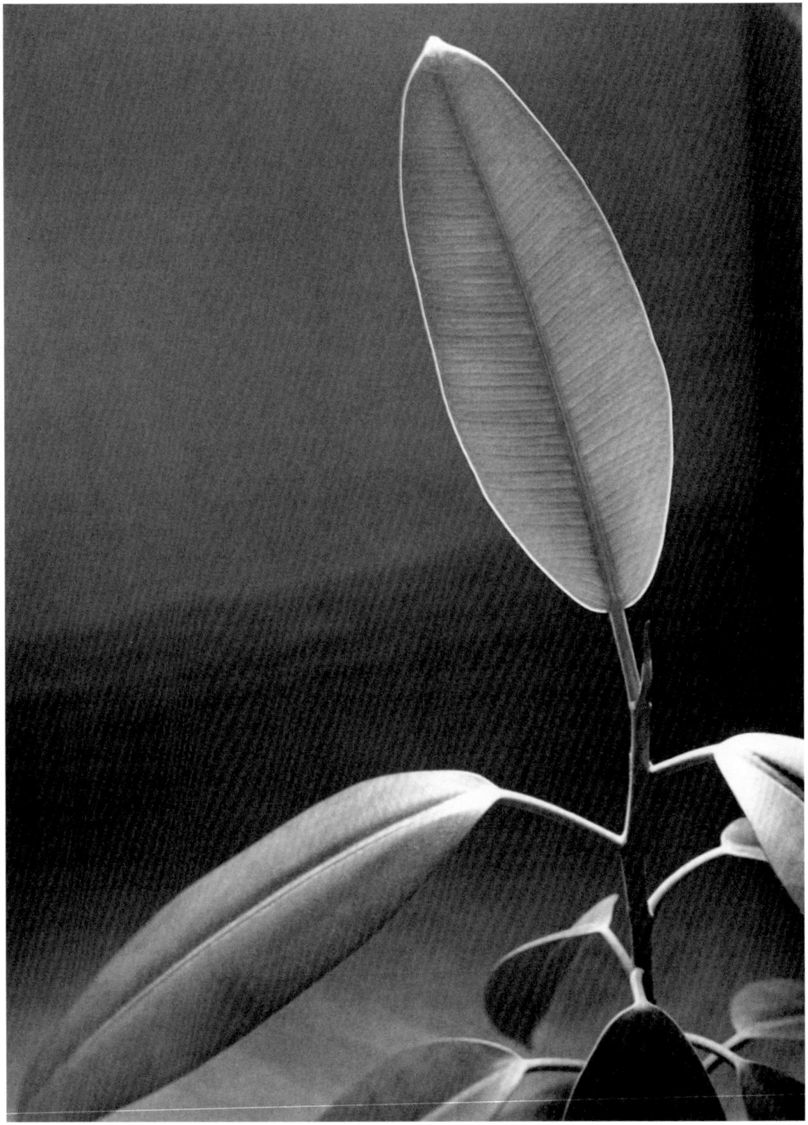

75 **Ficus / Fíkus** 1950s / 50. léta

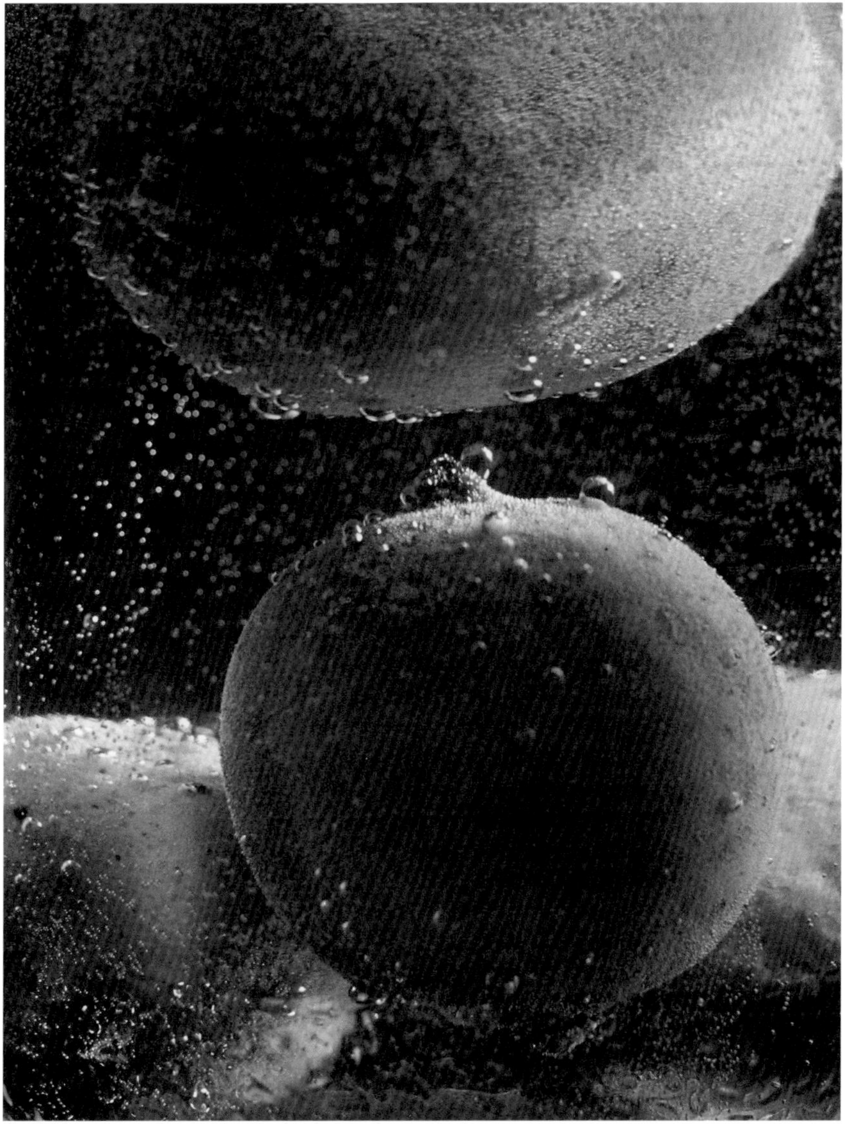

76 **Lemons / Citróny** 1956

Biographical Chronology

1888 On 20 September, born in the town of Dvůr Králové nad Labem, Bohemia, the second son of Alois Wiškovský, director of the general hospital in Dvůr Králové, before his marriage a professional soldier, and Eugenie Wiškovská, née Hotovcová. His elder brother was Alois (b. 1887), and he would soon have two other brothers, Otakar (b. 1890) and Bedřich (b. 1891).

1902 His father gave him his first camera, a 9 × 12 cm for sheet film.

1906 Matriculated from the *gymnasium* in Dvůr Králové, and began to study French, German, and psychology at the Czech University of Prague.

1909 Spent the winter semester on a scholarship at the University of Geneva.

1910 Graduated from university.

1910–12 Taught at the *realgymnasium* in the Prague district of Žižkov and in Prague II.

1912 Began teaching at the *realgymnasium* in Kolín.

1914–17 Fought as a soldier in the Austro-Hungarian army at the front in Italy and Russia. After being wounded twice he was transferred behind the lines to the town of Česká Lípa, north Bohemia.

1917 On 28 April, married Anna Streitová, who was born in Gródek, Galicia, on 8 August 1893. Briefly interested in photography again.

1918 On 23 March, Eugen and Anna Wiškovský's first child, Eva, was born. She would grow up to become a doctor.

1919 Returned to teaching at the *realgymnasium* in Kolín, and would remain there till 1937.
On 9 June, Eugen and Anna Wiškovský's second daughter, Hana, was born.

1928 Made his first mature photographic portraits, which involve experimenting with composition, lighting, and shadows.

1928–29 Made his first photographs of static objects in the style of New Objectivity, including *Collars* (later called *Lunar Landscape*), *Eggs*, *Insulator*, and *Pipes*. Worked together on photographs with his former pupil at the *gymnasium* Jaromír Funke.
In the 12th issue of *Foto*, 1929, published his first article on theory, "O obrazové fotografii" (Concerning pictorial photography), and then published nothing till eleven years later.

1930 Showed photographs in the "New Photography" exhibition in the gallery of the Aventinum publishing house (Aventinská mansarda or Aventinum Garret), in Purkyňova ulice, Prague, organized by Alexandr Hackenschmied, the first Prague group exhibition of avant-garde photography. He would then participate in a similar exhibition the following year.

1930–34 With Funke often took photographs of motifs from the building-site of the Functionalist ESSO power station in Kolín.

1933 Had work in the "Exhibition of Social-documentary Photography" in the Palais Metro, Prague, organized by the Cinema–Photography (Film–foto) group of the Left Front (Levá fronta) led by Lubomír Linhart. (The exhibition then moved on to Brno.) Made different versions of the photograph of the insulator.

1936 Five of his photographs were shown in the "International Exhibition of Photography" in the Mánes gallery, Prague. This was the most important exhibition of modern photography in interwar Czechoslovakia. Also exhibited with the Amateur Photographic Society of Kolín in the Kolín Municipal Library.

1937 Moved with his family from Kolín to Prague, where he taught at the *realgymnasium* in Ječná ulice. Began to take photographs of the landscape and landscape details on the outskirts of Prague. Made friends with Josef Ehm, a photographer and teacher at the State School of Graphic Art, Prague.

1939 Made his most important landscape photograph, called *Wheat* (later renamed *Disaster*).

1940–41 In the magazine *Fotografický obzor*, edited by Ehm and Funke, published a number of photographs and four theoretical essays in which he applied his knowledge of Gestalt psychology to the theory of photography, and developed his views on the potential of photography to stylize.

1945 In early May, did photojournalism of the building of the barricades during the Prague Uprising against the German occupation.

1946–48 In the magazines *Fotografie*, *Československá fotografie*, and *Zpravodaj fotografů*, published another six essays on theory. His work appeared in the "Modern Photography in Czechoslovakia" exhibition in Vienna and Zurich and at the "Fourth International Photographic Salon" in Prague.

1948 After the Communist takeover in late February, stopped teaching at the *realgymnasium* in the Prague district of Libeň, and went into retirement. Stopped exhibiting his photos and stopped writing on photography.

1950 On 27 April his daughter Eva gave birth to his only grandchildren, Jiří and Jan.

1950–54 Worked mainly on the large series "From the Old Jewish Cemetery in Prague," but also made landscape photographs, details of plants, and photographs of Prague.

1957 After years in oblivion, his life and work were recalled by Jiří Jeníček in an article in the April issue of *Československá fotografie*.

1963 The photography historian and theorist Anna Fárová published a set of twelve postcards with his works in the Profily series of Orbis publishing house.

1964 On 15 January, Eugen Wiškovský died in Prague. Anna Fárová's book about him and his work was published in the Státní nakladatelství krásné literatury a umění (State Publishing House for *Belles-lettres* and Art – SNKLU), Prague, in June of that year.

Životopisná data

1888 20. září přichází na svět ve Dvoře Králové nad Labem jako druhý syn Aloise Wiškovského, správce všeobecné zemské nemocnice ve Dvoře Králové, který byl před svatbou vojákem z povolání, a Eugenie Wiškovské, rozené Hotovcové. Bratři Alois (* 1887), Otakar (* 1890) a Bedřich (* 1891).

1902 Od otce dostává první fotoaparát na desky formátu 9 x 12 cm.

1906 Maturuje na gymnáziu ve Dvoře Králové, začíná studia francouzštiny, němčiny a psychologie na Filosofické fakultě české univerzity Karlo-Ferdinandovy v Praze.

1909 Zimní semestr tráví jako stipendista na univerzitě v Ženevě.

1910 Ukončuje vysokoškolská studia.

1910–12 Vyučuje na reálkách v Praze-Žižkově a v Praze II.

1912 Začíná svou pedagogickou činnost na Státním reálném gymnáziu v Kolíně.

1914–17 Bojuje jako voják rakousko-uherské armády na italské a ruské frontě, po dvojím zranění je převelen k týlovému vojsku do České Lípy.

1917 28. dubna se žení s Annou Streitovou, narozenou 8. srpna 1893 v Gródku v Haliči. Krátkodobě se obnovuje jeho zájem o fotografování.

1918 23. března se manželům Wiškovským narodila první dcera Eva, pozdější lékařka.

1919 Vrací se na Státní reálné gymnázium v Kolíně, kde působí jako profesor až do roku 1937. 9. června se narodila druhá dcera Hana.

1928–29 Vznikají první vyzrálejší fotografické portréty, v nichž experimentuje s obrazovou skladbou, osvětlením a vrženými stíny.

1929 Vytváří první fotografie statických objektů ve stylu nové věcnosti: Límce (později Měsíční krajina), Vejce, Izolace, Roury aj. Fotograficky spolupracuje se svým bývalým žákem z gymnázia Jaromírem Funkem.

Ve 12. čísle časopisu *Foto* z roku 1929 publikuje první teoretický text O obrazové fotografii, další následují až po jedenácti letech.

1930 Účastní se výstavy *Nová fotografie* v Aventinské mansardě v Purkyňově ulici v Praze, organizované Alexandrem Hackenschmiedem, na níž se poprvé v české metropoli skupinově představuje fotografická avantgarda. Obdobné výstavy se zúčastňuje i v následujícím roce.

1930–34 Společně s Jaromírem Funkem často fotografuje motivy ze stavby funkcionalistické elektrárny ESSO v Kolíně.

1933 Je zastoupen na *Výstavě sociální fotografie* v paláci Metro v Praze, organizované Film–foto skupinou Levé fronty pod vedením Lubomíra Linharta (repríza v Brně). Vznikají varianty fotografií izolátoru.

1936 Pět jeho fotografií je přijato na *Mezinárodní výstavu fotografie* v pražském Mánesu, nejvýznamnější přehlídku moderní fotografie v meziválečném Československu. Vystavuje s kolínským Klubem fotografů amatérů v Městské knihovně v Kolíně.

1937 Stěhuje se s celou rodinou z Kolína do Prahy, kde učí na reálce v Ječné ulici. Začíná fotografovat krajiny a krajinářské detaily v okolí Prahy. Navazuje přátelství s fotografem a pedagogem Státní grafické školy v Praze Josefem Ehmem.

1939 Vytváří svou nejznámější krajinářskou fotografii Obilí (později přejmenovanou na Katastrofa).

1940–41 Ve *Fotografickém obzoru*, redigovaném Josefem Ehmem a Jaromírem Funkem, publikuje řadu fotografií a čtyři teoretické stati, v nichž aplikuje poznatky z tvarové psychologie do oblasti teorie fotografie a rozvíjí své názory na stylizační možnosti fotografie.

1945 Vytváří reportážní snímky ze stavby barikád během Pražského povstání.

1946–48 V časopisech *Fotografie*, *Československá fotografie* a *Zpravodaj fotografů* uveřejňuje dalších šest teoretických statí. Je zastoupen na výstavě *Moderní fotografie v Československu* ve Vídni a v Curychu a na *4. mezinárodním fotografickém salonu* v Praze.

1948 Po převzetí moci komunisty ukončuje své pedagogické působení na reálném gymnáziu v Praze-Libni a odchází do důchodu. Stahuje se i z veřejného fotografického života.

1950 Dceři Evě se 27. dubna narodili jeho jediní vnuci Jiří a Jan.

1950–54 Pracuje především na rozsáhlém cyklu Ze Starého židovského hřbitova v Praze, vytváří však i krajinářské snímky, detaily rostlin a snímky z prostředí Prahy.

1957 Po letech zapomnění připomíná Jiří Jeníček jeho tvorbu v medailonu v dubnovém čísle *Československé fotografie*.

1963 Historička a teoretička fotografie Anna Fárová vydává v edici Profily v nakladatelství Orbis soubor dvanácti pohlednic s reprodukcemi Wiškovského fotografií.

1964 15. ledna umírá v Praze na zánět pobřišnice. Monografie, připravená Annou Fárovou, vychází ve Státním nakladatelství krásné literatury a umění v Praze až posmrtně v červnu téhož roku.

Solo Exhibitions / Samostatné výstavy

1985 Galleria d'Arte Narciso, Torino Fotografia '85, Torino
1988 Technické muzeum, Brno
1988 Krajská galerie, Hradec Králové
1992 Pražský dům fotografie / Prague House of Photography, Praha

Selected Group Exhibitions / Skupinové výstavy (výběr)

1930 *Nová fotografie*, Aventinská mansarda, Praha
1930 *1. členská výstava Klubu fotografů amatérů v Kolíně*, Kolín
1931 *Nová fotografie 2*, Aventinská mansarda, Praha
1933 *Výstava sociální fotografie*, palác Metro, Praha (Brno)
1936 *Mezinárodní výstava fotografie*, SVU Mánes, Praha
1936 *Výstava Klubu fotografů amatérů v Kolíně*, Městská knihovna, Kolín
1947 *Das moderne Lichtbild in der Čechoslowakei*, Der Kunstgewerbe Verein, Wien (Zürich)
1948 *4. mezinárodní fotografický salón*, Praha (Brno, Bratislava, Ostrava)
1965 *Memoriál Eugena Wiškovského*, Kulturní dům ROH, Hradec Králové
1966 *Edice Umělecká fotografie v SNKLU*, Výstavní síň Fotochema, Praha (Plzeň)
1966 *Surrealismus a fotografie*, Kabinet fotografie Jaromíra Funkeho, Dům pánů z Kunštátu, Brno (Essen, Praha, Bratislava)
1967 *Československá fotografie mezi dvěma světovými válkami*, Obecní dům, Praha (Brno, Bratislava, Ostrava)
1973 *Československá krajina*, Interkamera, Bruselský pavilon, Praha
1973 *Osobnosti české fotografie I*, Galerie výtvarného umění, Roudnice nad Labem (Praha, Brno)
1981 *Česká fotografie 1918–1938*, Moravská galerie, Brno (Praha)
1983 *Photographes tchèques 1920–1950*, Musée national d'art moderne, Centre Georges Pompidou, Paris
1983 *Tschechoslowakische Fotografen 1900–1940*, Leipzig
1984 *Tschechische Fotografie 1918–1938*, Museum Folkwang, Essen (Frankfurt am Main, Wien)
1985 *Ursprung und Gegenwart tschechoslowakischer Fotografie*, Fotografie Forum Frankfurt, Frankfurt am Main
1985 *Czeska Fotografia 1918–1938*, Muzeum Sztuki, Łódź
1986 *Fotografie, plakát, typografie ze sbírek UPM*, Výstavní síň Emauzy, Praha
1988 *Tschechische Kunst der 20er und 30er Jahre*, Mathildenhöhe, Darmstadt
1988 *Linie, barva, tvar v českém výtvarném umění třicátých let*, Dům U Kamenného zvonu, Galerie hlavního města Prahy, Praha (Pardubice, Hluboká nad Vltavou)
1989 *Cesty československé fotografie*, Dům U Kamenného zvonu, Galerie hlavního města Prahy, Praha
1989 *Co je fotografie – 150 let fotografie / What is Photography – 150 Years of Photography*, Mánes, Praha
1989 *Česká amatérská fotografie 1945–1989*, Bruselský pavilón, Praha
1989 *Sto padesát fotografií. Fotografická sbírka Moravské galerie v Brně*, Moravská galerie, Brno
1989 *Czech Modernism 1900–1945*, The Museum of Fine Arts, Houston (New York, Akron)

1990 *Aventinská mansarda – Otakar Štorch Marien a výtvarné umění*, Dům U Kamenného zvonu, Galerie hlavního města Prahy, Praha

1990 *Les avant-gardes tchèques, Rencontres internationales de la photographie*, Palais de l'Archevêché, Arles

1992 *Photographien aus der Tschechoslowakei der 30er und 40er Jahre*, Galerie Carla Stützer, Köln

1993 *El arte de la Vanguardia en Checoslovaquia / The Art of the Avant-Garde in Czechoslovakia 1918–1938*, IVAM Centre Julio Gonzales, Valencia

1993 *Umění pro všechny smysly – Meziválečná avantgarda v Československu*, Valdštejnská jízdárna, Národní galerie, Praha

1993 *Czech and Slovak Photography from Between the Wars to the Present*, Fitchburg Art Museum, Fitchburg (Boston, Middlebury, Seattle, Monaco)

1997 *Prague 1900–1938. Capitale secrète des avant-gardes*, Musée des Beaux-Arts, Dijon

1998–99 *Bellesa moderna. Les avantguardes fotogràfiques txeques 1918–1948 (Modern Beauty. Czech Photographic Avant-Garde 1918–1948)*, Museu Nacional d'Art de Catalunya, Barcelona (Paris, Lausanne, München)

1999 *Moderní krása. Česká fotografická avantgarda 1918–1948*, Dům U Kamenného zvonu, Galerie hlavního města Prahy, Praha

2000 *Tschechische Avantgarde-Fotografie der zwanziger und dreissiger Jahre aus der Sammlung des Kunstgewerbemuseums in Prag*, Tschechisches Zentrum, Berlin

2000 *Cseh Avantgárd Fotográfia 1918–1938*, Magyar Fotográfusok Háza, Mai Manó House, Budapest

2000 *Fotografie v Mánesu*, Mánes, Praha

2001 *Tvář naší země*, Tereziánské křídlo Pražského hradu, Praha

2003 *Maestri della Fotografia dell'Avanguardia Ceca negli anni Venti e Trenta / Masters of Czech Avant-Garde Photography of the 1920s and the 1930s*, CRAF – Centro di Ricerca e Archiviazione della Fotografia, Lestans

2004 *Česká fotografie 1840–1950. Příběh moderního média*, Galerie Rudolfinum, Praha

2005 *La fotografía en la collección del IVAM*, Instituto Valenciano de Arte Moderno, Valencia

2005 *Česká fotografie 20. století / Czech Photography of the 20th Century*, Uměleckoprůmyslové museum, Galerie hlavního města Prahy – Dům U Kamenného zvonu, Městská knihovna, Praha

2005 *Zrození múzy*, Galerie 4, Cheb

Represented in Public Collections / Zastoupení ve veřejných sbírkách

Instituto Valenciano de Arte Moderno, Valencia
J. Paul Getty Museum, Los Angeles
Moravská galerie, Brno
Musée national d'art moderne, Centre Georges Pompidou, Paris
Museum of Modern Art, New York
Národní technické muzeum, Praha
National Gallery of Art, Washington
Pražský dům fotografie / Prague House of Photography, Praha
San Francisco Museum of Modern Art, San Francisco
The Museum of Fine Arts, Houston
Uměleckoprůmyslové museum, Praha

Literature on Eugen Wiškovský (A Selection) / Literatura o Eugenu Wiškovském (výběr)

Jeníček, Jiří: Eugen Wiškovský, *Československá fotografie*, 1957, č. 4, s. 40–43.
Fárová, Anna: *Eugen Wiškovský* (12 postcards / 12 pohlednic), Praha, Orbis 1963.
Fárová, Anna: Imaginární rozhovor s Eugenem Wiškovským, *Československá fotografie*, 1964, č. 5, s. 150–154.
Fárová, Anna: *Eugen Wiškovský*, Praha, SNKLU 1964.
Fárová, Anna: Ze sbírek UPM: Eugen Wiškovský, *Československá fotografie*, 1972, č. 9, s. 404–405.
Anděl, Jaroslav: Teoretické přístupy a interpretace. Eugen Wiškovský. *Československá fotografie*, 1974, č. 1, s. 6–8, č. 2, s. 56–57.
Birgus, Vladimír: Eugen Wiškovský. *Revue Fotografie*, 1984, č. 4, s. 62–69.
Birgus, Vladimír: Eugen Wiškovský, in: *Torino Fotografia 1985*, Modena, Edizioni Panini, s. 19–22.
Birgus, Vladimír: Dobrodružství zraku, *Tvorba*, 1988, č. 39, s. 22.
Birgus, Vladimír: Sto let od narození Eugena Wiškovského, *Československá fotografie*, 1988, č. 11, s. 488–492.
Birgus, Vladimír: Krajiny Eugena Wiškovského, in: *4. bienále fotografie přírody*, Brno, Krajské kulturní středisko 1988.
Šejn, Miloš: *Eugen Wiškovský. Fotografie*, Hradec Králové, Krajská galerie 1988.
Birgus, Vladimír: *Eugen Wiškovský 1988–1964*, Praha, Pražský dům fotografie / Prague House of Photography 1992.
Sobek, Evžen: *Teoretické práce Eugena Wiškovského*, bakalářské teoretická diplomová práce, Opava, Institut tvůrčí fotografie 1998.

Portfolios / Portfolia

Eugen Wiškovský. 10 Photographs, limited-edition portfolio of 10 prints printed from original negatives, text Vladimír Birgus, Praha, Pražský dům fotografie / Prague House of Photography 1992.
Reconstructing the Original. Czech Abstractions 1922–35, limited-edition portfolio of new prints from original negatives by Czech photographers, text Jaroslav Anděl, New York, Gary Schneider 1994.

Other Literature / Další literatura

Books / Knihy

Jeníček, Jiří: *Fotografie jako zření světa a života*, Praha, Československé filmové nakladatelství 1947.
Ehm, Josef & Štech, V. V.: *Krásy plná, slávou i kletbou bohatá...Praho!* Praha, Družstevní práce 1948.
Kainar, Josef: *Fotografie 1928–1958*, Praha, SNKLHU 1959.
Tausk, Petr: *Hlavní vývojové cesty československé fotografie*, Praha, Ústřední dům lidové umělecké tvořivosti 1969.

Anděl, Jaroslav: *Analýza vývoje české fotografické teorie*, závěrečná teoretická práce, Praha, FAMU 1972.
Tausk, Petr: *Die Geschichte der Fotografie im 20. Jahrhundert*, Köln, DuMont 1977.
Tausk, Petr: *Současný stav fotografie*, Praha, Státní pedagogické nakladatelství 1977.
Tausk, Petr: *Photography in the 20th Century*, London, Focus 1980.
Mrázková, Daniela & Remeš, Vladimír: *Tschechoslowakische Fotografen*, Leipzig, VEB Fotokinoverlag 1983.
Baran, Ludvík: *Praha objektivem mistrů*, Praha, Panorama 1983.
Birgus, Vladimír: Fotografie, in: *Informatorium 2*, Praha, Mladá fronta 1984.
Vojtěchovský, Miroslav: *Vývoj československé teorie fotografie 20. století*, Praha, Státní pedagogické nakladatelství 1985.
Hlaváč, Ľudovít: *Dejiny fotografie*, Martin, Osveta 1986.
Tausk, Petr: *Přehled vývoje československé fotografie od roku 1918 až po naše dny*, Praha, Státní pedagogické nakladatelství 1986.
Mrázková, Daniela & Remeš, Vladimír, *Jakou barvu má domov. Česká a slovenská krajina očima fotografů v proměnách století*, Praha, Mladá fronta 1988.
Mrázková, Daniela & Remeš, Vladimír: *Cesty československé fotografie*, Praha, Mladá fronta 1989.
Opasek, Anastáz: *Dvanáct zastavení*, Praha, Torst 1992.
Encyklopedie českých a slovenských fotografů, Praha, ASCO 1993.
Král, Petr: *Fotografie v surrealismu*, Praha, Torst 1994.
Horová, Anděla (ed.): *Nová encyklopedie českého výtvarného umění*, Praha, Academia 1995.
Birgus, Vladimír: Tschechische Fotografie der Avantgarde 1918–1938. In: *Stifter Jahrbuch. Neue Folge Band 11*, München, Adalbert Stifter Verein 1997, s. 70–80.
Vilgus, Petr: *Fotografie v období protektorátu Čechy a Morava*, bakalářská teoretická diplomová práce, Opava, Institut tvůrčí fotografie, Slezská univerzita 1997 (www.itf.cz).
Dufek, Antonín: Fotografie třicátých let, in: *Dějiny českého výtvarného umění IV*, Praha, Academia 1998, s. 320–353.
Dusíková, Michaela: *Fotografický obzor ve 30. a 40. letech*, magisterská diplomová práce, Opava, Institut tvůrčí fotografie, Slezské univerzita 1998.
Birgus, Vladimír (ed.): *Česká fotografická avantgarda 1918–1948*, Praha, KANT 1999.
Birgus, Vladimír & Scheufler, Pavel: *Fotografie v českých zemích 1839–1999*, Praha, Grada 1999.
Birgus, Vladimír (ed.): *Tschechische Avantgarde-Fotografie 1918–1948*, Stuttgart, Arnoldsche 1999.
Heiting, Manfred (ed.): *At the Still Point. Photographs from the Manfred Heiting Collection*, Volume II, Part I, Los Angeles & Amsterdam, Cinubia 2000.
Birgus, Vladimír (ed.): *Czech Photographic Avant-Garde 1918–1948*, Cambridge, Mass. & London, The MIT Press 2002.
Birgus, Vladimír: Die Tschechische Avantgarde-Fotografie zwischen den zwei Weltkriegen / Czech Avant-garde Photography Between the Two World Wars, in: Jäger, Gottfried (ed.): *Die Kunst der Abstrakten Fotografie / The Art of Abstract Photography*, Stuttgart, Arnoldsche 2002, s. 138–161.
Birgus, Vladimír: Novaja fotografija, in: *Češskoje iskusstvo i literatura XX vek*. Moskva & Sankt-Peterburg, Gosudarstvennyj institut iskusstvoznanija & Aleteja 2003, s. 203–221.
Kuneš, Aleš & Pospěch, Tomáš: *Čítanka z teorie fotografie*, Opava, Slezská univerzita 2003.
Sobek, Evžen: *Teoretické práce české fotografické avantgardy*, Opava, Slezská univerzita 2004.

Anděl, Jaroslav: *Nová vize. Avantgardní architektura v avantgardní fotografii: Československo 1918–1938*, Praha, Slovart 2005.
Moucha, Josef: *Retrospektiva Galerie 4 / Gallery 4 Retrospective*, Cheb, Galerie 4 2005.
Dufek, Antonín: Fotografie 1939–1948, in: *Dějiny českého výtvarného umění V (1939–1958)*, Praha, Academia 2005.

Group Exhibition Catalogs / Katalogy skupinových výstav

Linhart, Lubomír: *Výstava sociální fotografie*, Praha, Film–foto skupina Levé fronty 1933.
Linhart, Lubomír: *Mezinárodní výstava fotografie*, Praha, S.V.U. Mánes 1936.
Teige, Karel: *Das moderne Lichtbild in der Čechoslowakei*, Praha, Orbis 1947.
Zykmund, Václav: *Surrealismus a fotografie*, Brno, Dům umění města Brna 1966.
Skopec, Rudolf: *Československá fotografie mezi dvěma světovými válkami*, Praha, Galerie hlavního města Prahy 1967.
Fárová, Anna: *Osobnosti české fotografie I*, Roudnice nad Labem, Galerie výtvarného umění 1973.
Fárová, Anna: *Osobnosti české fotografie I*, Praha, Uměleckoprůmyslové museum 1974.
Dufek, Antonín (ed.): *Česká fotografie 1918–1938 ze sbírek Moravské galerie v Brně*, Brno, Moravská galerie 1981.
Dufek, Antonín (ed.): *Česká fotografie 1918–1938*, Praha, Uměleckoprůmyslové museum 1982.
Dufek, Antonín & Kirschner, Zdeněk & Klaricová, Kateřina & Sayag, Alain: *Photographes tchèques 1920–1950*, Paris, Centre Georges Pompidou – Musée national d'art moderne 1983.
Dufek, Antonín & Eskildsen, Ute: *Tschechische Fotografie 1918–1938*, Essen, Museum Folkwang 1984.
Dufek, Antonín & Czartoryska, Urszula: *Czeska fotografia 1918–1938*, Łódź, Muzeum Sztuki 1985.
Fárová, Anna: *Ursprung und Gegenwart tschechoslowakischer Fotografie*, Frankurt am Main, Album 1985.
Rousová, Hana (ed.).: *Linie, barva, tvar v českém výtvarném umění třicátých let*, Praha, Galerie hlavního města Prahy 1988.
Anděl, Jaroslav, & Tucker, Anne (ed.): *Czech Modernism 1900–1945*, Houston, The Museum of Fine Arts 1989.
Dufek, Antonín: *Sto padesát fotografií. Fotografická sbírka Moravské galerie v Brně*, Brno, Moravská galerie 1989.
Klimpl, Petr: *Česká amatérská fotografie 1945–1989*, Praha, ÚKVČ 1989.
Krimmel, Bernd & Kotalík, Jiří: *Tschechische Kunst der 20er + 30er Jahre. Avantgarde und Tradition*, Darmstadt, Mathildenhöhe 1989.
Mrázková, Daniela (ed.): *Co je fotografie. 150 let fotografie / What is Photography. 150 Years of Photography*, Praha, Videopress 1989.
Bydžovská, Lenka & Srp, Karel (ed.): *Aventinská mansarda. Otakar Štorch-Marien a výtvarné umění*, Praha, Galerie hlavního města Prahy 1990.
Anděl, Jaroslav (ed.): *El arte de la Vanguardia en Checoslovaquia 1918–1938 / The Art of the Avant-garde in Czechoslovakia 1918–1938*, Valencia, IVAM Centre Julio Gonzales 1993.
Anděl, Jaroslav (ed.): *Umění pro všechny smysly. Meziválečná avantgarda v Československu*, Praha, Národní galerie 1993.
Forbes, Murray & Dufek, Antonín & Macek, Václav & Birgus, Vladimír: *Czech and Slovak*

Photography from Between the Wars to the Present, Boston, The Navigator Foundation 1993.
Anděl, Jaroslav & Starcky, Emmanuel (ed.): *Prague 1900–1938. Capitale secrète des avant-gardes*, Dijon, Musée des Beaux-Arts 1997.
Birgus, Vladimír & Bonhomme, Pierre: *Beauté Moderne, Les avant-gardes photographiques tchèques 1918–1948*, Paris & Praha, Mission du Patrimoine photographique & KANT 1998.
Dufek, Antonín & Teplá, Jana: *Česká fotografie 1939–1958 ze sbírek Moravské galerie v Brně*, Brno, Moravská galerie 1998.
Birgus, Vladimír & Bonhomme, Pierre: *Moderní krása. Česká fotografická avantgarda 1918–1948/ Modern Beauty. Czech Photographic Avant-garde 1918–1948*, Praha, Galerie hlavního města Prahy & KANT 1999.
Moucha, Josef & Kotalík, Jiří T.: *Fotografie v Mánesu*, Praha, S.V.U. Mánes 2000.
Birgus, Vladimír & Mlčoch, Jan: *Cseh Avantgárd Fotográfia 1918–1938*, Budapest, Magyar Fotográfusok Háza 2000.
Birgus, Vladimír & Zuckriegl, Margit: *Maestri della fotografia dell'avanguardia ceca negli anni Venti e Trenta / Masters of the Czech Avant-Garde Photography of the 1920s and the 1930s*, Milano, Silvana Editoriale 2001.
Bárta, Jaroslav & Dejmalová, Kateřina & Kotalík, Jiří T.: *Tvář naší země – krajina domova*, Lomnice nad Popelkou & Praha, Studio JB & Česká komora architektů 2001.
Anděl, Jaroslav: *Česká fotografie 1840–1950. Příběh moderního média*, Praha, KANT 2004.
Casabán, Consuelo Císcar & Flórez, Fernando Castro: *La fotografía en la collección del IVAM*, Valencia, Instituto Valenciano de Arte Moderno 2005.
Birgus, Vladimír & Mlčoch, Jan: *Czech Photography of the 20th Century*, Praha, KANT & Uměleckoprůmyslové museum 2005.
Birgus, Vladimír & Mlčoch, Jan: *Česká fotografie 20. století*, Praha, KANT & Uměleckoprůmyslové museum 2005.

Articles (A Selection) / Články (výběr)

Berka, Ladislav Emil: Aventinská výstava nové české fotografie, *Rozpravy Aventina*, 1929–1930, č. 34, s. 434.
Hackenschmied, Alexandr: K výstavě nové české fotografie v Aventinské mansardě, *Pestrý týden*, 1930, č. 12.
Linhart, Lubomír: Moderní fotografie a její výstava v Mánesu, *Tvorba*, 1936, č. 14, s. 221–223.
Hermann, Karel: Učme se vidět fotograficky, *Fotografie*, 1940, s. 307–398, 323–325, 332–333.
Teige, Karel: Cesty československé fotografie, *Blok*, 1948, č. 6, s. 77–86.
Mrázková, Daniela: Fotografické dědictví – vývojové proudy v české meziválečné fotografii, *Československá fotografie*, 1978, č. 6, s. 260–269.
Tausk, Petr: The Roots of Modern Photography in Czechoslovakia, *History of Photography*, 1979, č. 3, s. 253–271.
Vojtěchovský, Miroslav: Vývoj české teorie fotografie, *Revue Fotografie*, 1979, č. 4, s. 14–18.
Czartoryska, Urszula & Dufek, Antonín: Międzywojenna fotografia czeska, *Fotografia*, 1982, č. 1, s. 13–19.
Horak, Jan-Christopher: The Czech Avant-Garde, *Afterimage*, 1984, Summer.
Dufek, Antonín: Z historie české fotografie (od r. 1918 do r. 1930), *Revue Fotografie*, 1985, č. 5, s. 36–43.
Horak, Jan-Christopher: Le photographie tchèque entre les deux guerres, *Photographies*, 1985, č. 7, s. 100–102.

Tausk, Petr: Půlstoletí od Mezinárodní výstavy fotografie v Mánesu, *Československá fotografie*, 1986, č. 7, s. 296–300.
Dufek, Antonín: Fotografie v Čechách a na Slovensku 1919–1945, *Revue Fotografie*, 1989, č. 3, s. 2–9.
Lechowicz, Lech: Fotografia w kręgu czeskiej awangardy międzywojennej, Łódź, *Acta universitatis lodziensis*, Folia scientiae artium et litterarium 1990, s. 125–146.
Birgus, Vladimír: Modern Beauty – Czech Avant-Garde Photography 1918–1948, *Imago*, 1998, č. 6, s. 58–60.
Ginart, Belén: El MNAC ofrece la primera gran exhibición de fotográfia checa de vanguardia, *El Pais*, 8. 4. 1998.
Spiegel, Olga: El MNAC presenta la efervescencia creativa de las vanguardias fotográficas checas, *La Vanguardia*, 8. 4. 1998.
Uberquoi, Marie-Claire: El MNAC acoge una exposición sobre la fotografía checa de vanguardia, *El Mundo*, 8. 4. 1998.
D'Hooghe, Alain: La Tchécoslovaquie révélée. Les avant-gardes tchèques à Paris, *Le Matin*, 6. 8. 1998.
Gautran, Jean-Claude: Beauté Moderne. Les avant-gardes photographiques tchèques, *Le Photographe*, 1998, č. 7–8, s. 10–11.
Lebhart, Walter: Poesie und Technik – böhmische Moderne, *Der Landbote*, 19. 11. 1998.
Kanyar, Helena: Licht-Schatten-Spiele: Tschechische Fotoavantgarde 1918–46, *Basler Zeitung*, 12. 12. 1998.
Birgus, Vladimír: Nová věcnost a konstruktivismus v české fotografii, *Ateliér*, 1999, č. 5, s. 4–5.
Kuneš, Aleš: Česká teorie fotografie a fotografická publicistika 1918–1948, *Ateliér*, 1999, č. 5, s. 6–7.
Boček, Jaroslav: Vychutnejte krásu české moderní fotografie, *Právo*, 5. 3. 1999.
Birgus, Vladimír: Česká fotografická avantgarda v mezinárodním kontextu, *Film a doba*, 2000, č. 2, s. 69–76.
Birgus, Vladimír: The New Objectivity and Constructivism in Czech Inter-War Photography, *Imago*, 2000, č. 9, s. 8–20.
Chuchma, Josef: Nakolik je ta krása moderní?, *Literární noviny*, 1999, č. 21, s. 12.
Kuneš, Aleš: Moderní krása. Česká fotografická avantgarda 1918–1948, *Týdeník Rozhlas*, 1999, č. 14.
Kuneš, Aleš: Po Paříži se česká avantgardní fotografie představí v Praze, *Lidové noviny*, 2. 3. 1999.
Podestát, Václav: Česká fotografická avantgarda, *Plzeňský deník*, 11. 5. 1999.
Pokorný, Marek: Do Prahy doputoval pokus o anatomii české avantgardní fotografie, *Mladá fronta Dnes*, 3. 3. 1999.
Pospěch, Tomáš: Česká fotografická avantgarda 1918–1948, *Ateliér*, 2000, č. 8, s. 7.
Dattenberger, Simone: Hemdkragenspitzen. Neue Sammlung: Tschechische Avantgarde-Fotografie, *Münchner Merkur*, 9. 6. 1999.
Meyer, Claus Heinrich: Kraftwerk der Bilder. Eine Ausstellung tschechischer Avantgarde-Photographie in der Münchner Neuen Sammlung, *Süddeutsche Zeitung*, 15. 7. 1999.

Rother, Hans-Jürgen: Als die süssen Jahre bitter wurden. Tschechische Fotografie zwischen Avantgarde und Realismus: Eine Doppelaustellung in Berlin, *Frankfurter Allgemeine Zeitung*, 23. 6. 2000.
Birgus, Vladimír & Mlčoch, Jan: Cseh avantgárd fotográfia 1918–1938, *Fotóművészet*, 2001, č. 1–2, s. 67–81.
Kłos, Agnieszka: Perspektywa czystych bromów. O czeskiej międzywojennej awangardzie fotograficznej, *Format*, 2002, č. 41, s. 73–77.
Cibulková, Michaela: Česká fotografie 20. století, *Foto Video*, 2005, č. 6, s. 20–27.
Pavelka, Zdenko: Fotografie se loučí s klasikou, in: *Salon – Literární příloha Práva*, 1. 9. 2005, s. 1–3.
Volf, Petr: Plynulá cesta, *Reflex*, 2005, č. 35, s. 34–41.
Chuchma, Josef: Čas nové energie a nového vidění. Nedotažená kniha o sepětí architektury a fotografie v meziválečném Československu, *Mladá fronta Dnes*, 9. 9. 2005.

List of Published Photographs

39 Untitled, 1930s (private collection)
40 Canoe, 1930s (private collection)
41 On the Embankment, 1930s (private collection)
42 Beggars, 1930s (UPM – GF 13100)
43 Sázava, 1934 (collection of Anna Fárová, Prague)
44 Way near Police nad Metují, before 1933 (Eugen Wiškovský Portfolio, Prague House of Photography)
45 Hlubočepy, c. 1940 (private collection)
46 Hlubočepy Cliffs, 1940 (private collection)
47 Hlubočepy, 1943–44 (UPM – GF 80)
48 Undulating Terrain II (Slapy), 1946 (private collection)
49 Impressions, 1942 (Galerie Kicken, Berlin)
50 Landscape near Prague (Hlubočepy), 1939 (private collection)
51 Water, 1938 (Moravian Gallery, Brno – MG 6630)
52 Texture, 1944 (Moravian Gallery, Brno – MG 6618)
53 Cliffs, 1946 (collection of Anna Fárová, Prague)
54 Little Lake, 1940s (collection of Anna Fárová, Prague)
55 Untitled, 1929 (Moravian Gallery, Brno – MG 6680)
56 Landscape near Kolín, 1933 (Moravian Gallery, Brno – MG 6629)
57 Contour Lines, 1940–41 (collection of Anna Fárová, Prague)
58 Shadow, 1940 (private collection)
59 Banner, 1944 (private collection)
60 Disaster (Wheat), 1939 (collection of Anna Fárová, Prague)
61 Untitled, undated (private collection)
62 Specters, 1939 (private collection)
63 Untitled, undated (private collection)
64 Wounded Statue, undated (private collection)
65 Barricade, Prague Uprising, 1945 (UPM – GF 13064)
66 German Women and Czech Collaborators Removing Barricades, Prague, 1945 (UPM – GF 13063)
67 After an Air Raid, 1945 (private collection)
68 At the New Town City Hall, undated (private collection)
69 Chestnuts, 1948 (private collection)
70 Lichens, 1954 (private collection)
71 The Old Jewish Cemetery, 1953 (Eugen Wiškovský Portfolio, Prague House of Photography)
72 The Old Jewish Cemetery (Sign), 1952 (collection of Anna Fárová, Prague)
73 The Old Jewish Cemetery, 1950–51 (collection of Anna Fárová, Prague)
74 On Charles Square, 1950s (Robert Koch Gallery, San Francisco)
75 Ficus, 1950s (Galerie Kicken, Berlin)
76 Lemons, 1956 (private collection, Praha)

UPM – Museum of Decorative Arts, Prague

Soupis publikovaných fotografií

s. 2 Eugen Wiškovský. Foto Jaromír Funke, 30. léta
1 Portrét komponisty, 1930 (sbírka Anny Fárové, Praha)
2 Portrét, 1928 (UPM – GF 04716)
3 Cívky, 1928 (sbírka Anny Fárové, Praha)
4 Vejce, 1929 (portfolio Eugen Wiškovský, Pražský dům fotografie)
5 Měsíční krajina I (Límce I), 1929 (soukromá sbírka)
6 Měsíční krajina II (Límce II), 1929 (portfolio Eugen Wiškovský, Pražský dům fotografie)
7 Roury, 1930 (portfolio Eugen Wiškovský, Pražský dům fotografie)
8 Cementové skruže, 1928–29 (UPM – GF 13087)
9 Vlnitý plech, 1934 (portfolio Eugen Wiškovský, Pražský dům fotografie)
10 Zátiší, 1929 (sbírka Anny Fárové, Praha)
11 Detail turbíny, 1932 (portfolio Eugen Wiškovský, Pražský dům fotografie)
12 Paprsky, 1930 (UPM – GF 13077)
13 Izolace, 1929 (portfolio Eugen Wiškovský, Pražský dům fotografie)
14 Železné pruty, 1928 (soukromá sbírka)
15 Spodek antény v Libicích, 30. léta (UPM – GF 68)
16 Šrouby, 1933–34 (UPM – GF 58)
17 Izolátor, 1933 (sbírka Anny Fárové, Praha)
18 Izolátor s pružinou, 1933–35 (portfolio Eugen Wiškovský, Pražský dům fotografie)
19 Zmrazky, 1930 (soukromá sbírka)
20 Nervatura listu, 1939 (sbírka Anny Fárové, Praha)
21 Odraz, 1935 (sbírka Anny Fárové, Praha)
22 Arabeska, 1931 (portfolio Eugen Wiškovský, Pražský dům fotografie)
23 Elektrárna II, 1934 (Moravská galerie v Brně – MG 9952)
24 Komín, 1932 (UPM – GF 62)
25 Elektrárna v Kolíně, 1932 (Robert Koch Gallery, San Francisco)
26 Detail elektrárny, 1932–33 (UPM – GF 13092)
27 Stavba elektrárny v Kolíně, 1929–32 (UPM)
28 Haldy (Uhlí), 1932 (UPM – GF 13090)
29 Terasy Barrandov I, 30. léta (soukromá sbírka)
30 Terasy Barrandov II, 30. léta (soukromá sbírka)
31 Lodě na řece, první polovina 30. let (UPM – GF 13089)
32 Funkcionalistická architektura, 30. léta (soukromá sbírka)
33 Bez názvu, 1932–36 (UPM – GF 4735)
34 Petřínská rozhledna v Praze, 1937 (soukromá sbírka)
35 Bez názvu, 1928–29 (soukromá sbírka)
36 Hra, 1929 (UPM – GF 53)
37 Stíny, 30. léta (soukromá sbírka)
38 Lodička, 30. léta (UPM – GF 13099)

39 Bez názvu, 30. léta (soukromá sbírka)
40 Kánoe, 30. léta (soukromá sbírka)
41 Na nábřeží, 30. léta (soukromá sbírka)
42 Žebráci, 30. léta (UPM – GF 13100)
43 Sázava, 1934 (sbírka Anny Fárové, Praha)
44 Cesta u Police nad Metují, před 1933 (portfolio Eugen Wiškovský, Pražský dům fotografie)
45 Hlubočepy, kolem 1940 (soukromá sbírka)
46 Hlubočepské skály, 1940 (soukromá sbírka)
47 Hlubočepy, 1943–44 (UPM – GF 80)
48 Zvlněný terén II (Slapy), 1946 (soukromá sbírka)
49 Imprese, 1942 (Galerie Kicken, Berlin)
50 Krajina u Prahy (Hlubočepy), 1939 (soukromá sbírka)
51 Voda, 1938 (Moravská galerie v Brně – MG 6630)
52 Struktura, 1944 (Moravská galerie v Brně – MG 6618)
53 Skála, 1946 (sbírka Anny Fárové, Praha)
54 Jezírko, 40. léta (sbírka Anny Fárové, Praha)
55 Bez názvu, 1929 (Moravská galerie v Brně – MG 6680)
56 Krajina u Kolína, 1933 (Moravská galerie v Brně – MG 6629)
57 Vrstevnice, 1940–41 (sbírka Anny Fárové, Praha)
58 Stín, 1940 (soukromá sbírka)
59 Prapor, 1944 (soukromá sbírka)
60 Katastrofa (Obilí), 1939 (sbírka Anny Fárové, Praha)
61 Bez názvu, nedatováno (soukromá sbírka)
62 Přízraky, 1939 (soukromá sbírka)
63 Bez názvu, nedatováno (soukromá sbírka)
64 Zraněná socha, nedatováno (soukromá sbírka)
65 Barikáda, Pražské povstání, 1945 (UPM – GF 13064)
66 Německé ženy a české kolaborantky při uklízení barikád v Praze, 1945 (UPM – GF 13063)
67 Po náletu, 1945 (soukromá sbírka)
68 U Novoměstské radnice, nedatováno (soukromá sbírka)
69 Kaštany, 1948 (soukromá sbírka)
70 Lišejníky, 1954 (soukromá sbírka)
71 Ze Starého židovského hřbitova, 1953 (portfolio Eugen Wiškovský, Pražský dům fotografie)
72 Ze Starého židovského hřbitova (Znak), 1952 (sbírka Anny Fárové, Praha)
73 Ze Starého židovského hřbitova, 1950–51 (sbírka Anny Fárové, Praha)
74 Na Karlově náměstí, 50. léta (Robert Koch Gallery, San Francisco)
75 Fíkus, 50. léta (Galerie Kicken, Berlin)
76 Citróny, 1956 (soukromá sbírka, Praha)

UPM – Uměleckoprůmyslové museum v Praze

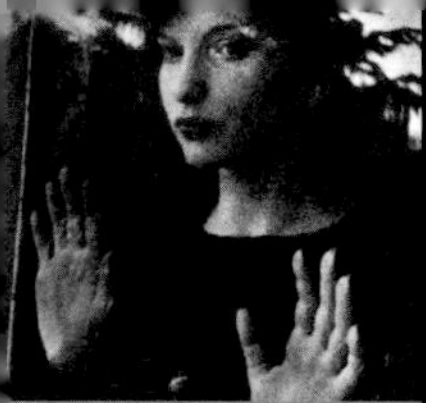
Alexandr **Hackenschmied**

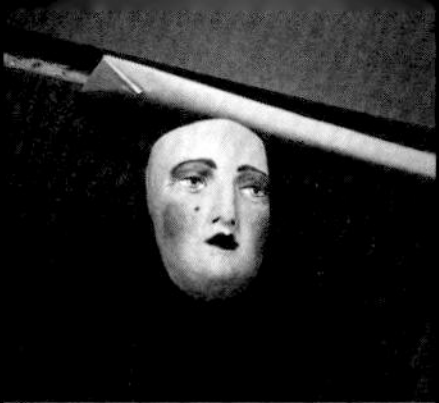
Jindřich **Štyrský**

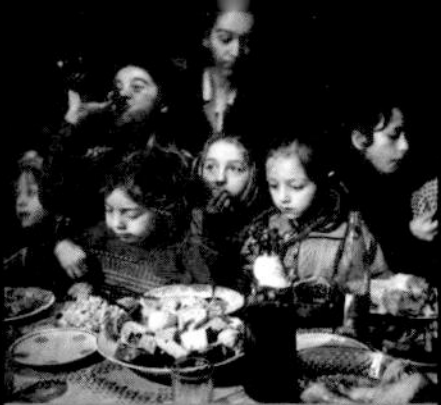
Karel **Cudlín**

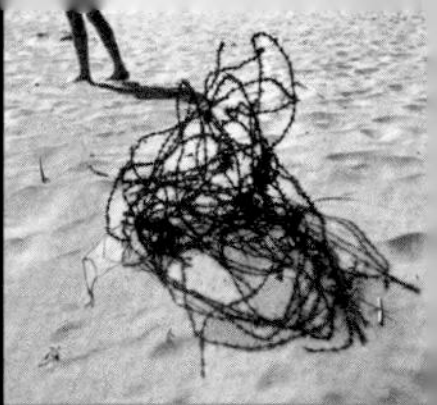
Josef **Koudelka**

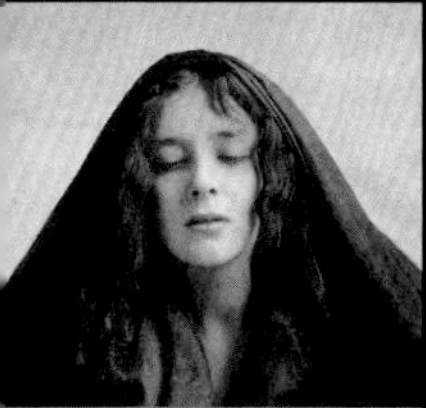
Alfons **Mucha**

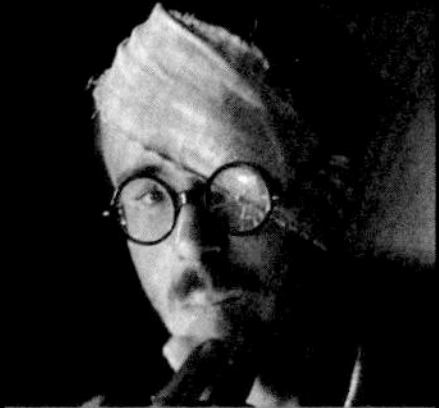
Zdeněk **Tmej**

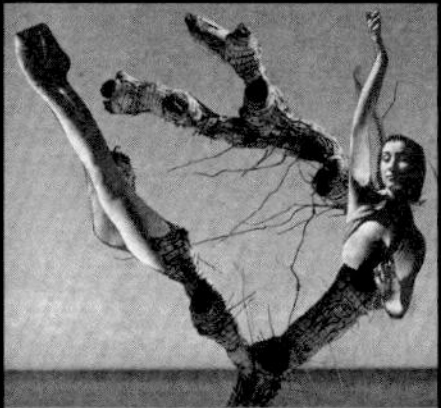
Karel **Teige**

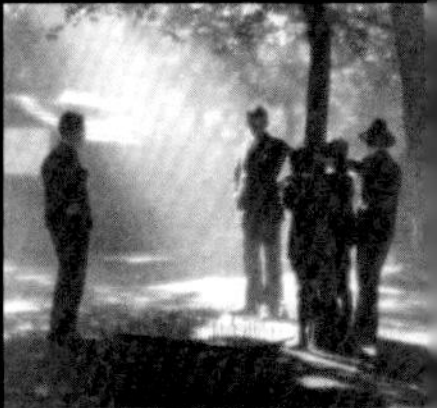
Josef **Sudek**

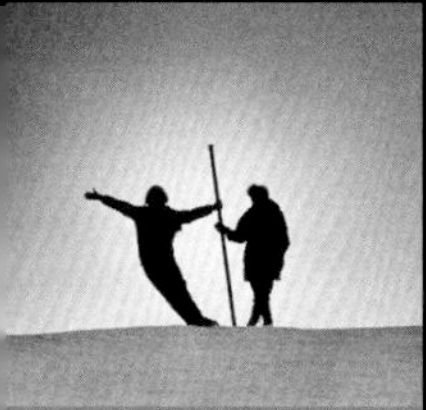
Bohdan **Holomíček**

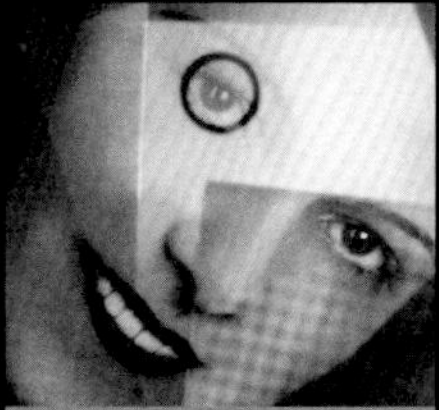
Jaroslav **Rössler**

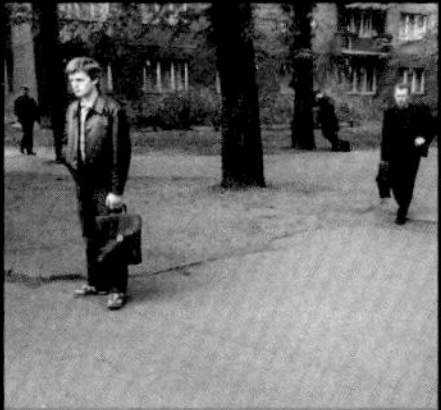
Viktor **Kolář**

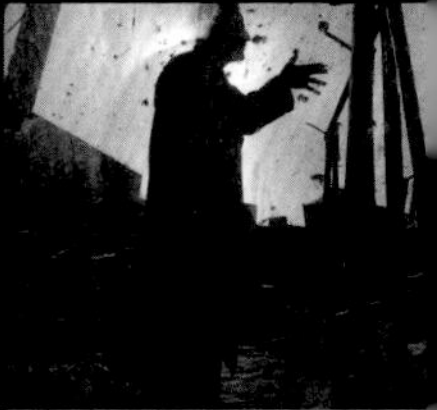
Antonín **Kratochvíl**

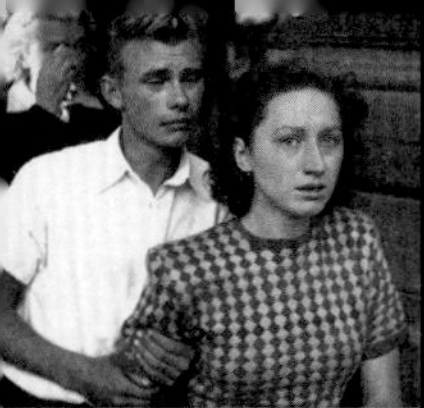

Jan **Lukas**

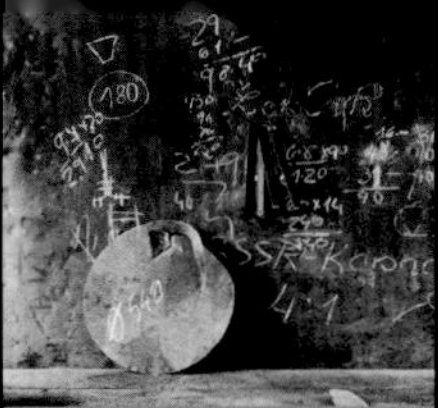

Ivo **Přeček**

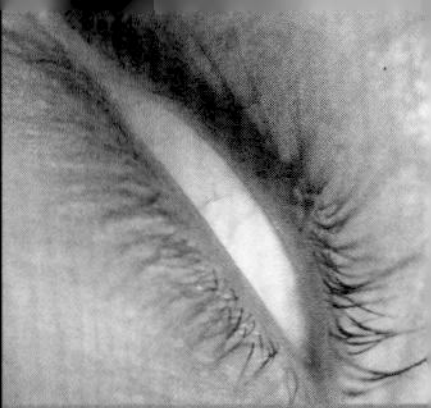

Tono **Stano**

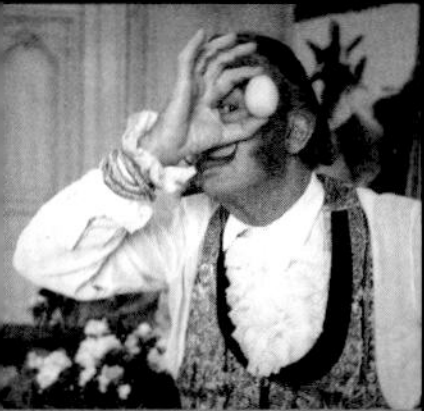

Václav **Chochola**

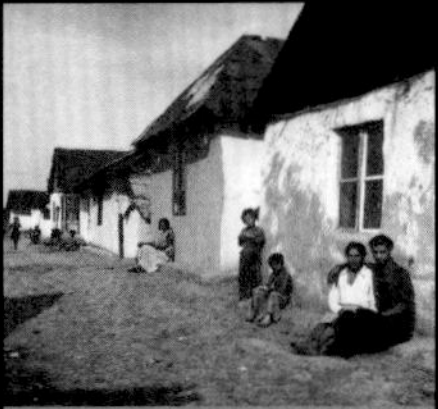

Eva **Davidová**

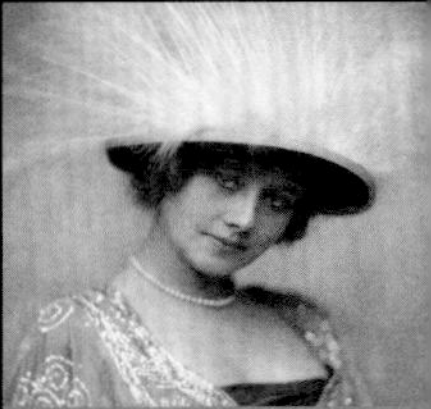

Jan **Langhans**

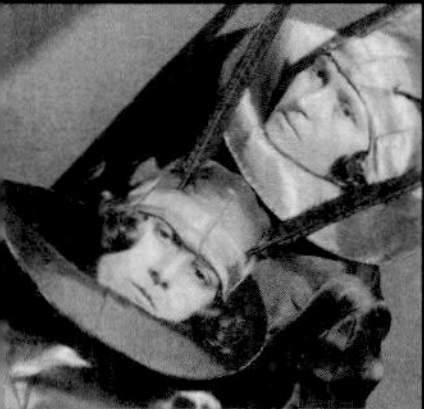

Jaromír **Funke**

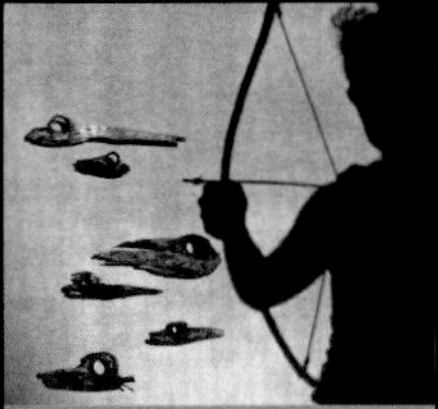

Emila **Medková**

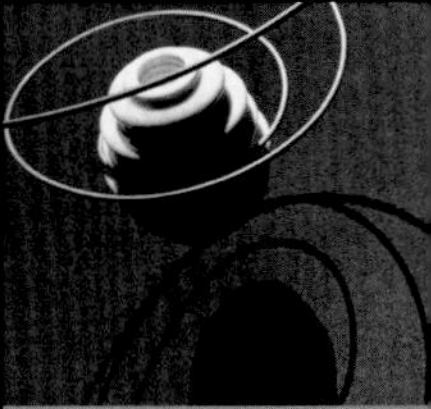

Eugen **Wiškovský**

FOTO**TORST**

Published to date / Dosud vyšlé svazky:

1 **Alexandr Hackenschmied**
2 **Bohdan Holomíček**
3 **Alfons Mucha**
4 **Jindřich Štyrský**
5 **Zdeněk Tmej**
6 **Jaroslav Rössler**
7 **Karel Cudlín** (Out of print / Vyprodáno)
8 **Karel Teige**
9 **Viktor Kolář**
10 **Josef Koudelka**
11 **Josef Sudek**
12 **Antonín Kratochvíl**
13 **Jan Lukas**
14 **Václav Chochola**
15 **Jaromír Funke**
16 **Ivo Přeček**
17 **Eva Davidová**
18 **Emila Medková**
19 **Tono Stano**
20 **Jan Langhans**

Soon to be published / Připravujeme:

Dušan Šimánek
Josef Binko
František Drtikol

Also available through D. A. P. / Distributed Art Publishers
155 Sixth Avenue, 2nd Floor, New York, N. Y. 10013, USA
Tel: ++1 (212) 627-1999 Fax: ++1 (212) 627-9484

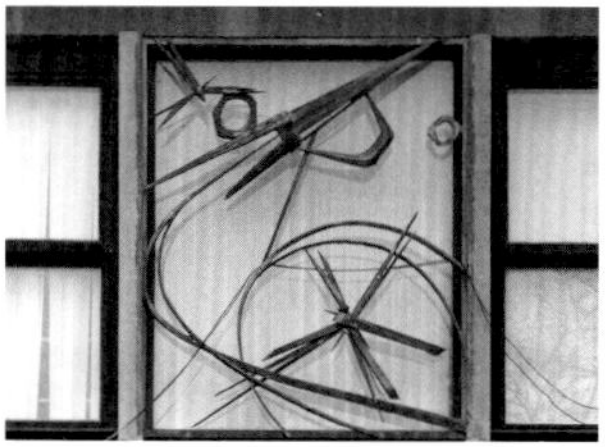

Dušan Šimánek

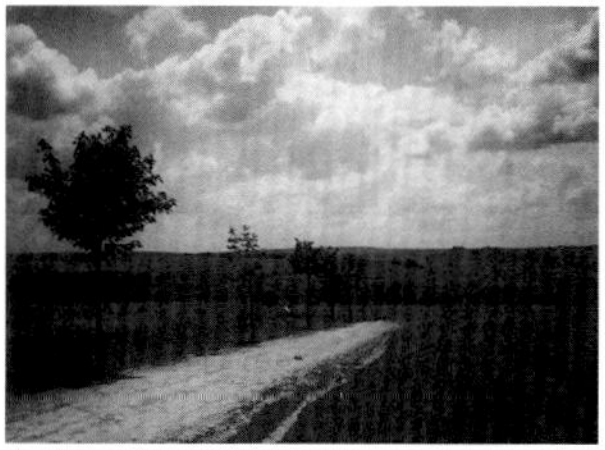

Josef Binko

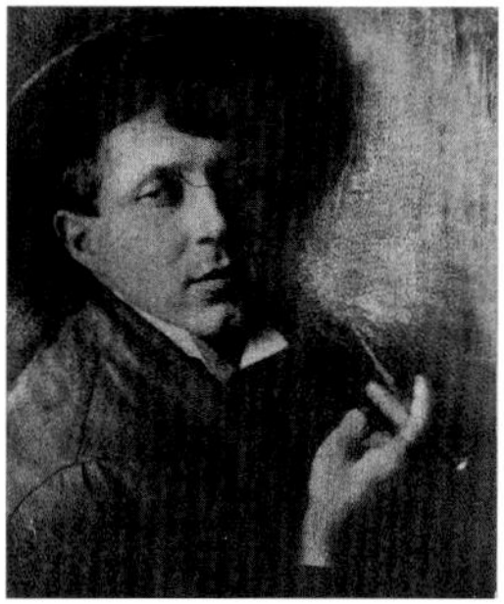

František Drtikol

Eugen Wiškovský

by Vladimír Birgus
Photo selection: Vladimír Birgus
Translation: Derek Paton
Graphic concept: Studio Najbrt, Prague
Graphic design: Pavel Lev, Studio Najbrt
Lithography: Art D, Prague
Printed by Trico, Prague
Copy editors: Jan Šulc, Lenka Urbanová, and Derek Paton
Published by TORST
Address: Opatovická 24, Prague 1
CZ-110 00, Czech Republic
foto@torst.cz
First edition, 2005

Also available through D. A. P./Distributed Art Publishers
155 Sixth Avenue, 2nd Floor, New York, N.Y. 10013, USA
Tel: ++1 (212) 627-1999 Fax: ++1 (212) 627-9484